D1486175

100
GARDEN
DESIGNS

100 GARDEN DESIGNS

JACK KRAMER AND ANDREW ADDKISON

Lyons & Burford Publishers

Distributed by:
Swan Hill Press
An imprint of Airlife Publishing Ltd.
101 Longden Road, Shrewsbury SY3 9EB, England

Printed in the United States of America

10 9 8 7 6 5 4 3 2 1

Library of Congress Cataloging-in-Publication Data

Addkison, Andrew R.
    100 garden designs / Andrew R. Addkison, Jack
  Kramer; perspective and plan drawings by Michael
  Valdez; botancial drawings by Robert Johnson.
        p.   cm.
    Rev. ed. of: 100 garden plans. 1st ed. 1977.
    Includes bibliographical references.
    ISBN 1-55821-255-8
    1. Landscape gardening.   2. Plants,
Ornamental.   3. Gardens—Design.   I. Kramer, Jack,
1927–   . II. Addkison, Andrew R.   100 garden
plans.   III. Title.   IV. Title: One hundred garden
designs.   V. Title: Garden designs.
SB473.A3   1993
712'.6—dc20   93-23824
                                                              CIP

Some of the plants referred to in this book, or appearing in
nature, may be poisonous. Any person, especially a novice
gardener, should exercise care in handling plants. The
publisher and the authors accept no responsibility for any
damage or injury resulting from the use or ingestion of,
or contact with, any plant discussed in this book.

ACKNOWLEDGMENTS

    The authors offer gracious thanks and gratitude to the
artists Robert Johnson and Michael Valdez. Each of them
went far and beyond the call of ordinary duty to give their
full and best cooperation in making this book "work."
    Our typist, Judy Smith, showed patience and did count-
less Saturday and Sunday work. And to Eva Strock, who
read and reread the script and did much of the editing, we
are forever thankful.
    Finally, we want to thank the many friends who allowed
us to use their gardens as conceptual ideas for some of our
plans. This includes people in California, Illinois, New York
and numerous other locations.

CONTENTS

INTRODUCTION

A GARDEN FOR EVERYONE

WHETHER you have the tiniest backyard, an apartment house terrace or a spacious property—whether you like roses or a rock garden, the elegance of ground cover or the practicality of vegetables, to get the results you want you need a specific plan. Every once in a while, casual planting, with a plant here and another there, can turn out well but usually the trial-and-error method of gardening is a waste of money and time. It is much better to plan your garden so that it conforms to your dreams.

This book has been arranged to help you avoid some of the problems of haphazard gardening. Without sensible plans, you are faced with choosing among thousands of plants, hundreds of plant families, countless species and varieties within each group. You may be bewildered by the conflict between space and function in garden design. For example, trying to install a rock garden on a level site simply won't work. Or, if you put a cutting garden on a hill, you will find that you harvest more exercise than flowers. And if you are a beginner and choose plants that are difficult to grow, you may become so discouraged that your first attempt will be your last.

This book presents one hundred plans for space from half an acre down to a 5-by-5 feet area. The gardens are illustrated so that you can see, pictorially, what you will come out with. Detailed plans are presented as well as information on what to expect from each setting. Armed with these plans, the layman can proceed like the good professional—knowing what he has to do to make his personal garden.

100
GARDEN
DESIGNS

One / Gardens, All Kinds

GARDENS can be arranged in many different shapes, sizes and designs—from a postage stamp-sized flower bed to a grand formal garden. And gardens can have many purposes: they can be places to grow vegetables, herbs, or berries; retreats in which to view flowers, meditate, or walk; utilitarian spots in which to eat or sunbathe. Gardens can be in wet places (for water plants), in natural sites (for native plants), in rocky areas (with charming wildflowers), in sleek terraces, or in lush atriums filled with tropical plants.

How do you decide the design, the purpose, the location of your garden? Simply choose a garden plan that fits your mode of life, and then scout the property to see what space is available and if it is suitable for the plan you want. Even in the city there are unexpected places for gardens on back porches, balconies, doorways, vertical areas, on in courtyards in condominiums.

Aim for a unified outdoor atmosphere instead of a mishmash of garden styles and functions on one property.

When you have considered where you want the garden or where you have to have it, decide on the mood and purpose: formal, viewing, utilitarian. Like houses, gardens have a feeling or character; they can be formal or informal, for viewing or cutting flowers or for practical purposes. It is important to use your land intelligently, but it is equally important to select a garden plan that pleases *you.* Only you can decide whether you want a garden purely for visual pleasure or for vegetables, herbs, or fruits.

Just remember that no matter what you grow, you have to take care of the plants; they do not grow by themselves. It is a waste of time and money to install gardens you will not or cannot take care of. If you are going to be a weekend gardener, an ornamental garden is the best; if you want to work at gardening, the produce garden is for you.

Do not just think of a garden as a place of plants; it is a particular arrangement planned to evoke a certain mood. Follow the 100 garden plans in this book and you will have the proper arrangement for your own needs.

ENTRANCE GARDENS

The entryway is the place where people get the first impression of your home and what is to come. Even if the space is limited, you can plan and plant to create a totally harmonious scene that will please the viewer. For example, the garden can be just a border of colorful perennials lining the front walk or the doorway area.

The entrance garden usually faces the street and has little privacy, but the right shrubs and plantings will provide a natural barrier. Consider hedges for screens. If you do not want to garden too much, use a few flowers and a lawn. Lawns create a luxurious, feeling and, once established, take care of themselves. If privacy is your prime concern, use decorative walls. Walls do not impart a prisonlike feeling if put within the site and draped with vines or other climbing plants.

If the entry is in shade, plant a small flower bed or a fern garden. Repeated plantings—not a lot of little plantings but two or three major groups of flowers—in a simple design, augmented with ground cover or a lawn and a few trees as the background, will highlight the entrance garden.

COURTYARD GARDENS

Corner lots can be difficult if the house is placed in the center of the lot, with little private space. A courtyard garden will utilize the front of the property to its fullest and will present a lovely setting to guests before they enter your home.

No matter what you do with the courtyard garden—and there are several plans in this book—use vining plants to cover the walls and to create old-world charm.

HILLSIDE GARDENS

A hillside garden can be a beautiful background for your home. This garden should be established with *permanent* planting for bloom every year because climbing and gardening on hillsides is arduous. You can help deal with this problem by terracing the site in a stair-step arrangement.

The hillside garden is a somewhat difficult plan to follow, and it takes time and patience, but it can be done.

LOW-MAINTENANCE GARDENS

Among the garden plans illustrated later are several designated as low mainte-nance. These are essentially gardens for the person who wants a handsome scene but does not want to spend a lot of time caring for plants. A gravel-and-plant garden is one solution, with most of the property planted with shrubs and a few islands of flowers and gravel used as decorative features.

Another low-maintenance garden plan involves incorporating wild flowers, native shrubs, and trees into the existing natural area. This is a popular type of garden because, once established, the plants fend for themselves. This natural garden will never look formal, but it has a special charm of its own.

A garden whose main feature is ground cover also requires little work. Once the plants are in place they grow steadily and easily, and when ground covers are interspersed with small drifts of flowers, the garden is quite handsome.

A water pool garden also needs little maintenance because, once installed, water plants can be left as they are—nature will do the rest. However, water pool gardens are expensive to construct and plants are also costly.

Two / What Do You Want?

LIKE houses, gardens have a feeling or character; they can be formal or informal, for viewing or for cutting flowers, or they can be utilitarian (a vegetable or herb garden, for example). For easy gardening and an attractive scene, there should be a theme. It is easier to achieve a complete entity when we have a specific idea in mind.

To some people, a garden is solely for beauty, perhaps a symmetrical plan with a touch of elegance. To some homeowners, a garden is a working one where they harvest crops; other people prefer to grow only flowers to cut for indoor decoration. There are also people who want the informal or casual ambience that is in a natural garden where there is no symmetrical plan. And finally, some garden plans take a little from each concept to make a total entity.

No matter what the site is—level, upslope, or downslope, you can have a garden and it may be done in various concepts but no matter what you choose and no matter how small or large the site, the garden should have a definite character and a definite purpose.

FORMAL GARDENS

The formal garden is symmetrical in design; each side mirrors the other. It usually has manicured hedges, and repeated lawn or flower spaces and flowers grown in color groups, without any shocking break of color rhythm. It is balanced and strikes the eye as a total picture, its elegance deriving from the very nature of repetition.

If you have sufficient space and if the exterior of your house is somewhat formal, this type of plan makes sense because it augments the design almost as an extension of the house. This is an easy garden to care for: your main task will be occasional pruning and clipping.

INFORMAL GARDENS

The informal garden is the most popular because you can use almost any type of plant and intersperse where necessary. There is no dividing line or mirror image, as in the symmetrical formal plan.

The informal garden repeats nature, with plants growing randomly but at the same time, coherently. This garden invariably takes a good deal of time to fulfill itself. Being natural, it must come together with time, more time than a month or a year.

The informal garden looks best when it is separated from the house by a patio or terrace, with paths and rocks added for a natural touch. It is the kind of garden that suits ranch homes, contemporary houses, cottages, and two-story buildings.

ORNAMENTAL GARDENS

The ornamental garden provides hours of visual beauty. This garden, which can be accommodated in a small space or backyard, usually has shrubs and trees as its backbone, with perennials and annuals as the striking feature. The ornamental garden can also be composed of just annuals and perennials, with no trees, or simply spring or summer bulbs. Any one of these three plans will produce a great deal in return for a little effort after the initial plantings are made. Ideally, however, the best ornamental garden plan combines trees, shrubs, flowers, and ground covers.

CUTTING GARDENS

The cutting garden is the mainstay of the English garden plan, where flowers are grown primarily to cut for indoor enjoyment. The cutting garden is traditionally placed apart from the main garden, but there is no reason why you cannot make it your main garden, with beautiful annuals, perennials, and bulbs. If it is large, there will always be flowers for cutting and viewing. (Indeed, a good cutting garden is both ornamental and useful.) And if you are a good or even fair gardener and follow the cutting-garden plans in this book, you can have three separate gardens—spring, summer, and fall—so you will have a succession of flowers to lift the spirits both indoors and out. But note that this takes lots of work and space.

PLEASURE GARDENS

You might find it hard to distinguish between the ornamental garden and the pleasure garden. The pleasure garden is sort of a secret place, a very personal garden. This is not a display or working garden but the place where you specialize in your finest plants. It could be a small fern garden off the bedroom, or a spot only for wildflowers. Rose gardens and iris or lily gardens are candidates too. Such a garden gives great satisfaction as a display of your own specialty, where you can putter and ponder, find a plant family that intrigues you and investigate it.

The 100 garden plans include several secret or pleasure gardens, including a fern garden and a handsome rose landscape.

SEASONAL GARDENS

I often see garden catalog pictures that portray the year-round garden, where an array of colorful bloom is ever present in one garden plot for spring, for summer, for all seasons. These gardens are possible, as mentioned, but only with intensive gardening and expertise.

The plans presented here are for a distinct season. Sometimes you will be lucky and the spring garden will overlap into the summer garden, or the summer garden into the fall, but this cannot be counted on. What you must do is decide which season is the most important for you, and then aim for that season's garden plan. As examples, if you are at home more in the summer, follow the summer garden plan, and be content with just a few flowering bulbs for spring. If spring is the time of the year when you must have color, then choose the spring garden plans. If you really like gardening, have one separate area for a spring garden and another separate area for a summer garden. Choose the garden plan for the season you like and have all pleasure, little work.

WORKING GARDENS

Does a working garden mean that you work a lot in it or that it works for you? Both—you get what you give. This kind of garden—vegetable, herb, berry, etc.—is wonderful if you have the time because you will get tasty, pure, and inexpensive food. But food plants, particularly vegetables, require more care than other plants: they need almost daily watering (unless your climate is rainy), good feeding, and a constant war against insects. Yet more people have vegetable, herb, and fruit gardens and would not be without them.

Vegetables are the "easiest" of all the food crops. If you really love vegetables, plan a small kitchen vegetable and herb garden near the house so you can easily and quickly get some vegetables for cooking. The kitchen garden requires frequent planting and needs almost perfect planning to get the most yield out of the least space.

Fruit trees take time and effort at first but eventually give a fine yield of fresh fruit. Be patient. Once established, fruit trees require minimal care and will usually produce year after year. Today there are improved varieties (and dwarf varieties for space-saving gardeners) of apples, peaches, plums, cherries, and pears.

Berry gardens yield a lot of fruit, and usually, after plants are established, must be controlled rather than encouraged. Berries can grow you out of space in a short time and need constant pruning and training on stakes and trellises. These are fine gardens for the energetic.

CONTAINER GARDENS

Growing Conditions

Almost any plant—tree, shrub, flowering—can be grown in containers. Container gardening enables you to have your garden where and when you want it. There is no need to wait for plants to grow or any reason to wonder if the soil around the house will support certain plants.

Where summers are short, plants in containers are the ideal answer to outdoor decoration. Among paths and walks or on patios, terraces, rooftops, and balconies, portable plants cannot be beat. When containers are on movable wooden dollies (sold at hardware stores or nurseries), they can be moved easily indoors in winter. The lemon tree that decorated the patio can go into the enclosed but unheated porch, the Norfolk pine that was on the terrace can become part of the living room scheme, and the tree-form azalea can grace an entry hall.

Container gardening entails no more work than any other type of plant growing. In fact, it is often easier because plants are in one area and so can be watered easily, and tubs and boxes can be moved according to light conditions.

Porches and Balconies

Porches and balconies use container gardens, but they are limited because these areas are usually long and narrow, with little space. It is best to grow some annuals and perennials on these, with one specimen shrub for a visual point of interest. Do not put any containers on the railings because they are likely to fall off.

The most practical plan of the long porch or balcony garden is U-shaped to leave the center area open for walking or seating. Put planters or other containers at least 28 inches off the ground so that tending plants will be easier. Use a triangular grouping of containers in one corner, and always try to have a few interesting or ornate pots.

Patios and Decks

The patio, an expanse of concrete about 16 by 20 feet, is rarely pleasing without plants. The patio is really an extension of the house, acting as an extra room. Thus it is important to make it a showplace because it is always on display.

The deck is about the same shape and size as the patio, but it has a wooden floor and its appearance is greatly enhanced with plants.

As with porches and balconies, you will have to plant in containers. Do not try to do too much to the patio or deck garden; rather, follow the principle of Japanese gardening, using little but making it look like a lot. Group plants in arcs, and use decorative round pots and rectangular redwood planters for handsome arrangements.

Three / Garden Construction

YOU need things like planter boxes, fences, screens and trellises to make a garden complete. Many of these structures can be bought, but it is usually better to make them yourself—to keep expenses down and to get exactly what you want. You also need to consider what materials to use to cover your paths, the ground of your patio, the base of your terrace, and similar areas. Though such jobs can be handled by professionals, there is a good deal of satisfaction to be had in doing them yourself.

We have listed below some of the home construction projects you might wish to undertake, with a few tips we've picked up over the years. Obviously, you will need more help than this to get started on such work, but you will find that your local lumberyard or home improvement center will be eager to help you. There are also some really good books available for the home handyman, including *The Outdoor Garden Build-It Book* by Jack Kramer (Scribners) and *The Outdoor How-to-Build-It Book* by Robert Lee Behme (Hawthorn).

• **Fences** Muscle and a rented post-hole digger are the main ingredients for successful fence building. Make sure that your holes are deep, at least 24 inches, and use 4-by-4 inch posts set in concrete.

• **Trellises** Trellises are fun to make and the most popular patterns are grid and diamond. Redwood or cedar lathing is usually sold in bundles of 50, in lengths of 8, 10, or 12 feet. A good-sized screen can be made in a weekend, even by a rank amateur.

• **Planters** Make sure you make friends with your lumber dealer before you start your planter boxes. Tell the dealer the size box you want and he will suggest the number of boards and the sizes needed. Rough redwood makes an inexpensive, easily maintained box that lasts from five to seven years even in severe weather. Place your planters on 2-inch wood blocks at the corners so that air can reach the plant roots.

• **Surfacing** Brick, concrete, or flagstone are the usual surfaces for outdoor flooring but if you want to save money, loose-fill materials like wood chips, lava rock, or crushed bricks can be used. Take into consideration weather conditions, wear, ease of maintenance, comfort for walking on, color, cost, and —most important—how easy the material is to install.

Concrete—Concrete meets most of the tests for suitable outdoor flooring. The appearance is a problem for some people but you can use color by painting or dying the top layer. Take a look at rough, textured, or aggregate concrete to see which pleases your eye. This is one job, though, which is only feasible for the home handy person to undertake in small areas. If you have a large place to cover, you'd better call a professional.

Concrete Blocks and Slate—These materials are easy to install and easy to move around. They are also familiar to everyone and it is just a question of choosing individual pieces that suit your fancy.

Tile—Brown or red tile is something that I love to use with green plants. It is also easy to clean and virtually impossible to stain. Though you can use a sand base, most tiles need a mortar bed so they will not crack. The mortar work should be done by a professional.

Flagstone—Flagstone is a hard, richly finished, lifetime surface that comes in lovely colors. You can lay it dry or in mortar. For dry laying, use 1½-inch thick stone, for masonry use 1-inch stone.

Fieldstone—The trick to laying fieldstone is to use flagstones for the upper sur-facing and to sink the irregularities into the bedding. Lay fieldstones dry on four inches of sand on top of compacted earth or on about eight inches of crushed gravel or stone.

Brick—The most popular paving material, brick, is attractive and very easy to use. If you make a mistake when you're laying it in sand, simply pick it up and begin again. The best bricks for surfacing are either the smooth or the rough-textured common brick. Try to buy hard-burned rather than green brick—it should be dark red rather than salmon color (which indicates an underburned process and less durability). If you live in an area of severe winters, ask for SW (Severe Weathering) brick and always make sure, whatever kind you're buying, that the dealer has a sufficient quantity of what you want because there are dimensional and color variations in different batches. Bricks can be set in sand but again, the mortar work really requires a professional. The trick to good sand installation is to make sure that you have a perfectly level sand base of 2–3 inches.

Wood Decks—Here, you should certainly consult some of the really handsome plans that are available for wood decks and you should ask your lumber dealer what wood he recommends, whether it needs a preservative, and how long it will last.

Patio Blocks—Pavers, or thick patio blocks, are fairly new on the market. They are made of concrete that has been vibrated under pressure. They are set directly on a sand base, thus making it easy for the homeowner to install and eliminating the cracking that can occur in a poured concrete floor. Because they are so easy to install, paving blocks are fast becoming a very popular patio ter-race flooring.

Wood Blocks and Rounds—These are wonderful in a woodland setting and are available in rounds about four inches thick or in square blocks. The problem with this material is that it is not permanent, even when it is coated with a preservative. Wood tends to crack in intense sun and to split in severe frost, and you will probably only get about five years' service from the wood. Still, it does look lovely.

Loose-Fill Material—You can use wood chips, lava rock, limestone, crushed brick, gravel, pebbles, and many other kinds of loose-fill. Some of them, like lava rock, are difficult to walk on. Others, like loose gravel and pebbles, need a high border edge of wood strips or bricks to keep them confined. Even so, loose-fills do wash out of place and pack down and you may have to replenish spots from time to time.

Four/Basic Garden Fundamentals

NO matter what plan you select, your garden and its plants have to be cared for: you have to know what kind of soil to use, how much water to give plants, what kind of fertilizer to use and how often, and how to fight insects and prevent diseases. The fundamentals of good gardening follow and though they involve work, there is nothing here one cannot cope with and, in fact, enjoy.

SOIL

Good soil is the most important part of the garden. If you are thinking of using your property's soil for your garden, think again. Most yard soil has few nutrients left, or the rich topsoil has been stripped away by bulldozers and tractors. In most cases, you have to mix new soil with what is already on your property.

To mix new soil with old, first break up or crumble the old soil. This is necessary to make it porous: if soil does not have porosity (tilth), water will not get to plant roots. This will be your hardest job. If you have a fair amount of land, or if your land is stony, consider having the soil professionally Rototilled. Otherwise, you could be in for a truly backbreaking job.

Now comes the new soil. This should be free of impurities but have nutrient additives. Buy the soil from reputable dealers by the truckload. Soil comes in 6-yard trucks, and is usually dumped onto your driveway. (Be prepared to spend some time shoveling or pushing wheelbarrows to your garden site.) Mix the new soil thoroughly with the crumbled-up soil, using a rake, hoe, or shovel to blend the soils well.

You can use packaged soil, but it is costly and generally not as good as screened bulk soil. However, if you are container gardening and need to fill only five or six pots, packaged soil is more economical that a 6-yard truck.

Once your soils are mixed together, add humus (decayed vegetable matter that will lend valuable microorganisms to your soil). Get humus from the woods, or buy bags of it. (It is quite expensive, but worthwhile.) Add humus until the soil feels porous and mealy, like a well-done baked potato, and smells earthy.

Now test the soil with a soil-testing kit from a garden-supply company. This will indicate whether the soil is acid, alkaline, or neutral. You will be testing the soil's pH scale; 7 is neutral, 1 to 6 acid, 8 and up is alkaline. Most plants thrive in a neutral soil, but some plants prefer an acid soil, and a few like an alkaline soil. If the pH is too high, mix one pound of ground sulfur to every 100 square feet of soil. This will lower the pH symbol about one point. If the pH is too low, mix ten pounds of ground limestone to every 150 square feet of soil. Apply sulfur or limestone every six or eight weeks.

FERTILIZER

Fertilizing is the next most important part of gardening. However, this does not mean that half your gardening days should be spent "stuffing" plants with food. Use plant foods discreetly. If your soil is good and prepared well, most annuals and perennials will need feeding about twice a month or less. Do not overdose: too much food will kill plants.

Plant foods contain nitrogen to make plants grow; phosphorous to promote strong stems and leaves; and potash to help plants resist disease. Plants' needs vary: flowers like a lot of phosphorous, for example, and lawns need much nitrogen. Any fertilizer you buy will have the elements marked in percentages, with nitrogen first, followed by phosphorous and potash. A 10–10–5 fertilizer is fine for most plants.

There are also fertilizers for specific plants, such as roses, azaleas and camellias. These are specially prepared and are perhaps more valuable for certain plants than the general fertilizers.

Because there are so many plant foods, you should know which ones will suit your garden. For example, if you want to feed a lawn, use a high nitrogen food like 20–20–10. For flower beds and blossoming plants, select a food with high phosphorus content like 12–12–12 or 5–10–5. If you want something to improve the soil structure and to release nutrients slowly, choose an organic food like blood meal or bone meal.

You can buy fertilizers in various forms. Granular is most popular, easy to apply (just sprinkle granules on the soil and add water), and some granular fertilizers contain insecticides or weed killers. Though powdered fertilizers are convenient, they can blow away on a windy day or stick to foliage, and if you store them in a damp place they will cake. But concentrated powders and tablets (mainly for houseplants) are fine. Diluted in water, they are then applied to the soil. Concentrated liquids, which also have to be diluted with water, are good fertilizers, but require spray equipment.

There are nitrogen-releasing fertilizers you can use. Quick-releasing nitrogen materials—ammonium sulfate, ammonium nitrate, urea, nitrate of soda, ammonium phosphate, calcium nitrate—are water-soluble. However, frequent light applications are necessary for uniform growth over a long period of time.

Slow-releasing available nitrogen materials fall into two groups: organic matter (sewerage sludge, animal and vegetable tankage, manures, cottonseed meal) and ureaform compounds (synthetic materials made by the chemical union of urea and formaldehyde).

WATERING

You *must* water the soil thoroughly to saturate the roots. And to water completely you will have to use mechanical watering devices. Hand watering isn't sufficient because water does not reach the roots for at least three hours—plant roots are deep and numerous. Also, sporadic waterings, no matter how long, are not enough. You have to water plants *regularly,* especially in the spring and summer, the growing seasons.

You can use the expensive automatic watering systems, the ultimate in ease and accuracy, but if you cannot or do not want to spend the money they entail, use good sprinklers. The Rain Bird waterer throws a 360-degree arc of water, but cheaper and just as good are sprinklers you set at different angles. Until you find the right location for your sprinklers you will have to keep moving them and experimenting. You most likely will need more than one unless you have a very small, single garden or you are prepared to move one sprinkler around every few hours.

When and How Much to Water

You can water any time of the day except in the late evening because then the soil will stay wet and invite fungus if the temperature falls. Rain will simplify a part of your watering schedule, but annuals, perennials, and vegetables especially need water every day during June, July, and August, particularly if summer rains are less than usual. Try not to skip days; if you do, your vegetable yield and flower blooms may suffer.

MULCHING

Mulching is the spreading of organic matter between and around plants to cover the soil. Mulching serves three useful functions: (1) it decreases the amount of moisture lost from the soil surface and keeps the soil cool; (2) it helps to minimize the harmful effects of thawing and freezing; and (3) it helps control weed development.

Apply mulches in the fall only after the ground has frozen and then thawed, or growth will stop because the soil will be cool. Or mulch in the spring, after the soil has warmed and growth has started.

The best mulches are composed of leaves, hay, straw, grass cuttings, sawdust, wood chips, and ground fir bark. Hay and straw are good because they decompose slowly and are weed-free. Grass cuttings should be mixed with wood chips to prevent matting. Mix sawdust and wood chips with peat.

CLIMATE

Climate affects your watering and feeding schedules. The sun's heat determines how much food plants can take in and how much water is needed. If the weather is hot and sunny, your plants will need more water. Study the weather in your area, but remember that there can be climatic differences even three or four miles away. Know *your* weather, not your friend's. Also study Department of Agriculture sunlight charts and rainfall maps for your area to see the moisture pattern and the sunlight percentages (available for a minimum charge from the United States Department of Agriculture, Washington, D.C.).

CULTURE

If you overwater or overfeed plants, or if your garden is too shady or too windy, your plants will let you know. Withering growth or brown or crisp edges on leaves indicate that plants are getting too much heat and that temperatures are fluctuating. Leaves can turn yellow if the soil lacks acidity, though some leaves naturally turn yellow and drop off. Brown or silvery streaks on leaves are a symptom of too much sun. Lifeless leaves lack water. Plants not blooming usually need more sun. And your plant is in too much shade and getting too much moisture if the stems turn soft and the leaves wilt.

INSECTS

If you do not meticulously follow proper culture rules, and if you are not alert to scouting parties of insects, bugs will infest your garden. Not all insects will harm your plants; for example, grasshoppers maintain the balance of nature, the larvae of the lacewing fly eat plant lice, ladybugs thrive on aphids, and tachina flies devour cutworms and caterpillars. But sucking and chewing insects, like aphids and scale, will pierce plant tissue and eat parts of the plant. And minute, hard-to-see insects like mites and root lice will devastate a garden. Insects love to lurk in debris. Clean and spray plants frequently with water to wash off larvae, and get rid of any refuse in the garden area. Watch for insects, and if you cannot identify the bad bugs, check with your local agricultural station for advice on what bugs you have. And be sure you welcome and encourage the good insects.

If good cultural rules and biological control do not work, apply contact poisons or insecticides. Ask your local nurseryman about insecticides, whether they are inorganic, botanical, or synthetic. Pyrethrum and rotenone, botanical preventatives derived from plants, are coming back into use. The synthetic chemicals include chlorinated hydrocarbons, carbonates, and organophosphates. Chlordane, lindane, and aldrin are hydrocarbon-type insecticides that should not be used because they are highly poisonous.

Read all instructions carefully before applying chemicals, and always use less than is recommended rather than more. Handle poisons with care. Keep them out of reach of children and pets. Repeated applications may be necessary.

DISEASES

Many destructive plant diseases are caused by bacteria, fungi, and viruses. Diseases are generally named for their dominant symptoms—blight, canker, leaf spot—or for the organism that causes the disease, such as rust and powdery mildew. Many times unfavorable conditions and poor cultural practices open the way for these agents to cause trouble. A poorly grown plant, like a human being in poor health, is more susceptible to bacteria and virus. Insects, too, spread diseases from one plant to another.

Moisture and temperature also play a part in the development of bacterial and fungal attacks. Moisture is necessary for the germination of the spores of the disease organisms and excessive moisture in the soil can lead to root rot. Plants in shade are more apt to develop disease than those in light.

PLANT HARDINESS

A hardy plant survives without injury the general climatic extremes of a given area. In our garden plan plant description lists I have indicated in degrees the minimal night temperatures for most plants. This way, you can determine at a glance whether the plant will survive in your area.

There is also a universal reference guide, called "the hardiness zone map," available from the Department of Agriculture in Washington, D.C. Based on minimal night temperatures determined by local weather stations, this map separates areas of the United States into temperature zones.

Hardiness of plants does influence your choice of plants but there are always exceptions. Some plants that are not supposed to survive in a particular area do very well, so there is some room for experimentation. Generally a difference of a few degrees one way or another won't make that much difference.

CONTAINER plants (see page 79) require special conditions if they are to grow well on your patio or terrace. For example, a good soil is important for all plants, but even more so for plants in containers. Here are some basic soil mixes I use:

For most plants
2 parts garden loam   1 part leaf mold
1 part sand   1 teaspoon bone meal for each 8-inch pot

For begonias and ferns
2 parts garden loam   2 parts leaf mold
2 parts sand

For bulbs
2 parts garden loam   1 part leaf mold
1 part sand

For cacti and succulents
2 parts garden loam   1 part leaf mold
2 parts sand   Handful of limestone

For successful potting, be sure the soil of the plant has been previously moistened so the root ball will come out intact. Put enough drainage material (broken pot pieces or crushed stones) in the bottom of the container so that excess water will drain off freely. Spread a layer of soil over the bottom of the tub. The bedding should be about three inches deep for a 16-inch container. Remove the plant from its nursery container and center it on the bed of soil. Put soil in and around the roots, pressing down with your fingers to eliminate any air pockets. Add more soil until the tub is filled to a few inches below the rim. Water thoroughly and place the plant in a partially shaded area for a few days; then move it to its permanent place.

Container plants exposed to the elements dry out more quickly than plants in the ground. And watering plants in containers depends on many conditions: the amount of rainfall, the size of the container (large ones dry out more slowly than small ones), and the material of the container (glazed urns and jugs without drainage holes need careful watering to avoid a stagnant soil; wooden tubs, boxes, and planters dry out slowly; and metal containers stay wet for days).

When you water plants, be sure the stream of water is not so strong that it washes away the soil. And *soak* the soil. Sparse watering results in pockets of soil becoming wet and eventually waterlogged. Water should run out of the drainage holes. A good rule to follow is to water soil thoroughly and then allow it to dry out before watering again.

Use a commercial soluble 10–10–5 fertilizer mixed weaker than the directions on the bottle indicate, but use it more often. Generally feed plants in large containers (18 to 26 inches in diameter) about once a week in the summer, and plants in smaller containers about once a month. Decrease feedings in the winter.

Five / The Plants

THE plants in our gardens are of many types, from water lilies to strawberries. There are almost one thousand plants from many plant groups. Not all plants grow the same way or have the same requirements, which is why it is important to become familiar with the various plant families—you must know how to grow what you select.

None of the following cultural requirements are really stringent, and none are impossible to master. Raising your plants successfully is just a matter of knowing the basic rules of care and then applying them. Even if you follow only half the directions, you should be able to grow the plants recommended in this book; if you are a perfectionist, all of them will grow spectacularly.

ANNUALS AND PERENNIALS

Annuals and perennials are the flowers of your gardens. Annuals produce flowers, mature, and then die within a year. Perennials bear flowers, die down in the winter, and then bloom again in the spring. Between these two groups are biennials, which bloom for two years.

Annuals are inexpensive and very colorful. They need only watering, good sun, and occasional feeding to bear abundant flowers. Annuals are not fussy about soil, as long as the soil contains some fertilizer.

Annuals, such as nasturtiums, are self-sowing, but some plants grown as annuals in severe winter climates are really frost-free, tender perennials. Wax begonias and coleus are in this group. Start annual seeds indoors for outdoor growing later, or start them outdoors directly in the ground once the weather and soil are warm. An easier method is to plant prestarted annuals in the garden. (Available from nurseries at seasonal times.)

Perennials need good soil, water, and sunlight. Add a complete plant food, like 10-5-5, every other watering to keep the plants in good health. Remember that some perennials bloom in spring, others bloom in summer, and still others bloom in fall. Also, perennials have to be started more carefully than the annuals. Be sure the soil beds are at least 18 inches deep, and add fresh topsoil every year. Perennials need no care in winter because that is when they rest. Start perennial seeds indoors, or plant prestarts outdoors.

The specific garden plans have descriptions and more care data for annuals and perennials.

BULBS

Bulbs (also called corms or tubers) are underground storehouses of energy. Many of the most beautiful spring-flowering bulbs, such as tulips and daffodils, need cold weather to multiply and so can be left in the ground year after year. Summer-flowering bulbs such as dahlias, most iris, and lilies can also be left in the ground from year to year.

Gladioli, tuberous begonias, caladiums, and cannas, must be dug up in the late fall and stored over the winter in most regions. They can be left in the ground only if temperatures do not drop below freezing. When foliage dies down in late summer or fall, dig up the bulbs and let them dry in an airy place. If bulbs have foliage, cut it back to about 5 inches. Remove all dirt from the bulbs, and store them in a dry cool place (50°F) in brown bags or boxes of sand.

Bulbs need a moisture-retaining but fast-draining soil of highly organic matter. They do not do well in clay soil, and few prosper in sandy soil.

Planting holes for bulbs must have concave bottoms so that air pockets form beneath the bulbs.

It is always confusing to know which end of the bulb goes into the ground first. Plant with the growing side up; in most instances this is the pointed end of the bulb or the end showing some growth. Plant the bulb to a 3-inch depth: that is, the top of the bulb, not the bottom, should be 3 inches below ground level. Firm the soil over the bulb; do not leave it loose.

Buy bulbs from reputable dealers; you are buying "unseen produce," so that you must rely on the reputation of the supplier. Only healthy bulbs will produce the flowers you want—bulbs that have laid around too long or have been bruised or injured rarely make successful plants.

Most bulbs can live off their own supply of food for some time, but once they are growing they need good watering and plant food every other watering. When flowers fade and foliage starts withering, decrease watering and then let the bulbs dry out somewhat, but never completely.

Specific descriptions and more care data are given in the garden plans.

WATER PLANTS

There are two types of water plants: those that cannot grow when submerged in water and those that can. The first type includes elephant ears, Egyptian paper plant, horsetail, plantain lily, and golden bamboo. Water plants that can grow when submerged in water include water hyacinth, water violet, water poppy, and the exotic water lotus.

The beautiful water lily is the most commonly used water plant. It comes in an enormous number of varieties: some tropical species have large flowers, up to 12 inches across; others bloom at night; many water lilies are fragrant; and some plants carry their blooms above the surface of the water.

The hardy water lilies bloom during the day and the flowers last about three days. At the first frost, these lilies die back and spend the winter safely under ice, if the pool bed is at least 30 inches deep.

In addition to requiring this depth, water lilies need ample sun, rich soil and, especially for the tropicals, plenty of fertilizer. Plants should not be grown directly in the bottom of the pool but should be set in 10-inch boxes, anchored to the bottom with wire or bricks. Do not use redwood boxes because the wood has harmful chemicals that could kill plants. Set the plants in equal amounts of soil and fertilizer. Do not use sand.

Suppliers carry hardy water lilies in mid-April as either a piece of rootstock with leaves and perhaps a few buds or just a section of rootstock. Tropicals are carried later, in June. Plant tropicals when the water temperature is above 70°F. Plant both kinds of lilies as soon as you get them; leaving them unplanted can be injurious.

VEGETABLES

Home-grown vegetables have delicious flavor and save you money. The secret to growing vegetables is to get them into the ground, and keep them growing, rapidly. This means plenty of water, good rich soil, and at least four hours of sun daily.

Warm-season vegetables like tomatoes and squash need warm weather to be at their best. Vegetables like peas and spinach need coolness to thrive. Thus, plant the warm-season vegetables in the spring so they will mature in the heat of summer, and start cool-season vegetables in the summer so they will mature in the coolness of the early fall.

Grow some beets, carrots, radishes, salad greens, spinach, and peas; perhaps squash and cucumbers if you have the space. There are hundreds of varieties of vegetables, some more flavorful than others. Your nurseryman will be able to tell you which varieties are best suited to your specific climate.

Generally, planting in rows will make weeding and harvesting easier, but if space is a problem, plant in a terrace-type design (see page 201). Keep weeds out of the vegetable garden, and harvest produce when it is young and tender. Insects love vegetables, so use the old-fashioned methods of control or, if absolutely necessary, the chemical means described in Chapter 4.

FRUIT TREES

If you do not grow a few fruit trees in your garden, you will be missing good eating and attractive foliage. Fruit trees are little trouble once they are established: they need only ample water, supplemental feeding, an occasional pruning, spraying with a dormant oil twice a year, and a watchful eye for insects.

Incorporate fruit trees into a standard garden plan, or consider a special fruit tree orchard, which can be grown in a small area if you use some of the many dwarf varieties. If you hesitate to grow them because it takes time for them to bear fruit, remember that some varieties now produce fruit five years from planting. This is hardly a long time, considering that once these trees produce, they bear fruit every year. Consult a reliable local nurseryman for the best information on what trees suit your specific climate.

GROUND COVERS

Ground covers are inexpensive; need little maintenance (just water and regular feeding); can decorate areas where you cannot have a lawn, such as hills or ravines; bind sandy soil; check erosion; cover unsightly areas; and will, depending on the plant, grow in shade or tolerate full sun and drought.

Obviously ground covers are tough plants, but there are some things to watch for. Shrubby ground covers can grow too high, in which case you just cut away the rampant growth. Many ground covers become a solid bed and will not tolerate foot traffic. Flat-growing ground covers do take some foot traffic, but you should put in stepping stones for heavy traffic.

Evergreen ground covers are attractive in summer and winter. There are many species for mild climates and even for regions with severe winters there are several handsome varieties.

Ground covers are sold in flats of eighty or one hundred plants. Start plants in the spring in cold-weather areas; start them in the spring or fall where winters are moderate. Plant ground covers in a rich soil. Space plants however you want, but note that the closer they are the quicker they will cover an area.

VINES

Vines are decorative and functional and most of them grow quickly. Dutchman's-pipe, clematis, and ivy are excellent for color, but more important perhaps, they cover mistakes. Any garden plan that lacks a feeling of lushness or a finished appearance can profit from vines. Use them to cover bare fences, disguise ugly walls, and to provide attractive foliage to "blank spots."

Some people are afraid to use vines because they need walls or fences or trellises for support. Trellises and even fences are relatively easy to make. Consult a home carpentry book for detail or speak to a reliable local lumberyard.

Vines need periodic thinning and retying to their supports to look their best but they are not difficult to maintain once they are established. Plant in a rich loamy soil and feed well during their growth period in the spring and summer. You *must* plant vines in deep (24-inch) holes; fill in and around plants with topsoil.

HERBS

Herbs add zest to food, can be used in teas, impart a nice fragrance when used in sachets or by themselves, and are attractive in the garden.

Herbs will grow in ordinary conditions in little space. Plant small prestarted herbs, or start herbs from seed. Use a quick-draining sandy soil, and give plants at least three hours of sun a day. Keep the soil moist. Prune plants occasionally.

Cut herbs just as the flowers are about to open, as this is when the essential oils are the most plentiful. To save the herbs for future use, cure and store them. Wash the leaves or stems in cold water, and then dry them thoroughly by spreading leaves over a wire mesh in a warm place. Or put them on a baking sheet in a 200° oven with the door open. When they are dry, strip the leaves from the stems and put them in airtight containers. Do not overdry the leaves; they should barely reach the crumbling stage. A nice old-fashioned way to dry herbs is to tie stems in bunches and hang them from the ceiling in an attic or other dark place until it is time to use them.

TREES AND SHRUBS

Trees and shrubs are essential parts of most gardens. Trees act as the vertical accent around which the garden is built. Wherever possible, work with existing trees or else plant those suited to your climate. In our garden plans, trees are specified only when they are an integral part of the plan. Do not, of course, cut trees down simply to "fit" a plan. If you need to buy trees, the nurseryman in your area can direct you to those best suited to your region.

Shrubs are the backbone of many gardens, and some flowering shrubs are gardens in themselves. The deciduous shrubs give real splashes of color in their season, and the evergreens provide year-round beauty. Generally, once shrubs are in place and started, they take care of themselves except for an occasional pruning.

The evergreen shrubs provide color all year: they are invaluable as entrance plantings and as background plants.

Evergreen shrubs are usually sold in containers or balled and burlapped. Deciduous varieties are sold bare root in their dormant season and planted in early spring, or they are sold, more expensively, in containers. Buy young shrubs and plant them with ample spacing because most shrubs grow quickly and fill out.

Use wide and deep planting holes for shrubs: spread out the roots when you put plants in the ground. Break up the soil in the bottom of the hole, and add fresh topsoil to it. A common mistake many people make in shrub planting is to bury the crown of the plant too low in soil. Set the bushes so the soil level is almost the same as it was when you bought the plant at the nursery.

Balled and burlapped shrubs are planted with the burlap on. Cut the strings and cover the roots and burlap with soil; eventually the burlap decays and becomes part of the soil.

WILDFLOWERS

Wildflowers have an informal charm and subtle beauty. Though getting them established requires time and patience, once they are growing wildflowers will bloom year after year.

Select an area about 10-by-20 feet with some natural rocks, or a stream or a niche to act as background. A shady place with deciduous trees to provide filtered light and protection from summer sun is best.

Clear the area and condition the old soil by digging it up and mixing it with rich humus, plenty of leaf mold and composted leaves. A slightly acid soil is preferable.

Be sure there is adequate drainage. If this isn't the case, install a layer of gravel under the soil or raise the surface of the wildflower garden somewhat by filling with soil so water drains freely.

As we have said, once established wildflowers will take care of themselves. You will not have to weed, fertilize or mulch them.

Wildflowers are protected by law in most states so don't dig them up for transplanting. Buy them from suppliers. Put the roots in deep holes in the ground the same day you get them; keep the soil moist and mulched with leaves until the plants become established.

STANDARDS OR TOPIARY

Standards are plants with one crown on a single stem trained to tree form. Many plants can be trained as standards but roses, fuschias, wisterias, and geraniums are most often used. The tree shape can assume many patterns, but the most popular is a single ball. Other patterns include double ball, pyramid, poodle trim, and so on. The idea is the same no matter which shape is selected: to create a neat, sculptural effect. Standards in the garden provide elegance and formality.

Most people buy standards already trained; but you can buy plants and, with time and patience, train them yourself. Early spring is the best time to start. Select a young plant with strong top growth and remove all side shoots as they form. Stake the plant when it is about 8 to 10 inches tall. When the trunk reaches the height you want, remove the main growing tips at the top so the branches can form. In a few months pinch out the branch tips to start shaping the top of the standard.

You can buy wire forms for standards at nurseries. These forms include the basic cone, ball, or pyramid shapes. Wire the forms to the tree and then train the stems of the plants to the forms. Tie the stems with tie-ons or string, and keep clipping and trimming the plant to the desired shape.

ESPALIER

The art of espalier—growing plants flat against a wall or fence—contributes in many ways to a distinctive garden. It saves space and, when well done, it is dramatic.

If possible, buy an espalier partially started. It is much easier to train such a tree or shrub than to initiate one yourself. Espaliers take time, but once established they require only occasional trimming.

You can train almost any shrub or small tree to espalier patterns, but when espalier was at its most popular fruit trees were generally used. The patterns for espalier work vary and include candelabra, vertical U- and horizontal T-shapes, and connecting arches.

Six / 100 Garden Plans

A GARDEN plan is a pattern for a harmonious, eye-pleasing arrangement. It shows how to use the available space to its best advantage to enhance the appearance of your home. Coincidentally this adds value to the property. Houses with barren grounds rarely sell. The garden plan relies on a pleasing composition of proportion, scale, unity, and balance—it incorporates vertical and horizontal design elements and mass and space.

ELEMENTS OF DESIGN

Plants should be in the right proportion, with a definite rhythm and balance. To achieve proportion you should consider the shapes and sizes of your plants as well as how the garden will look in relation to the house. For example, how will a dogwood, with its horizontal lines, look with spreading ivy or vertical hollyhocks? A large house looks incongruous with too small a garden, as does a small house with an elaborate court and garden. A large paved terrace and a small garden can be in proportion, but to make both areas the same size probably would prevent the areas from complementing each other. In addition to proportion, consider rhythm—repeating the same groups of plants—and balance—plants of similar size and form—to create a unified whole of form, color, and textures.

OUR GARDEN PLANS

The following 100 plans include garden layouts in alphabetical order for porches, patios, balconies, decks, flower gardens, vegetable or berry gardens, and so forth. The plans are designed to utilize the maximum space to the best advantage. All plans are a combination of color, form, function, and design to please the eye and to suit particular needs.

We have not specified actual footage or dimensions because most of these plans can be adapted to areas of various sizes. If your area is small, reduce the number of plants; if your area is larger, plant more of what is suggested.

The plans can be used for both new and old gardens. As we have discussed, in most cases we have not designated trees, assuming that they will already be in background areas. We have concentrated on small- to medium-sized easily assembled gardens, stressing flowers, bulbs, shrubs, and vines.

The plants specified have certain forms or colors that are necessary to create a harmonious garden plan. Wild, hybridized, and variety plants have been used. A species name is designated in italics, such as *Cornus florida;* a variety name is shown in single quotes, such as *C. florida* 'Rainbow,' a man-made hybrid known for its spectacular coloring.

Wherever it was possible to ascertain we have included the species name along with the variety. However, most plant suppliers usually list only the variety name.

If you cannot get the specific plant designated in the plans from your suppliers, use a plant of similar color or form. New varieties appear frequently, and it is not difficult to find a plant similar in color and shape.

The plans are arranged with a perspective drawing above, to show the garden as it would look, and a plan drawing below to help you visualize the space. Drawings of each plant appear on the accompanying page so you will know exactly what the plant looks like.

The text describes the height, color, and season of bloom of the plants, as well as miscellaneous notes on the gardens themselves. About one thousand plants are detailed.

To see how an overall color scheme of a plan looks, place a piece of tracing paper on the black-and-white garden plan. Make outlines of the plant forms. Now check the flower color in the plant descriptions and with colored pencils color in the plant groups. This will give you a color rendition of each garden plan.

NOTES ON PLANT DESCRIPTIONS

The descriptions show the technical name and/or the name under which the plant appears in most garden catalogs, and the common name of plants (if they have one). The descriptions also tell whether the flowers are annual or perennial and the time of year they bloom. For trees and shrubs we have shown the minimum temperature at which they will grow well.

100 GARDEN PLANS

(Alphabetical)

1 / Annual Garden

As a "spot" garden with vibrant color, this yellow and white garden is simple but handsome. Its basic plan is a cross with islands of flowers. Zinnias are used as a focal point of color. Note the repeated island design, which can be used in any small area to turn a barren spot into an attractive one.

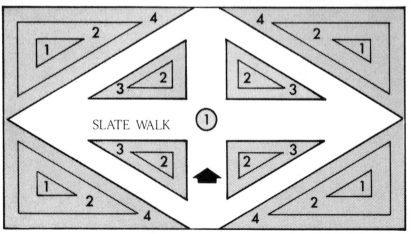

SLATE WALK

32

1. **_Zinnia_ 'Snow Time'**
   Annual
   Summer
   To 16 inches; cactus form;
   flowers large and white. Good
   cut flowers.

2. **_Tagetes_ 'Diamond Jubilee'**
   Marigold
   Annual
   Summer/Fall
   To 24 inches; flowers large
   and yellow. The Jubilee group
   are almost spherical.

3. **_Lobularia_**
   'Carpet of Snow'
   Sweet Alyssum
   Annual
   Summer
   To 6 inches; low growing;
   flowers fragrant, tiny and
   white, in mounds. Bloom
   prolifically.

4. **_Begonia_ 'Viva'**
   Wax Begonia
   Annual
   Summer
   To 8 inches; leaves glossy
   green; flowers white, in
   masses. Use leaf mold in soil.
   Provide good drainage and
   water frequently.

1. Zinnia 'Snow Time'

2. Tagetes 'Diamond Jubilee'

3. Lobularia 'Carpet of Snow'

4. Begonia 'Viva'

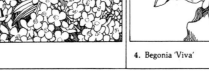

33

2 / Atrium Garden

This garden enclosed within a house is open to the sky. The large slab stepping stones are handsome and provide an easy walk-through. A small pool further complements the plan.

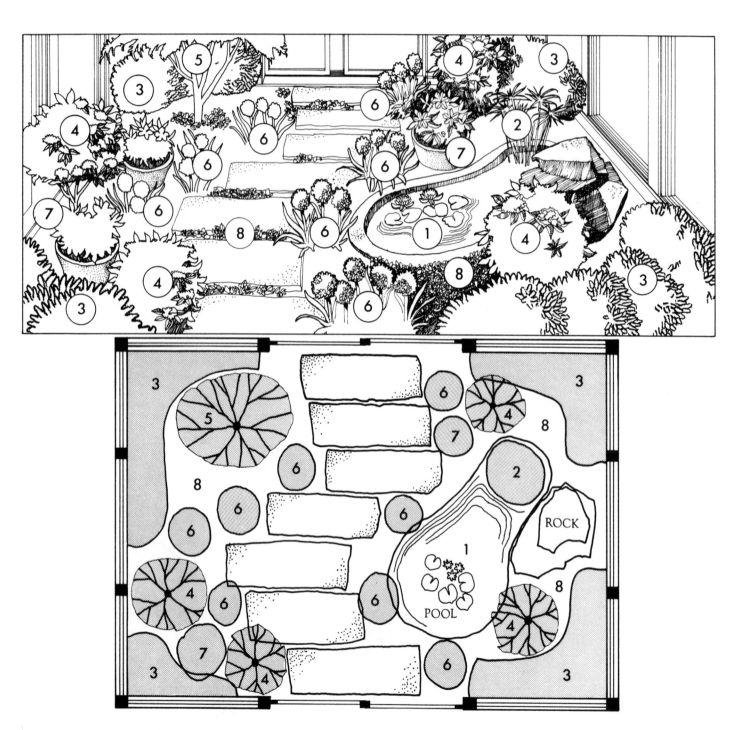

1. *Nymphaea 'Rose Arey'*
    Water lily
    Perennial
    Summer
    Leaves 3 to 5 inches wide, flowers large, pink-white. Highly recommended for small pools.

2. *Cyperus alternifolius*
    Umbrella Plant
    Perennial
    Summer
    To 48 inches; flower clusters above long leaves give umbrellalike appearance. Needs wet location.

3. *Picea abies 'Repens'*
    Norway Spruce
    Tree/Evergreen
    Hardy to −35F
    Low tree to 30 feet, with arching branches; leaves needle-like, with drooping papery cones. Tends to lose lower branches, but extremely hardy.

4. *Azalea 'Helen Curtis'*
    Shrub/Deciduous
    Hardy to −35F
    If this variety is difficult to find in your area, use an evergreen double white.

5. *Acer palmatum*
    'Burgundy Lace'
    Tree/Deciduous
    Hardy to −10F
    To 20 feet; beautiful red cut leaves. Needs good soil, proper light, no direct sun, and even moisture.

6. *Armeria maritima*
    laucheana
    Thrift
    Perennial
    Spring/Summer
    To 6 inches; narrow leaves grow to 6 inches long; rose flowers in hemispherical heads. Does best in light sandy soil with minimal feeding.

7. *Browallia 'Blue Bells'*
    Annual
    Fall/Winter
    To 8 inches; leaves small and oblong; flowers blue. Grows in most soils, needs even moisture.

8. *Ajuga genevensis*
    Geneva Bugle
    Ground Cover/Evergreen
    Hardy to −35F
    To 8 inches; toothed, oblong leaves; blue flowers in whorls on spikes. Grows well in almost any soil, in sun or partial shade.

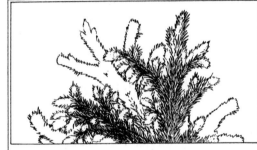

1. Nymphaea 'Rose Arey'

2. Cyperus alternifolius

3. Picea abies 'Repens'

4. Azalea 'Helen Curtis'

5. Acer palmatum 'Burgundy Lace'

6. Armeria maritima laucheana

7. Browallia 'Blue Bells'

8. Ajuga genevensis

3 / Backporch Garden

With the use of a wood ramp and trellises this porch has been transformed into a lovely housing for a garden. Wooden boxes and planters are custom-made to accommodate plants, but you can also make them yourself with the help of a good home carpentry book and your local lumberyard. The garden relies heavily on climbing roses, with color throughout the warm months. Containers of dwarf red dahlias are used as spot accents.

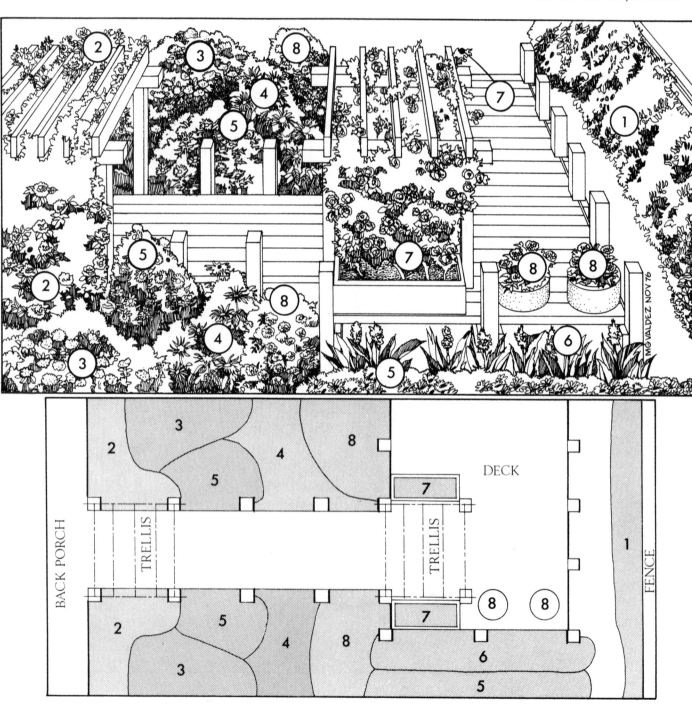

1. *Lonicera sempervirens*
   'Magnifica'
   Trumpet Honeysuckle
   Vine/Semievergreen
   Perennial
   Hardy to —35F
   Summer
   To 20 feet; leaves oblong; flowers orange-red with yellow interior; fruit red. Vigorous; needs little care.

2. *Rosa* **'White Dawn'**
   Shrub/Deciduous
   Hardy to —10F
   Climbs to 96 feet; everblooming white rose with fragrant double flowers. Long season of bloom.

3. *Viburnum carlcephalum*
   Snowball Bush
   Shrub/Deciduous
   Hardy to —10F
   To 72 inches; leaves broad and ribbed; flowers white in large globe-shaped clusters. Tolerates poor soils; rarely attacked by insects.

4. *Monarda didyma*
   Beebalm
   Perennial
   Summer/Fall
   To 24 inches; leaves oblong; flowers fragrant and bright red. Easily grown.

5. *Chrysanthemum*
   'Thomas Killin'
   Shasta Daisy
   Perennial
   Summer/Fall
   To 24 inches; leaves narrow and toothed; flowers white. Does well in Pacific and Eastern regions. Dislikes hot and dry climate.

6. *Canna*
   'Pfitzer's Cherry Red'
   Bulb/Hardy
   Summer
   To 28 inches; leaves large, arising from base of stem, flowers large, red, prolific and bright.

7. *Rosa* **'Blaze'**
   Shrub/Deciduous
   Hardy to 10F
   Climbs to 10 feet; leaves dark; many red flowers. Very popular and dependable.

8. *Dahlia* **'Fred Springer'**
   Bulb/Hardy
   Summer
   To 16 inches; leaves oval and toothed; flowers brightly colored, double, semidouble, or single. Dwarf type.

1. Lonicera sempervirens 'Magnifica'

2. Rosa 'White Dawn'

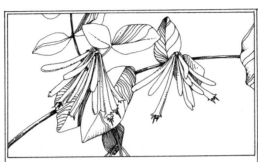

3. Viburnum carlcephalum

4. Monarda didyma

5. Chrysanthemum 'Thomas Killin'

6. Canna 'Pfitzer's Cherry Red'

7. Rosa 'Blaze'

8. Dahlia 'Fred Springer'

4 / Balcony Garden

This small balcony garden has a pair of planter boxes with coneflowers at front, and a long bin in rear brimming with fire-orange flowers. Tubs of plants are used to balance the scene. There is a fine blend of mass, scale, and proportion to create a visual treat. (For apartment, condominium or any small balcony.)

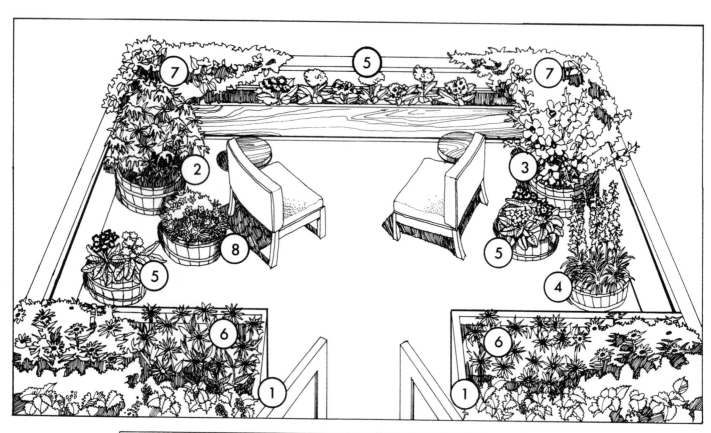

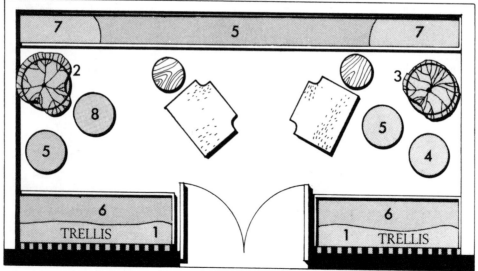

TRELLIS

TRELLIS

1. *Ampelopsis*
    brevipedunculata
    Boston Ivy
    Porcelian Ampelopsis
    Vine/Deciduous
    Perennial
    Hardy to −10F
Climbs to 40 feet; leaves ivy-shaped; small flowers; blue berries. Vigorous. Needs well-drained soil.

2. *Pieris japonica*
    Japanese Andromeda
    Shrub/Evergreen
    Hardy to −20F
To 84 inches; leaves toothed; flowers quite small. Related to rhododendron. Requires acid soil, excellent drainage.

3. *Althaea* 'Blue Bird'
    Hollyhock
    Biennial
    Summer
To 48 inches; leaves toothed and lobed; flowers large, flat and blue. Grows in almost any soil, likes sun.

4. *Lobelia cardinalis*
    Cardinal Flower
    Perennial
    Summer/Fall
To 24 inches; leaves narrow; flowers bright red in spikes. Likes moisture; mulch plants in winter.

5. **Polyanthus (Pacific Giant type)**
    Primula
    Annual
    Summer
To 18 inches; leaves green and oblong; flowers in many colors. Plant early in loamy soil. Water often; easily grown.

6. **Echinacea 'The King'**
    Coneflower
    Perennial
    Summer
To 48 inches; narrow leaves grow to 8 inches long; flowers lavender and conical. Likes sun and sandy soils; tolerates wind.

7. *Campsis tagliabuana*
    'Mme Galen'
    Clinging Vine
    Vine/Semievergreen
    Perennial
    Hardy to −10F
    Summer/Fall
To 30 feet; leaves green and small; flowers fiery red-orange and trumpet-shaped. Also called Bignonia. Must have sun.

8. *Lithospermum diffusa*
    'Heavenly Blue'
    Gromwell
    Shrub/Evergreen
    Hardy to −10F
To 10 inches; leaves narrow; flowers blue. Likes clayey, somewhat acid soil. Sometimes listed as *Lithodora diffusa.*

1. Ampelopsis brevipedunculata

2. Pieris japonica

3. Althaea 'Blue Bird'

4. Lobelia cardinalis

5. Polyanthus (Pacific Giant type)

6. Echinacea 'The King'

7. Campsis tagliabuana 'Mme Galen'

8. Lithospermum diffusa 'Heavenly Blue'

5 / Bath Garden (walled; spring)

A garden off the bathroom is lovely to look at and makes the bathroom seem larger. Almost any type of shrub can be used for the frame of this garden and the bulbs make a massive color display in spring. This garden is suitable for almost any small area where tile floor can be used.

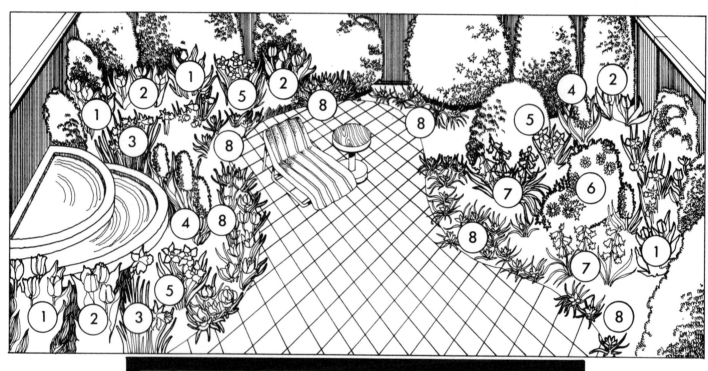

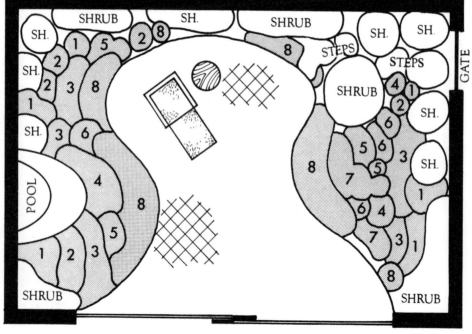

1. **Tulipa 'William Tell'**
Bulb/Hardy
Spring
To 26 inches; long basal leaves; rose-colored flowers on central stem. Darwin type. Plant 5 inches deep.

2. **Tulipa 'Inga Hume'**
Bulb/Hardy
Spring
To 24 inches; long basal leaves; flowers yellow inside, pink with white edges outside. Plant 5 inches deep.

3. **Narcissus 'Louise de Coligny'**
Bulb/Hardy
Spring
To 24 inches; long basal leaves; fragrant flowers with white petals and pink cups. Plant 6 inches deep in soil fertilized with bone meal.

4. **Hyacinthus 'Lady Derby'**
Bulb/Hardy
Spring
To 12 inches; long narrow leaves; pink flowers on central stalk. Plant 3 inches deep.

5. **Narcissus 'White Cheerfulness'**
Bulb/Hardy
Spring
To 24 inches; long basal leaves; flowers fragrant and white with some yellow in cup. Plant 6 inches deep. Good for a bouquet.

6. *Anemone blanda* **Greek Anemone**
Bulb/Hardy
Spring
To 4 inches; leaves deeply cut; bright blue flowers 2 inches wide. Low growing. Plant 2 inches deep. Blooms early.

7. **Scilla 'Rose Beauty'**
Bulb/Hardy
Spring
To 12 inches; leaves narrow and long; bell-shaped pink flowers on central stalk. Plant 4 inches deep.

8. **Crocus 'Striped Beauty'**
Bulb/Hardy
Spring
To 6 inches; narrow basal leaves, blue-striped white flowers on short stalks. Plant 2 inches deep.

1. Tulipa 'William Tell'

2. Tulipa 'Inga Hume'

3. Narcissus 'Louise de Coligny'

4. Hyacinthus 'Lady Derby'

5. Narcissus 'White Cheerfulness'

6. Anemone blanda

7. Scilla 'Rose Beauty'

8. Crocus 'Striped Beauty'

6 / Bath Garden (walled; summer)

A variation of the bath garden showing color through summer to replace spring bulbs. Irish moss has been added between the slate squares and a wall provides privacy. Begonias are used as the edging plants and colorful clematis and daphne for highlights. This garden requires minimum watering.

GREEN IRISH MOSS BETWEEN 6x6 SLATE SQUARES

POOL

GATE

GLASS DOORS TO BATH

1. *Syringa patula*
   Lilac
   Shrub/Deciduous
   Hardy to −10F
   To 10 feet; 4-inch leaves are oval and hairy; lilac flowers in 5-inch spikes. Needs fertile, rather moist soil.

2. *Clematis patens*
   'Nelly Moser'
   Vine/Deciduous
   Perennial
   Hardy to −35F
   Summer
   To 20 feet; dark green oblong leaves; large pink and blue flowers, each petal with a red stripe. Needs alkaline or limestone soil, some shade, morning sun.

3. *Chamaecyparis pisifera*
   'Plumosa Aurea'
   False Cypress
   Tree/Evergreen
   Hardy to −35F
   To 72 feet; leaves scalelike, golden-yellow when young, glossy green when mature. Good color throughout the year. This can be cut and shaped to suit your needs.

4. *Daphne genkwa*
   Lilac Daphne
   Shrub/Deciduous
   Hardy to −10F
   To 36 inches; 2-inch leaves; lilac flowers appear before the leaves; white fruit. Flowers on growth made previous year. Difficult to transplant.

5. **Anemone 'Robustissima'**
   Perennial
   Summer/Fall
   To 36 inches; leaves five-lobed; flowers pink, 2 inches wide. Needs rich sandy soil, some shade. Magnificent cut flowers. Water often, mulch each year.

6. **Ampelopsis 'Lowi'**
   (*Parthenocissus tricuspidata*)
   Boston Ivy
   Vine/Deciduous
   Perennial
   Hardy to −10F
   Climbs to 10 feet; leaves, purplish when young, grow to 1½ inches. Grows in almost any soil.

7. **Delphinium 'Bellamosa'**
   Garland Larkspur
   Perennial
   Summer/Fall
   To 72 inches; leaves small and narrow; flowers blue, with spur. Likes cool weather; needs lots of ground watering and some bone meal. Stake as soon as spikes appear.

8. **Begonia 'Danica'**
   Wax Begonia
   Annual
   Summer/Fall
   To 12 inches; leaves large and broad; flowers red to white, 1 inch wide. Grows in almost any soil. Allow to dry out between waterings. Responds to light feeding.

9. *Sagina subulata*
   Corsican Pearlwort
   Ground Cover/Evergreen
   Hardy to −10F
   Bright green spreading ground cover; forms a mat. Likes moisture and sandy soil.

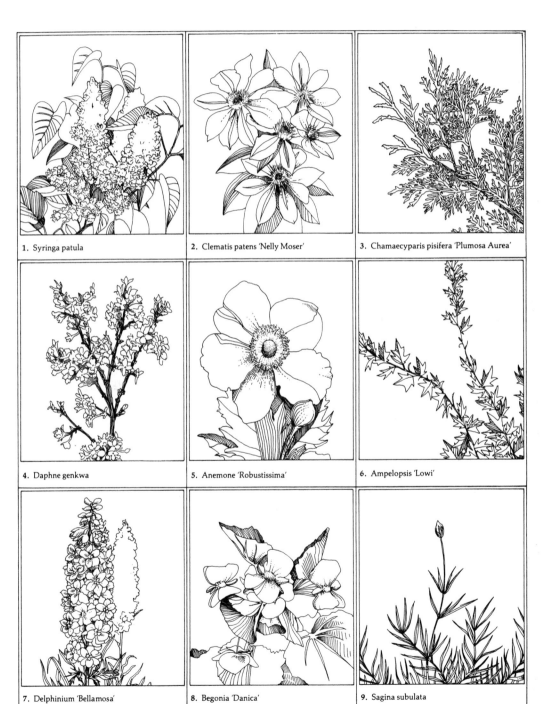

1. Syringa patula

2. Clematis patens 'Nelly Moser'

3. Chamaecyparis pisifera 'Plumosa Aurea'

4. Daphne genkwa

5. Anemone 'Robustissima'

6. Ampelopsis 'Lowi'

7. Delphinium 'Bellamosa'

8. Begonia 'Danica'

9. Sagina subulata

7 / Beginner's Garden

Specially selected for the beginner, these plants, once started, almost take care of themselves. This rather large garden is also convenient because of its cold frame. The raised planters and pathways give it a lovely style.

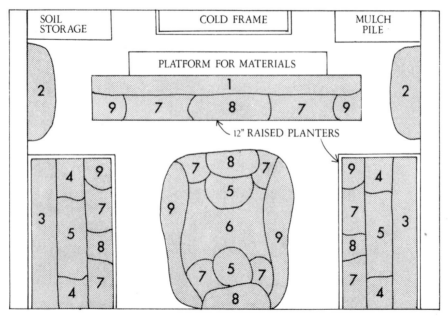

SOIL STORAGE

COLD FRAME

MULCH PILE

PLATFORM FOR MATERIALS

12" RAISED PLANTERS

1. *Ilex crenata* **'Green Lustre'**
    Japanese Holly
    Shrub/Evergreen
    Hardy to −5F
    To 48 inches; dwarf with lustrous dense green foliage. Needs excellent drainage; relatively free of pests.

2. *Forsythia intermedia* **'Spring Glory'**
    Shrub/Deciduous
    Hardy to −10F
    To 72 inches; abundant large yellow flowers. Prune only after blooming.

3. *Pyracantha coccinea* **'Lalandei'**
    Firethorn
    Shrub/Semievergreen
    Hardy to −10F
    To 96 inches; small foliage; white flowers and red berries.

4. *Althaea rosea*
    Hollyhock
    Biennial
    Summer
    To 72 inches; leaves toothed and hairy; abundant yellow, pink or red flowers on tall spikes.

5. **Antirrhinum 'Madame Butterfly'**
    Snapdragon
    Annual
    Summer
    To 40 inches; profuse fire-red or orange double flowers on tall stems.

6. **Cosmos 'Sensation'**
    Annual
    Summer/Fall
    To 48 inches; grassy foliage; bright pink, lavender and red flowers with yellow eye. Spectacular bloom from July until frost. Easy to grow, likes water, good drainage essential.

7. **Aster (Princess type)**
    Annual
    Fall
    To 24 inches; flowers red, purple, lavender, or pink. Old-fashioned favorites with improved stems.

8. **Zinnia 'Peter Pan'**
    Annual
    Fall
    To 12 inches; low massed foliage; red blooms. Lovely cutting flowers.

9. **Portulaca 'Sunkiss'**
    Annual
    Summer/Fall
    To 6 inches; fleshy stems and leaves; dense masses of red, pink, rose, orange, and yellow flowers. Big and showy, hybrids easily grown.

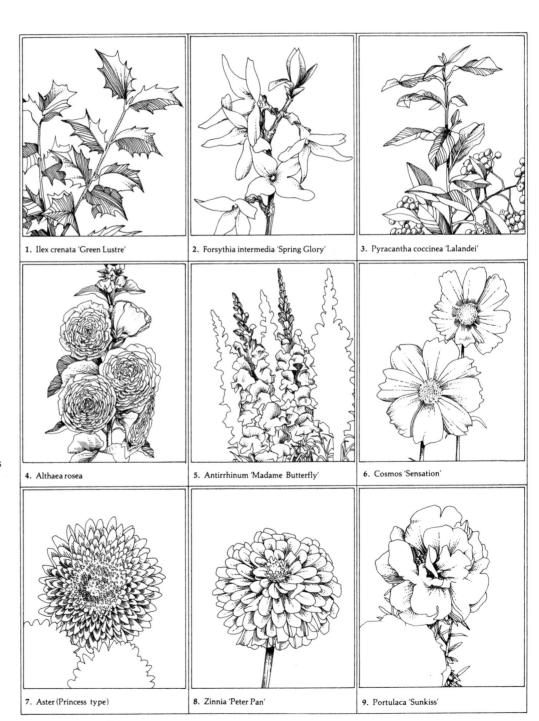

1. Ilex crenata 'Green Lustre'   2. Forsythia intermedia 'Spring Glory'   3. Pyracantha coccinea 'Lalandei'

4. Althaea rosea   5. Antirrhinum 'Madame Butterfly'   6. Cosmos 'Sensation'

7. Aster (Princess type)   8. Zinnia 'Peter Pan'   9. Portulaca 'Sunkiss'

8 / Berry Garden

Tiered circles of corrugated metal and planter boxes are used to house berries. Trellises provide vertical lines to balance the circular design—as well as to make the berries easy to cultivate and harvest. In the center are two tree-type currents. High bushes of blueberries are at each side.

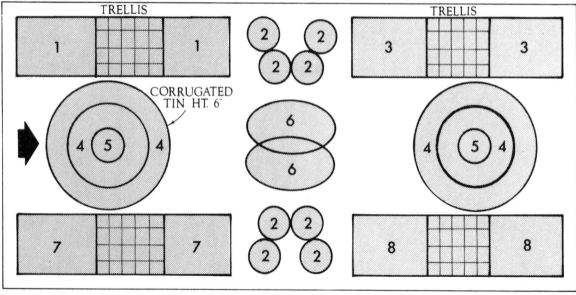

1. **Blackberry 'Darrow'**
 Hardy to −5F
Improved variety, ripens in mid-June, vigorous bushes. Plant two or more different varieties for cross-pollination. Needs acid soil. Rambles; contain in boxes.

2. **Blueberry 'Earliblue'**
 Hardy to −10F
Best for eating; profuse berries. Substitute 'Pemberton' if unavailable. Plant two or more different varieties for cross-pollination. Needs acid soil. Rambles; contain in boxes.

3. **Red Raspberry 'Newburgh'**
 Hardy to −10F
One of the best home varieties. Delicious flavor. Rambles; contain in boxes.

4. **Strawberry 'Premier'**
 Hardy to −10F
Good size and abundant yield. Self-pollinating. Set plants with crowns just above surface of soil. Needs sun.

5. **Strawberry 'Alpine'**
 Hardy to −10F
Good edging plant and excellent producer. Self-pollinating. Set plants with crowns just above surface of soil. Needs sun.

6. **Red Currant 'Red Lake'**
 Hardy to −20F
Grown in bush form; one of best for home use. Heavy feeder. Let soil dry out between waterings. Prune annually in spring for maximum production.

7. **Black Raspberry 'Allen'**
 Hardy to −10F
Reliable and rich producer. Prune when new shoots are 18 inches tall.

8. **Dewberry 'Thornless Gardenia'**
 Hardy to −10F
Sprawling growth. Large, delicious black fruit. Treat same as blackberries. Tolerates drought.

1. Blackberry 'Darrow'

2. Blueberry 'Earliblue'

3. Red Raspberry 'Newburgh'

4. Strawberry 'Premier'

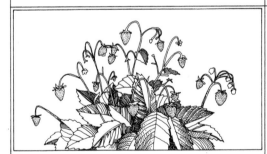
5. Alpine Strawberry 'Alpine'

6. Red Currant 'Red Lake'

7. Black Raspberry 'Allen'

8. Dewberry 'Thornless Gardenia'

9 / Bird Lover's Garden

If it is birds you like, that's what you will get with this interesting plan. Using a lawn as an island for accent, cotoneaster, pyracantha, and viburnum (all splendid with berries in autumn) comprise the main part of the garden. The six-foot-high wire fence surrounding the entire garden is designed to keep out cats, and throughout the garden there are suitable bird baths and feeders.

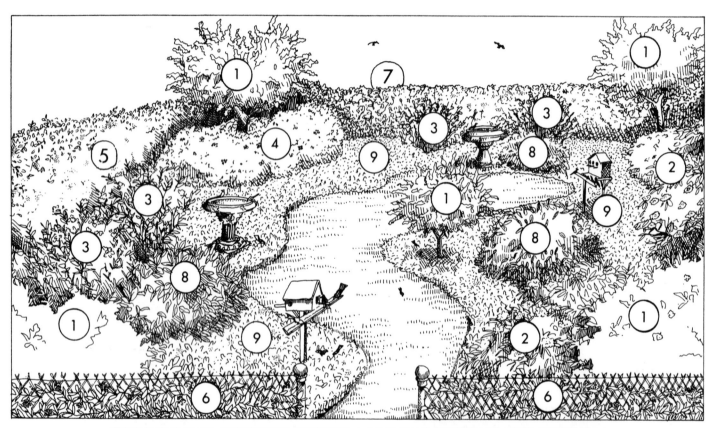

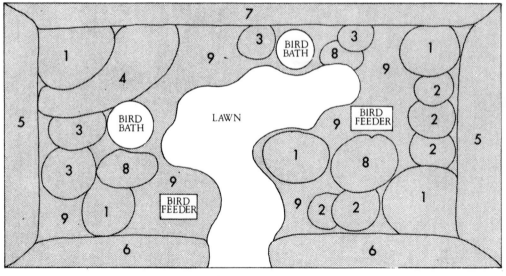

1. *Pyrus calleyrana* **'Bradford'**
   Bradford Pear
   Tree/Deciduous
   Hardy to −25F
   To 30 feet; foliage turns red in winter; lovely white flowers in spring. Thornless and columnar. Keep moist. Birds like the fruit.

2. *Viburnum opulus* **'Compacta'**
   European Cranberry Bush
   Shrub/Deciduous
   Hardy to −35F
   To 48 inches; leaves small and three-lobed; berries red in fall. Tolerant of almost any soil; dependable and rarely bothered by insects.

3. *Aronia arbutifolia* **'Erecta'**
   Red Chokeberry
   Shrub/Deciduous
   Hardy to −20F
   To 10 feet; leaves toothed; flowers white; berries red. Showy bloom, attractive fruit in fall.

4. *Ligustrum obtusifolium regelianum*
   Regal Privet
   Shrub/Evergreen
   Hardy to −35F
   To 72 inches; yellow flowers with blue-black berries. Vigorous and fast growing. Tolerates most soils.

5. *Cotoneaster multiflorus*
   Large-Flowering Cotoneaster
   Shrub/Deciduous
   Hardy to −10F
   To 36 inches; leaves oval and shiny green; flowers white; berries waxy red. Will flourish even under adverse conditions.

6. *Pyracantha coccinea* **'Lalandei'**
   Firethorn
   Shrub/Semievergreen
   Hardy to −10F
   To 92 inches; leaves oblong; flowers white; berries red.

7. *Cotoneaster bullata* **'Firebird'**
   Shrub/Evergreen
   Hardy to −20F
   To 72 inches; leaves oval and shiny green; flowers red. Leaves turn bright red in fall.

8. *Euonymus fortunei*
   Wintercreeper
   Shrub/Evergreen
   Hardy to −10F
   Climbs to 60 inches; leaves simple; orange fruit in fall. Spectacular autumn color. Plants susceptible to scale and must be sprayed.

9. *Pachysandra terminalis*
   Japanese Spurge
   Ground Cover/Evergreen
   Hardy to −10F
   To 12 inches; leaves simple and toothed; flowers white. Likes shade and moisture. One of the most amenable ground covers.

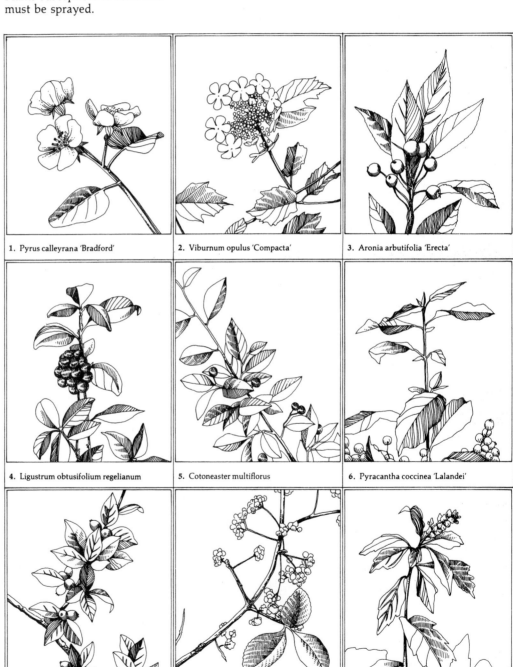

1. Pyrus calleyrana 'Bradford'

2. Viburnum opulus 'Compacta'

3. Aronia arbutifolia 'Erecta'

4. Ligustrum obtusifolium regelianum

5. Cotoneaster multiflorus

6. Pyracantha coccinea 'Lalandei'

7. Cotoneaster bullata 'Firebird'

8. Euonymus fortunei

9. Pachysandra terminalis

49

10 / Bog Garden

Using a simplified border plan with accent trees, this garden is built around a bog or pond. Iris furnish the vertical accent in the foreground with cattail at the rear; other water plants such as skunk cabbage and marsh marigold are used to complement the scene. Water lilies float on the pond and existing trees frame the garden. a simple but distinctive use of a swampy location.

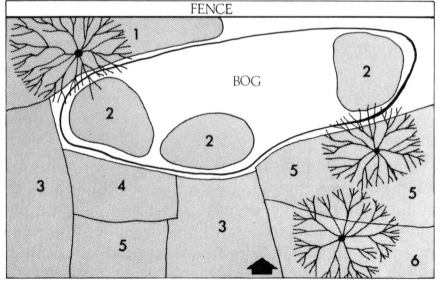

1. *Typha latifolia*
   Cattail
   Perennial
   Summer
   To 48 inches; leaves sword-like; flowers brown. Use flowers for dried arrangements. Likes boggy conditions; grows like a weed.

2. *Nymphaea odorata*
   Fragrant Water Lily
   Perennial
   Summer
   Leaves 4 to 10 inches wide; flowers waxy white with pinkish hue. Many varieties.

3. *Iris versicolor*
   Blue Flag
   Perennial
   Summer
   To 36 inches; leaves grasslike; blue flowers splashed with yellow. Grows easily in wet soils.

4. *Caltha palustris*
   Marsh Marigold
   Perennial
   Spring
   To 30 inches; leaves heart-shaped; flowers bright yellow. Grows easily in wet conditions.

5. *Symplocarpus americanus*
   Skunk Cabbage
   Perennial
   Spring
   To 20 inches; leaves broad; flowers clublike. Good bog plant.

6. *Arisaema triphyllum*
   Jack-in-the-Pulpit
   Perennial
   Spring
   To 16 inches; leaves compound; pulpit-shaped flowers green and purple. Likes rich mucky soil but also grows in drier humusy locations.

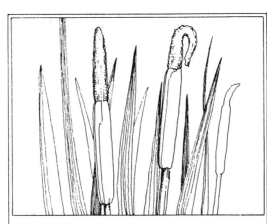
1. Typha latifolia

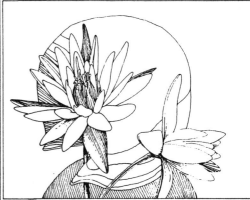
2. Nymphaea odorata

3. Iris versicolor

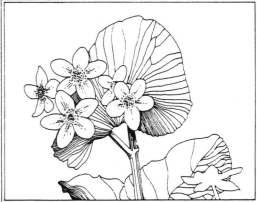
4. Caltha palustris

5. Symplocarpus americanus

6. Arisaema triphyllum

11 / Box Garden

There is a feeling of motion and rhythm throughout this charming garden. Blue and pink are the dominant colors and impatiens and sweet peas are the flowers in this multi-level planter box garden. There is a shady area to sit in and a lawn for green serenity.

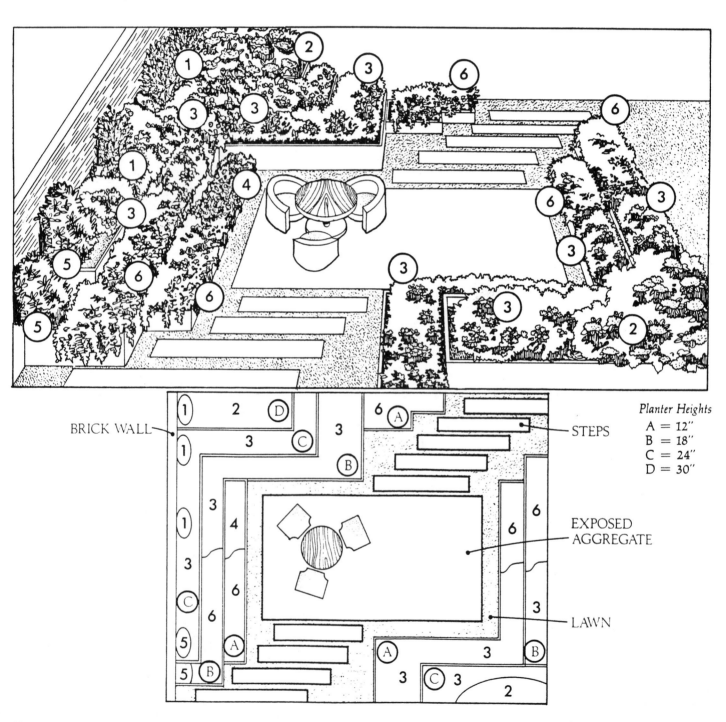

BRICK WALL

STEPS

Planter Heights
A = 12"
B = 18"
C = 24"
D = 30"

EXPOSED
AGGREGATE

LAWN

1. *Hydrangea petiolaris*
   Climbing Hydrangea
   Vine/Deciduous
   Perennial
   Hardy to —10F
   Summer
   To 20 feet; broad leaves;
   white flowers in clusters.

2. *Hydrangea macrophylla*
   'All Summer Beauty'
   Shrub/Deciduous
   Summer/Fall
   Hardy to —10F
   To 30 inches; profuse violet-
   blue flowers all summer.
   Likes acid soil and grows or-
   derly.

3. **Impatiens 'Crazy Quilt'**
   Annual
   Summer
   To 24 inches; toothed green
   leaves; glowing pink-red
   blooms with white blotches.
   Responds well to 15–30–15
   fertilizer. Water freely.

4. *Gentiana septemfida*
   Gentian
   Perennial
   Summer
   To 10 inches; tiny bright
   green leaves; small vivid blue
   flowers. Rich loamy soil is es-
   sential. Easy to grow.

5. *Clematis montana*
   'Tetra Rosa'
   Anemone Clematis
   Vine/Semievergreen
   Perennial
   Hardy to —10F
   Spring
   Climbs to 10 feet; oval leaves;
   open-faced pink flowers that
   bloom prolifically in spring.
   Likes lime.

6. **Lathyrus 'Knee-Hi'**
   Sweet Pea
   Annual
   Summer
   To 30 inches; sparse foliage;
   abundant pink-to-purple
   flowers.

1. Hydrangea petiolaris

2. Hydrangea macrophylla 'All Summer Beauty'

3. Impatiens 'Crazy Quilt'

4. Gentiana septemfida

5. Clematis montana 'Tetra Rose'

6. Lathyrus 'Knee-Hi'

12 / Bulb Garden (spring)

This typical early spring bulb garden uses old favorites such as tulips, hyacinths, and daffodils and is relatively easy to care for. By June this garden has finished blooming and other plans can be adapted.

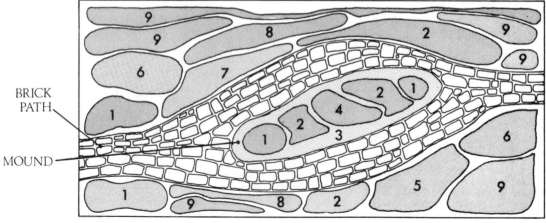

BRICK PATH

MOUND

1. *Hyacinthus azureus (ciliatus)*
   Hyacinth
   Bulb/Hardy
   Spring
   To 24 inches; leaves narrow and basal; flowers blue, on tall stalk. Plant 5 to 6 inches deep, 9 inches apart.

2. *Tulipa saxatilis*
   Cliff Tulip
   Bulb/Hardy
   Spring/Summer
   To 12 inches; leaves narrow; flowers mauve with yellow bottoms; fragrant. Plant 8 inches apart, 4 inches deep.

3. *Tulipa pulchella*
   Bulb/Hardy
   Spring/Summer
   To 6 inches; leaves narrow; flowers mauve-red, yellow at bottom. Plant 5 inches apart, 4 inches deep.

4. *Narcissus bulbocodium*
   Petticoat Daffodil
   Bulb/Hardy
   Spring
   To 20 inches; leaves basal; flowers yellow with cuplike centers, surrounded by flat petals. Not particular about soil. Plant 4 inches apart, 2 inches deep.

5. **Tulipa 'Pink Supreme'**
   Bulb/Hardy
   Spring
   To 24 inches; leaves narrow; flowers pink. Use good rich soil, no manure.

6. **Narcissus 'Lady Bird'**
   Bulb/Hardy
   Spring
   To 24 inches; leaves at base of stalk; flowers pink and white and large, surrounded by flat petals. Let foliage grow after flowers fade. Plant 5 inches apart, 4 inches deep.

7. *Muscari armeniacum*
   Grape Hyacinth
   Bulb/Hardy
   Spring
   To 12 inches; leaves linear and basal; flowers blue, in dense heads on stalk. Plant in early fall, 3 inches apart, 2 inches deep.

8. *Anemone blanda airocoerulea*
   Blue Anemone
   Bulb/Hardy
   Spring/Fall
   To 12 inches; leaves dissected; flowers showy and blue. Needs rich, well-drained soil. Plant 4 inches apart, 3 inches deep.

9. **Tulipa 'Aristocrat'**
   Bulb/Hardy
   Spring
   To 24 inches; leaves narrow; flowers pink. Needs rich soil, no manure.

1. Hyacinthus azureus (ciliatus)

2. Tulipa saxatilis

3. Tulipa pulchella

4. Narcissus bulbocodium

5. Tulipa 'Pink Supreme'

6. Narcissus 'Lady Bird'

7. Muscari armeniacum

8. Anemone blanda airocoerulea

9. Tulipa 'Aristocrat'

13 / Bulb Garden (summer)

This bulb garden relies heavily on two colorful areas framed with a solid mass of blue iris. The rest of the garden is designed to provide bloom through summer and fall. This garden requires more work and space than most, but is well worth th* time and effort for the bou* y of color.

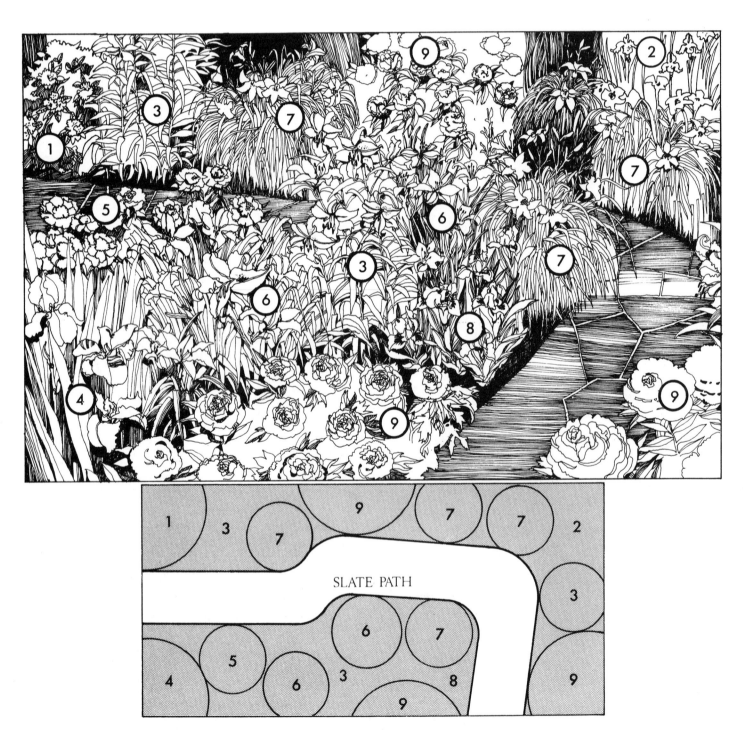

SLATE PATH

1. **Azalea (Exbury hybrid)**
Shrub/Deciduous
Hardy to −10F
To 60 inches; leaves oblong and ribbed; flowers very large, yellow or orange. Needs cool, moist, acid soil; let soil dry out between waterings.

2. **Iris 'Deep Space'**
Bulb/Hardy
Spring/Summer
To 40 inches; leaves long and narrow; flowers deep blue. Work leaf mold and fertilizer well into the soil before planting and feed after plant blooms. Replant every 3 years.

3. **Lilium**
'Pink Glory Strain'
Lily
Bulb/Hardy
To 60 inches; leaves long and narrow; flowers salmon pink and 8 inches in diameter. This giant is an oriental hybrid.

4. *Iris* **'Far Out'**
Bulb/Hardy
Spring/Summer
To 18 inches; leaves long and narrow; flowers yellow. Requires same culture as Deep Space.

5. **Paeonia 'Pink Lemonade'**
Anemone Flowered
   Peony
Deciduous
Summer
Hardy to −10F
To 40 inches; leaves large and compound; flowers showy. Use slightly acid soil and keep well drained. 'Glowing Candles,' yellow and white, also recommended.

6. **Hemerocallis**
'Flaming Dawn'
Day Lily
Perennial
Spring/Summer/Fall
To 30 inches; leaves long and narrow; flowers large and orange. Add compost and steer manure to soil before planting.

7. **Hemerocallis**
'Little Papoose'
Day Lily
Perennial
Spring/Summer/Fall
To 36 inches; leaves long and narrow; flowers large and red. Great for cuttings. Yellow 'Primrose Mascotte' also suggested.

8. **Iris 'Banbury Ruffles'**
Bulb/Hardy
Spring/Summer
To 18 inches; leaves long and narrow; flowers blue. If you prefer yellow iris, substitute 'Clap Hands.'

9. **Paeonia 'Judy Ann'**
Peony
Shrub/Deciduous
Hardy to −10F
To 24 inches; leaves large; flowers pink. Needs a somewhat acid, well-drained soil.

1. Azalea (Exbury hybrid)

2. Iris 'Deep Space'

3. Lilium 'Pink Glory Strain'

4. Iris 'Far Out'

5. Paeonia 'Pink Lemonade'

6. Hemerocallis 'Flaming Dawn'

7. Hemerocallis 'Little Papoose'

8. Iris 'Banbury Ruffles'

9. Paeonia 'Judy Ann'

14 / Cacti and Succulent Garden

A cacti and succulent garden is built on a slight upslope using stone steps and four large boulders. The rosette form of the agaves dominates the plan, and low plantings of sedum and sempervivums provide ground color. For all its plants and seemingly complex form, this is an easy garden to tend.

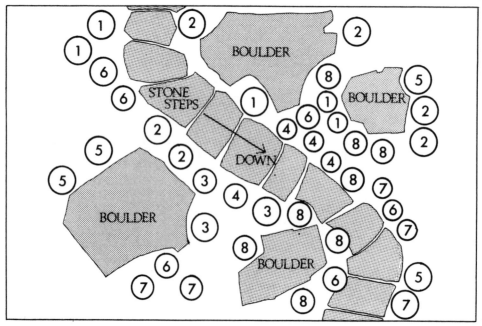

1. *Lemairocereus spachianus*
   Torch Cactus
   Hardy to −30F
   To 60 inches; columnar and ribbed; bright green with sparse spines. Dramatic accent.

2. *Yucca filamentosa*
   Adam's Needle
   Hardy to −10F
   To 12 feet; leaves to 2½ feet long, 1 inch wide; white flowers to 2 inches long. Grows easily in dry sandy soil.

3. *Euphorbia grandicornus*
   Cow's Horn Cactus
   Hardy to −30F
   To 72 inches; branches to 6 inches thick; leaves scalelike; flowers borne between branch spines. More bizarre than beautiful. Difficult to grow.

4. *Echinocactus grusoni*
   Golden Barrel Cactus
   Hardy to −30F
   To 48 inches, 30 inches in diameter; light green with golden spines which turn white with age; yellow flowers open in daylight.

5. *Agave attenuata*
   Century Plant
   Hardy to −20F
   To 60 inches; leaves grayish, to 30 inches long and 10 inches wide at base; flowers greenish-yellow on 10-foot spikes.

6. *Sedum album*
   'Indian Chief'
   Ground Cover/Semievergreen
   Hardy to −10F
   To 10 inches; leaves fleshy and gray-green; flowers red, in clusters at stem tips. Makes good ground cover.

7. *Sedum spectabile*
   Showy Sedum
   Perennial
   Summer/Fall
   To 15 inches; leaves gray-green; flowers red, in clusters. Tolerates shade. Keep evenly moist.

8. *Sempervivum (hybrid)*
   Houseleek
   Perennial
   Hardy to −10F
   To 10 inches; succulent, thick leaves, often grow in rosette habit; flowers green, white, rose, yellow, or purple. Many varieties.

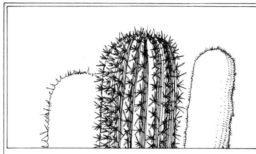
1. Lemairocereus spachianus

2. Yucca filamentosa

3. Euphorbia grandicornus

4. Echinocactus grusoni

5. Agave attenuata

6. Sedum album 'Indian Chief'

7. Sedum spectabile

8. Sempervivum (hybrid)

15 / Children's Secret Garden

This garden of sunflowers and gourds, pumpkins and peanuts will be a joy for kids. There is a teepee hideaway in the center and a bark path makes maintenance easy. The design is simple—an octagon with a walkway around it—and it can be planned in a small or large area.

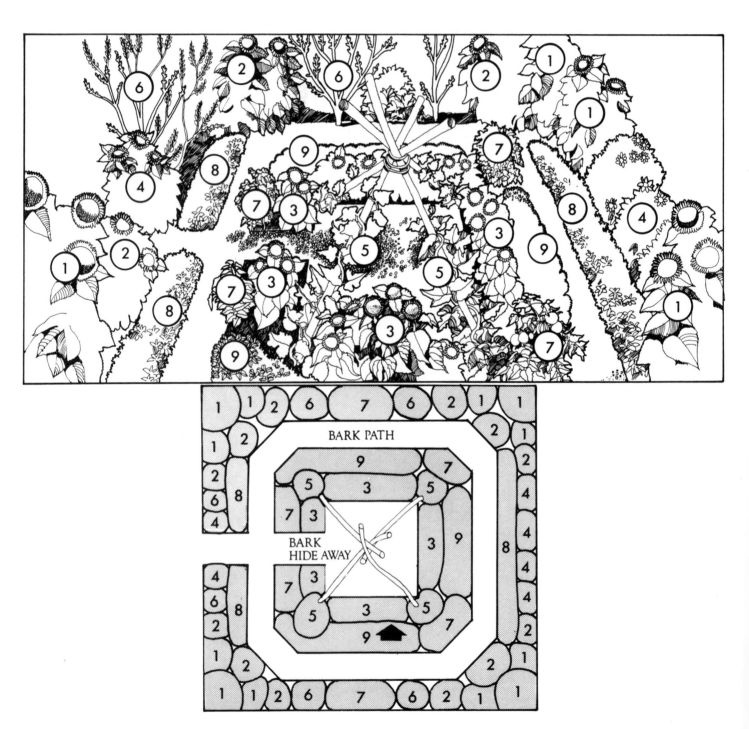

BARK PATH

BARK HIDE AWAY

1. **Helianthus 'Grey Stripe'
   Sunflower**
   Annual
   Summer
   To 72 inches; leaves heart-shaped; flowers striped. Easily grown giant, whose head follows the sun.

2. **Helianthus 'Sungold'
   Sunflower**
   Annual
   Summer
   To 72 inches; leaves heart-shaped; flowers yellow. Easily grown. Not as large as 'Grey Stripe,' but with more yellow petals.

3. **Helianthus 'Sungold'
   Sunflower**
   Annual
   Summer
   To 15 inches; leaves heart-shaped; flowers golden-yellow, and bright double blooms are always looking for the sun. Easily grown.

4. **Tithonia 'Torch'
   Mexican Sunflower**
   Annual
   Summer
   To 36 inches; leaves long and narrow; flowers bright orange-red. Good vigorous background plant. Not true sunflowers.

5. **Cucurbita
   Ornamental Gourd**
   Summer/Fall
   On spreading vines with lacy leaves, gourds come in a variety of shapes, sizes, and colors. Needs long growing period but prospers in most soils.

6. **Salix 'French Pink'
   Pussy Willow**
   Tree/Deciduous
   Hardy to −10F
   To 10 feet; narrow leaves; silvery-pink catkins. Will grow in poor dry soil but prefers moist soils.

7. **Cucurbita 'Pepo'
   Pumpkin**
   Summer/Fall
   Spreading vine with spiny stems; large triangular leaves; fruit in many shapes and sizes. Needs much space so plant 40 inches apart. Do not step on the vines. Have the carving knife ready for Halloween.

8. **Nepeta cataria
   Catnip**
   Perennial
   Spring
   To 20 inches; leaves oblong; flowers whitish or lilac. Makes good herb tea.

9. **Arachis hypogaea
   Peanut**
   Summer
   To 20 inches; leaves divided into four leaflets; flowers yellow; seed pods (peanuts) underground. Likes heat and good moisture.

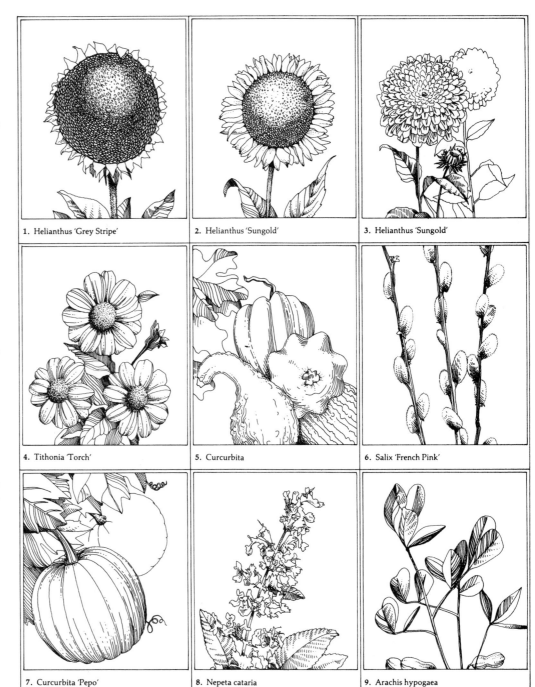

1. Helianthus 'Grey Stripe'

2. Helianthus 'Sungold'

3. Helianthus 'Sungold'

4. Tithonia 'Torch'

5. Curcurbita

6. Salix 'French Pink'

7. Curcurbita 'Pepo'

8. Nepeta cataria

9. Arachis hypogaea

16 / City Garden I (apartment)

There is more going on in this plan than first meets the eye. An angular design makes this garden quite handsome, and the benches against a brick floor create a distinctive beauty. Angular lawns also complement the plan as do the sparse plantings. Flowing frilly plants are used to soften the angles.

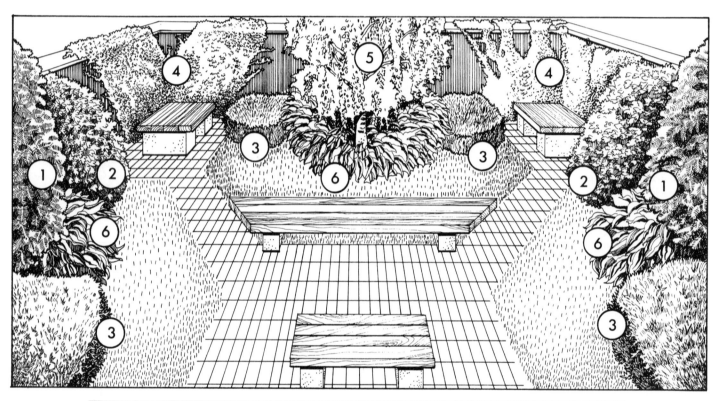

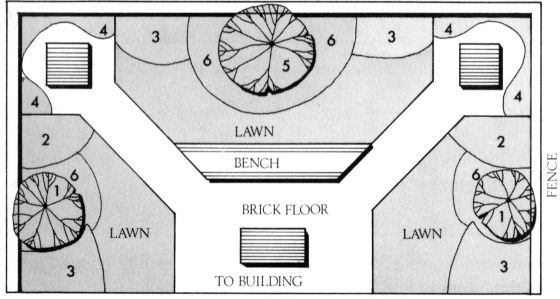

1. *Picea pungens*
   Colorado Spruce
   Tree/Evergreen
   Hardy to −35F
   To 75 feet; stiffly branched, sharp bluish-green needles. Grows to 30 feet in cultivation.

2. *Acer campestre*
   Hedge Maple
   Tree/Deciduous
   Hardy to −20F
   To 12 feet; dense growth; bright green, lobed leaves. Trim to 8 feet.

3. *Salix purpurea* 'Nana'
   Purple Osier
   Shrub/Deciduous
   Hardy to −10F
   To 10 feet; slender branching habit; mass of silvery-blue leaves. Likes moist conditions.

4. *Hedera helix*
   Ivy
   Vine/Evergreen
   Perennial
   Hardy to −5F
   Climbs to 20 feet; masses of large lobed green leaves. Likes shade, grows in most soils.

5. *Betula pendula* 'Gracilis'
   Cut Leaf European Birch
   Tree/Deciduous
   Hardy to −10F
   To 60 feet; pendulous habit, small green leaves. Will thrive in wet or dry soil; transplant only in spring.

6. *Hosta lancifolia*
   albomarginata
   Plantain Lily
   Perennial
   To 10 inches; large broad green leaves edged in white. Needs rich soil and light shade. Easily grown.

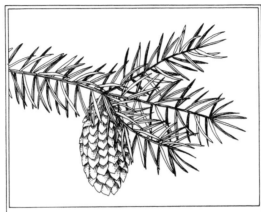

1. Picea pungens

2. Acer campestre

3. Salix purpurea 'Nana'

4. Hedera helix

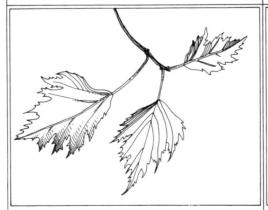

5. Betula pendula 'Gracilis'

6. Hosta lancifolia albomarginata

17 / City Garden II (dog run)

This garden is strictly for the dogs and how city animals will love it! The U-shaped run which borders the garden is fenced; within, there is a small planting area and benches for resting. Two areas of lawn define the garden and an aggregate concrete floor makes it easy to clean. Planter boxes create visual interest and Fido has his own house. In fact, even without a dog, by eliminating the fence area, this is a charming little garden.

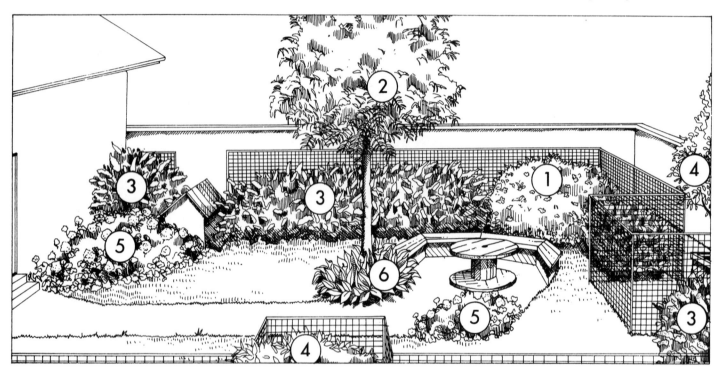

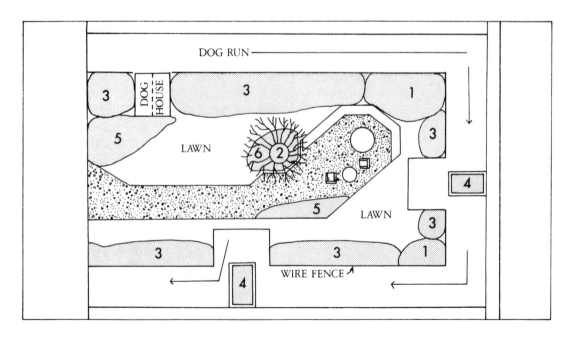

1. *Weigela florida* **'Bristol Ruby'**
   Shrub/Deciduous
   Hardy to −10F
   To 72 inches; leafy, masses of red flowers. Needs plenty of water and good drainage.

2. *Gleditsia triacanthos* **'Rubylace' Honey Locust**
   Tree/Deciduous
   Hardy to −10F
   To 100 feet; thornless, dark purplish-red foliage turns bronze-green at maturity. Grows in almost any type of soil.

3. *Spiraea nipponica tosaensis* **'Snowmound'**
   Shrub/Deciduous
   Hardy to −10F
   To 60 inches; a mass of small white flowers. Vigorous, not particular about soil nor demanding about light.

4. **Malus 'Strathmore' Pyramidal Crabapple**
   Tree/Deciduous
   Hardy to −10F
   To 20 feet; abundant bright red-pink flowers, beautiful pyramidal shape.

5. **Geranium (Carefree type)**
   Perennial
   Summer
   To 18 inches; typical geranium leaf; profuse clusters of popular red-pink flowers.

6. *Zantedeschia rehmanni* **Pink Calla Lily**
   Bulb/Hardy
   Summer
   To 16 inches; lanceolate leaves; fine large pink flowers. Likes wet soil; good for cut flowers.

1. Weigela florida 'Bristol Ruby'

2. Gleditsia triacanthos 'Rubylace'

3. Spiraea nipponica tosaensis 'Snowmound'

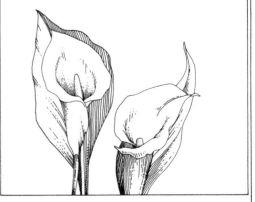

4. Malus 'Strathmore'

5. Geranium (Carefree type)

6. Zantedeschia rehmanni

18 / City Garden III (formal)

The circle upon circle design creates formality here and the central area works as a sunken platform clothed in a luxurious green lawn. Spirea and lilac are at the center in three circles and pots of color are furnished by red phlox. Six-inch steps further emphasize the circular plan.

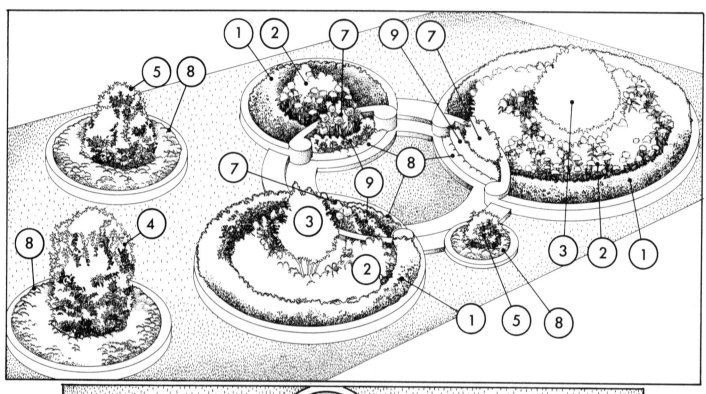

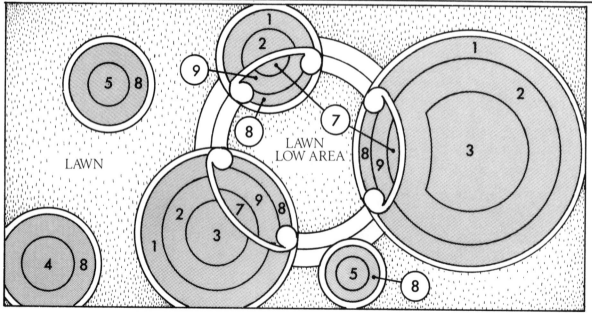

1. **Cotoneaster divaricata**
Spreading Cotoneaster
Shrub/Deciduous
Hardy to −10F
To 72 inches; small leaves; pink flowers in clusters of three; red berries. Grows easily in most conditions but does not like shade. Prune to 36 inches.

2. *Spiraea macrothyrsa*
Japanese Spiraea
Shrub/Deciduous
Hardy to −10F
To 48 inches; compact masses of pale lilac flowers. Easy to grow and transplant; thin out somewhat in spring.

3. *Syringa sweginflexa*
Lilac
Shrub/Deciduous
Hardy to −10F
To 72 inches; leaves oblong; flower masses long-tubed, fragrant and pink. Prune every few years to keep plants vigorous.

4. *Ilex aquifolium*
Pyramidal Holly
Tree/Evergreen
Hardy to −10F
To 20 feet; small leaves; many handsome hybrids. Can be shaped to pyramidal form. Female trees produce berries when a male is nearby.

5. *Ilex aquifolium*
    'Luteo-Variegata'
Dwarf Holly
Shrub/Evergreen
Hardy to −5F
To 24 inches; leaves small, green and yellow; berries red. Stellar variety.

6. *Ficus pumila*
Creeping Fig
Shrub/Evergreen
Hardy to −20F
Creeping vine; leaves oblong and thick; flowers inconspicuous. Likes shade and good moisture.

7. *Phlox* 'Starfire'
Perennial
Summer
To 48 inches; leaves oblong; red and purple flowers in showy head.

8. *Lobularia* 'Royal Carpet'
Sweet alyssum
Annual
Summer
To 6 inches; leaves small; purple flowers in clusters.

9. *Erigeron annuus*
Fleabane
Annual
Summer/Fall
To 16 inches; narrow leaves; pink daisy-like flowers with yellow eyes. Needs well-drained soil.

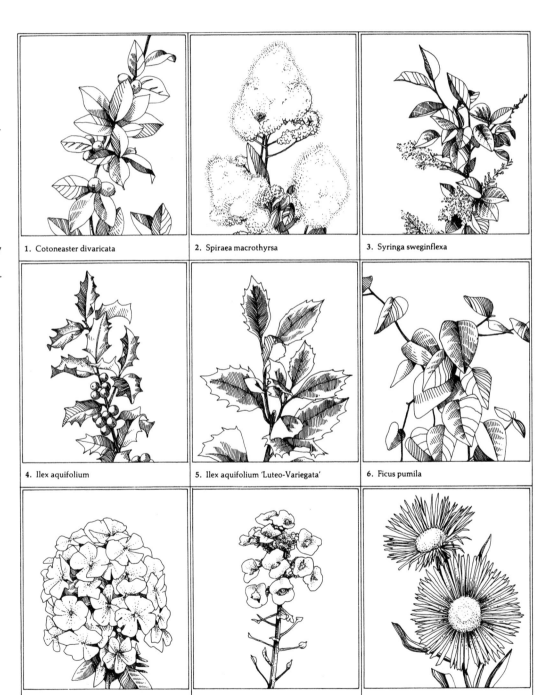

1. Cotoneaster divaricata   2. Spiraea macrothyrsa   3. Syringa sweginflexa

4. Ilex aquifolium   5. Ilex aquifolium 'Luteo-Variegata'   6. Ficus pumila

7. Phlox 'Starfire'   8. Lobularia 'Royal Carpet'   9. Erigeron annuus

19 / City Garden IV (low maintenance)

Bright blazing color is the keynote of this casual city garden. The flowers have been selected for varying height and color. The round concrete steps also work well as a design element. This versatile plan can be used at the rear of the house, at front or on sides.

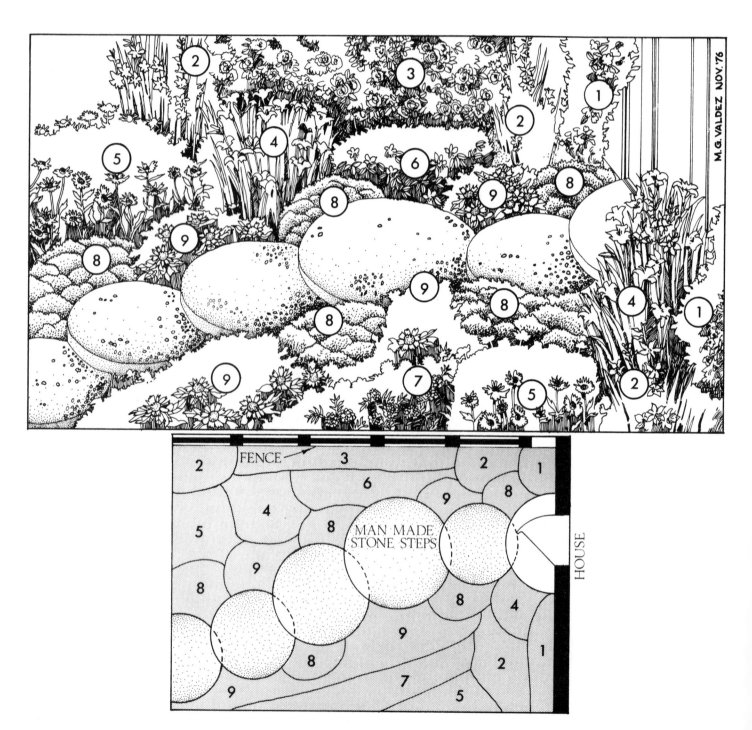

M.G. VALDEZ NOV. '76

1. **Campsis tagliabuana 'Mme Galen'**
   Vine/Semievergreen
   Perennial
   Summer/Fall
   Hardy to —10F
   Climbs to 30 feet; dense foliage; fiery orange-red, trumpet-shaped flowers. Also called Bignonia. Must have sun.

2. **Montbretia crocosmiiflora**
   Bulb/Hardy
   Summer
   To 48 inches; grassy foliage; bright orange flowers. Easily grown. Separate every third year.

3. **Rosa 'Gold Rush'**
   Shrub/Deciduous
   Hardy to —10F
   To 20 feet; handsome large orange flowers.

4. **Hemerocallis 'Illustrous'**
   Bulb/Hardy
   Summer
   To 40 inches; grassy foliage; large orange flowers.

5. **Helenium 'Coppersfield Orange'**
   Perennial
   Summer
   To 48 inches; large orange flowers with dark brown centers. Lovely autumn colors.

6. **Hypericum calcyinum Aaron's Beard**
   Ground Cover/Semievergreen
   Hardy to —10F
   To 12 inches; 3- to 4-inch green leaves; bright yellow 3-inch flowers. Excellent for sandy soil and semishaded locations.

7. **Tagetes 'Firelight'**
   Annual
   Summer/Fall
   To 12 inches; narrow and scalloped leaves; dark reddish-orange flowers. One of the dwarf double group. Easily grown.

8. **Antirrhinum 'Floral Carpet' Snapdragon**
   Annual
   Summer
   To 8 inches; excellent dwarf with pink, red, rose, orange and yellow flowers. A carpet of color.

9. **Gaillardia 'Sun Dance' Blanketflower**
   Perennial
   Summer
   To 12 inches; large leaves; bright orange flowers, tipped red. Add leaf mold and some sand to soil.

1. Campsis tagliabuana 'Mme Galen'   2. Montbretia crocosmiiflora   3. Rosa 'Gold Rush'

4. Hemerocallis 'Illustrous'   5. Helenium 'Coppersfield Orange'   6. Hypericum calcyinum

7. Tagetes 'Firelight'   8. Antirrhinum 'Floral Carpet'   9. Gaillardia 'Sun Dance'

20 / City Garden V (narrow lot)

To accomodate a narrow lot this aggregrate surfaced garden relies on ivy in the foreground and a foil of azaleas. In the rear, a fern and a palm give vertical thrust. Ophiopogon is used as ground cover around the open area and a fence provides privacy. This garden is best suited to an all-year temperate climate.

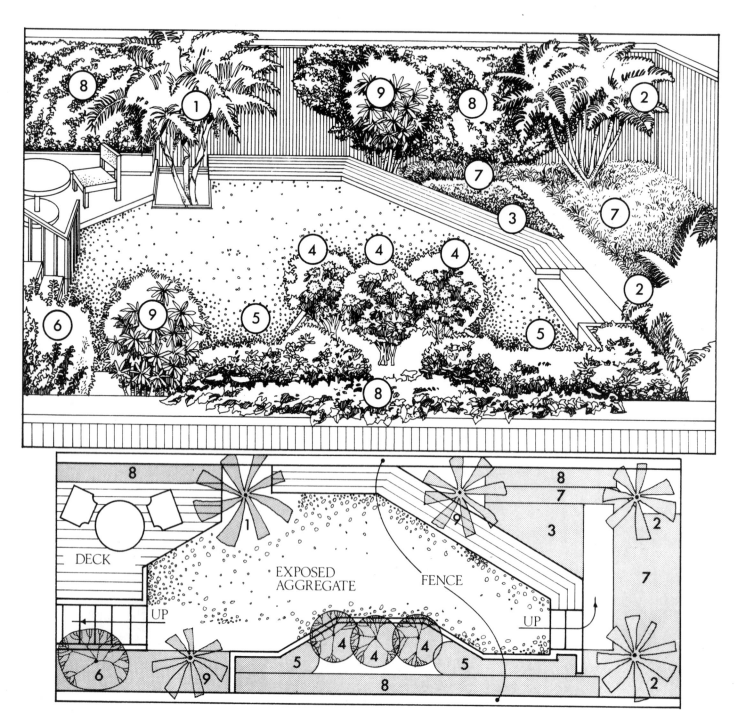

1. **Chrysalidocarpus lutescens**
Butterfly Palm
To 10 feet; graceful arching fronds of bright green; multi-branch habit.

2. **Dicksonia antarctica**
Tasmanian Tree Fern
To 15 feet; shiny green arching fronds. Likes moisture and some shade.

3. **Hedera helix**
Ivy
Vine/Evergreen
Perennial
Hardy to −5F
Climbs to 10 feet; small lobed, dark green leaves. Likes moisture and shade.

4. **Azalea (hybrid)**
Shrub/Deciduous
Hardy to −10F
To 60 inches; small leaves and brightly colored flowers in spring. Many varieties and colors. For this plan, use red or orange variety.

5. **Veronica spicata**
Speedwell
Perennial
Spring/Summer
To 16 inches; lovely blue flowers on erect stems. Needs full sun and well-drained soil.

6. **Ilex cornuta**
Chinese Holly
Shrub/Evergreen
Hardy to −10F
To 8 feet; squarish dark green leaves. Does well in shade.

7. **Ophiopogon japonicus**
Dwarf Lilyturf
Ground Cover/Evergreen
Hardy to −5F
To 10 inches; leaves long and narrow; lilac flowers on short spikes. Grows in sun or shade.

8. **Hedera canariensis**
Algerian Ivy
Vine/Evergreen
Perennial
Hardy to −5F
To 10 feet; very large lobed leaves with burgundy hue. Likes shade and moisture.

9. **Livistona chinensis**
Chinese Fan Palm
Hardy to −10F
To 25 feet; glossy green fronds, fan-shaped leaves.

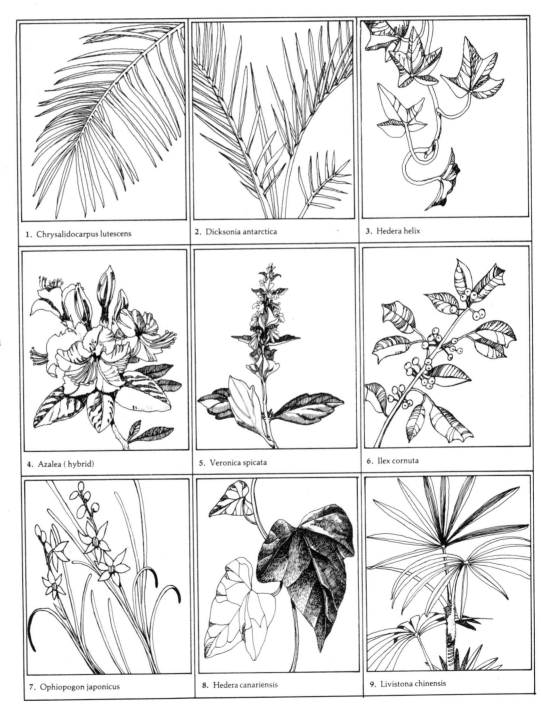

1. Chrysalidocarpus lutescens

2. Dicksonia antarctica

3. Hedera helix

4. Azalea (hybrid)

5. Veronica spicata

6. Ilex cornuta

7. Ophiopogon japonicus

8. Hedera canariensis

9. Livistona chinensis

71

21 / City Garden VI (pool)

Sophisticated in approach, this garden plan based on an island design uses a handsome pool as its accent. Viburnum is planted against the fence and the green and white color scheme creates a cool elegance. Brick paving is used as surfacing and there is ample space for tending plants and walking through the garden. A brick wall affords privacy.

POOL

UP

STEPS

BRICK WALL

1. *Stewartia pseudo-camellia*
Japanese Stewartia
Shrub/Deciduous
Hardy to —10F
To 10 feet; pyramidal habit; large green leaves; beautiful camellia-type white flowers; colorful flaking bark. Needs rich humus soil and plenty of moisture.

2. *Sorbus aucuparia*
'White Wax'
Mountain Ash
Tree/Deciduous
Hardy to —35F
To 20 feet; small toothed leaves; white berries in fall. Can tolerate sun or shade. Is subject to borers, especially in Eastern states.

3. *Viburnum plicatum*
'Mariesii'
Japanese Snowball
Shrub/Deciduous
Hardy to —10F
To 72 inches; bright green leaves; bowers of white flowers; red berries. Dependable. Rarely attacked by insects. Grows in almost any soil; can take light shade.

4. **Petunia 'Super White'**
Annual
Summer
To 12 inches; extra large flowering white petunia. Spreads and reblooms when cut.

5. *Astilbe arendsii*
'Bridal Veil'
Meadowsweet
Perennial
Summer
To 24 inches; leafy with plumes of small pink flowers. Loves shade and moisture; responds to constant but very light feeding.

6. **Caladium**
'White Christmas'
Bulb/Tender
To 24 inches; leaves heart-shaped, white and green. Needs loamy soil and lots of water. Keep out of sun.

7. **Begonia 'Viva'**
Wax Begonia
Annual
Summer
To 8 inches; waxy leaves; small white flowers. Needs loamy soil, good drainage. Likes morning sun.

8. **Nymphaea 'Missouri'**
Water Lily
Perennial/Hardy
Summer
Large white flowering water lily. Stellar variety.

9. **Iris 'Gold Bound'**
Japanese Iris
Bulb/Hardy
Spring
To 48 inches; grassy foliage; fine white flowers. Needs good rich loam; fertilize only after bloom.

1. Stewartia pseudo-camellia

2. Sorbus aucuparia 'White Wax'

3. Viburnum plicatum 'Mariesii'

4. Petunia 'Super White'

5. Astilbe arendsii 'Bridal Veil'

6. Caladium 'White Christmas'

7. Begonia 'Viva'

8. Nymphaea 'Missouri'

9. Iris 'Gold Bound'

22 / Community Garden

A "Y" design makes this garden easy to tend. The steps are an integral part of the plan and the blue spruce serves as a Christmas tree in the center; the planting of crab apples creates an attractive circular design. Drifts of petunias surround the crab apples. Sectioned in three areas, this garden works well for three families.

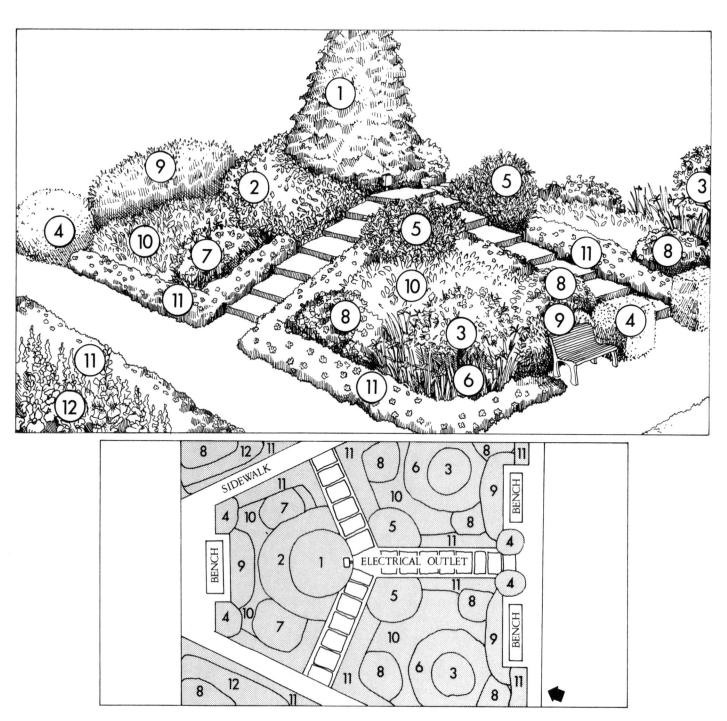

1. **Picea pungens**
   Colorado Spruce
   Tree/Evergreen
   Hardy to −35F
   To 100 feet; stiffly branched; sharp blue-green needles. Good pyramidal shape.

2. **Ilex vomitoria**
   Yaupon
   Shrub/Evergreen
   Hardy to −10F
   To 24 feet; leaves 1½ inches long; small red fruits on previous year's growth. Drought resistant.

3. **Malus 'Crimson Beauty'**
   Crab Apple
   Tree/Deciduous
   Hardy to −20F
   To 20 feet; bright red flowers. Good small crab apples; spraying not necessary.

4. **Ribes alpinum**
   Alpine Currant
   Shrub/Deciduous
   Hardy to −35F
   To 84 inches; small 2-inch leaves; fruits scarlet red. Excellent for hedges. Foliage appears early in season.

5. **Berberis thunbergii**
   'Crimson Pygmy'
   Japanese Barberry
   Shrub/Evergreen
   Hardy to −20F
   To 12 inches; red foliage; profuse flowers. Requires sun for bright color; younger foliage is brightest. Good low hedge. Needs no pruning. Thorny.

6. **Hemerocallis 'Helios'**
   Day Lily
   Bulb/Hardy
   To 24 inches; brilliant flame-red flowers, golden center.

7. **Cosmos 'Diablo'**
   Perennial
   Summer
   To 30 inches; lobed leaves; wiry stems with vibrant rust-red single flowers, yellow center. Likes water and good drainage.

8. **Petunia 'Beacon'**
   Annual
   Summer
   To 18 inches; showy and large bright red flowers with yellow center.

9. **Salix purpurea**
   'Gracilis'
   Purple Osier
   Shrub/Deciduous
   Hardy to −20F
   To 100 inches; narrow leaves; slender shape; dense habit. Good in moist conditions.

10. **Ajuga reptans**
    'Bronze Beauty'
    Carpet Bugle
    Ground
    *   Cover/Semievergreen*
    Hardy to −20F
    To 4 inches; tiny bronze leaves form a tight mass.

11. **Dianthus 'Zing'**
    Maiden Pink
    Perennial
    Summer
    To 12 inches; dense mounds of foliage, red or pink flowers. Mulch well in winter.

12. **Antirrhinum**
    'Sweetheart'
    Snapdragon
    Annual
    To 30 inches; leaves lanceolate; flowers on tall spikes.

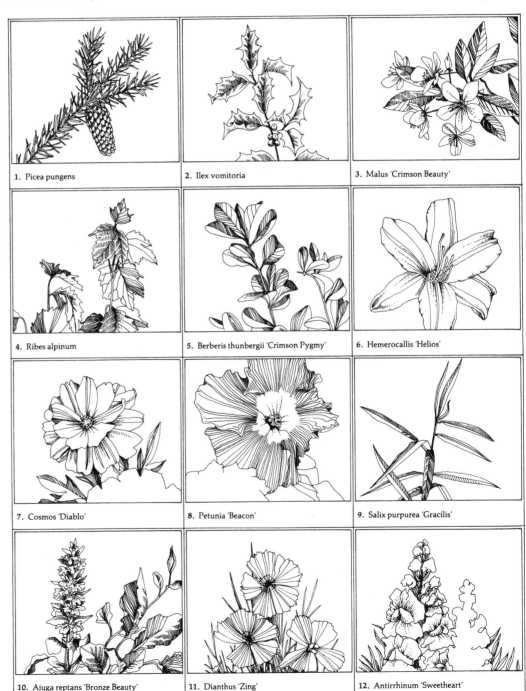

1. Picea pungens

2. Ilex vomitoria

3. Malus 'Crimson Beauty'

4. Ribes alpinum

5. Berberis thunbergii 'Crimson Pygmy'

6. Hemerocallis 'Helios'

7. Cosmos 'Diablo'

8. Petunia 'Beacon'

9. Salix purpurea 'Gracilis'

10. Ajuga reptans 'Bronze Beauty'

11. Dianthus 'Zing'

12. Antirrhinum 'Sweetheart'

23 / Condominium Garden

Using plants in an L-shape, this is a lovely small private garden for a condominium owner. Pachysandra and azaleas are at one side and in the foreground, a massive planting of bearberry furnishes ample color. A Japanese black pine tree adds an almost oriental effect, and a tile floor complements the scene.

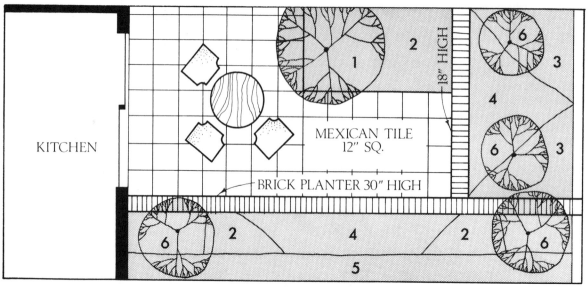

KITCHEN

MEXICAN TILE 12" SQ.

BRICK PLANTER 30" HIGH

18" HIGH

1. *Pinus thunbergii*
   Japanese Black Pine
   Tree/Evergreen
   Hardy to −5F
   To 90 feet; dark green stiff needles; dense branching habit. A durable tree.

2. *Paxistima canbyi*
   Cliff Green
   Shrub/Evergreen
   Hardy to −10F
   To 12 inches; oblong 1-inch leaves. Needs well-drained soil. Makes a shining carpet.

3. *Pachysandra terminalis*
   Japanese Spurge
   Ground Cover/Evergreen
   Hardy to −20F
   To 8 inches; clustered sawtooth leaves. Forms lush carpet. Likes a very rich soil.

4. *Vinca 'Minor'*
   (Bowles variety)
   Periwinkle
   Ground Cover/Evergreen
   Hardy to −20F
   To 6 inches; rich glossy green foliage; lavender-blue flowers. Prefers half-shade.

5. *Arctostaphylos uva-ursi*
   Bearberry
   Ground Cover/Evergreen
   Hardy to −35F
   To 8 inches; shiny dark green leaves; tiny pink flowers in spring followed by red berries. Likes a well-drained, acid soil.

6. *Azalea 'Elizabeth'*
   Shrub/Deciduous
   Hardy to −10F
   To 36 inches; small leaves; masses of pretty red flowers. Needs acid soil.

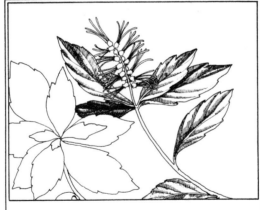

1. Pinus thunbergii

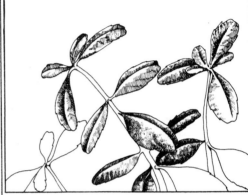

2. Paxistima canbyi

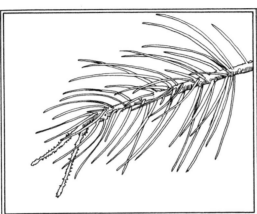

3. Pachysandra terminalis

4. Vinca 'Minor' (Bowles variety)

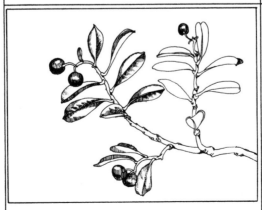

5. Arctostaphylos uva-ursi

6. Azalea 'Elizabeth'

24 / Container Garden (spring)

The dining and living areas of this house open to a small, colorful picture of narcissus and iris. White iris and pink tulip border one area and a flat stone walk provides an interesting path. At the corner of the house a tall blue hydrangea is the accent.

LIVING AREA

STONE WALK

1. *Viburnum opulus* 'Nanum'
   European Cranberry
   Bush
   Shrub/Deciduous
   Hardy to —35F
   To 48 inches; small leaves;
   pink flowers; red berries.
   Grows in almost any soil, tol-
   erates light shade.

2. *Hydrangea macrophylla*
   'Mariesii'
   Shrub/Deciduous
   Spring/Summer
   Hardy to —10F
   To 60 inches; exquisite white-
   edged leaves; clusters of violet
   flowers. Commonly called
   Lace Cap.

3. **Iris**
   'Ochroleuca Gigantea'
   Bulb/Hardy
   Spring
   To 48 inches; grassy leaves;
   large well-branched stalks
   with four to six fine white
   and yellow flowers. Needs
   acid conditions.

4. **Tulipa 'Inga Hume'**
   Bulb/Hardy
   Spring
   To 36 inches; lance-shaped
   leaves; pink flowers. Plant 1
   inch deep.

5. *Paeonia moutan*
   Peony
   Shrub/Deciduous
   Hardy to —10F
   To 48 inches; bushy, with
   dense leaves; large pink flow-
   ers. Needs good humusy soil
   and full sun.

6. **Narcissus 'Jeanne d'Arc'**
   Butterfly Narcissus
   Bulb/Hardy
   Spring
   To 18 inches; grassy foliage;
   large yellow flowers.

7. **Iris 'Lemon Flare'**
   Bulb/Hardy
   Spring
   To 12 inches; grassy foliage;
   small white flowers, splotched
   lemon on the falls. A prolific
   semi-dwarf.

8. **Hyacinthus 'Lady Derby'**
   Bulb/Hardy
   Spring
   To 12 inches; grassy foliage;
   large clusters of clear pink
   flowers. Plant 3 inches deep.

9. *Convallaria majalis*
   Lily-of-the-Valley
   Bulb/Hardy
   Spring
   To 12 inches; broad dark
   green leaves; pendulous, tiny
   fragrant white flowers. Needs
   lots of moisture; likes crowd-
   ing. Use some manure in soil
   just before first snowfall.

1. Viburnum opulus 'Nanum'

2. Hydrangea macrophylla 'Mariesii'

3. Iris 'Ochroleuca Gigantea'

4. Tulipa 'Inga Hume'

5. Paeonia moutan

6. Narcissus 'Jeanne d'Arc'

7. Iris 'Lemon Flare'

8. Hyacinthus 'Lady Derby'

9. Convallaria majalis

25 / Cookout Garden

Planned with plenty of space for dining activities, this garden uses raised planter beds in the foreground. At the rear corners are two massive islands of plants. Low zinnias form the back edging and there are radishes and tomatoes as a surprise harvest for guests. This garden will fit into the average concrete or brick patio area.

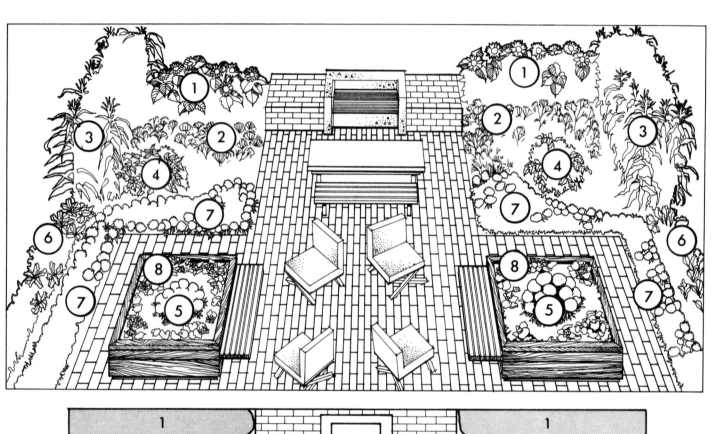

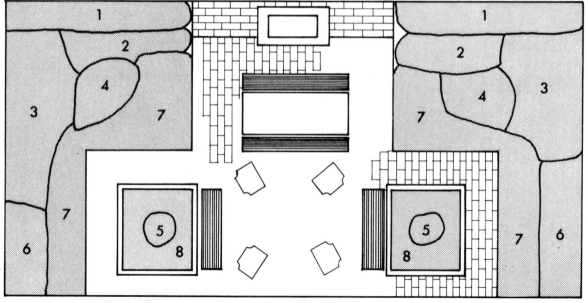

1. **Helianthus 'Piccolo'**
   Sunflower
   Perennial
   Summer
   To 48 inches; leaves long, heart-shaped; flowers 4 inches wide, yellow with dark center. Grows easily in any soil; likes lots of water and sun.

2. *Anethum graveolens*
   Dill
   Annual
   Summer
   To 36 inches; leaves very finely divided into threadlike leaflets; small, yellow flowers. Prune well to insure branching out.

3. **Corn**
   'Golden Cross Bantam'
   To 72 inches; matures in 83 days; small ears. One of the sweetest and best for home gardens. Be sure this is planted in a clump: breezes cross-pollinate it and a straight row will result in very few ears.

4. **Tomato 'Patio'**
   Climbs to 24 inches; medium-sized red fruit; matures in 70 days. Hardy and easily grown. Water freely. Likes loose soil and full sun.

5. **Tagetes 'First Lady'**
   Marigold
   Annual
   Summer
   To 18 inches; green leaves divided into leaflets; yellow flowers to 3½ inches wide, long stems. Cut for bouquets; long blooming.

6. **Radish 'Tendersweet'**
   To 12 inches; leaves green, mature in 25 days. An easy variety. Replant as you harvest; grows fast.

7. **Zinnia (Paint Brush type)**
   Annual
   Summer
   To 16 inches; leaves oblong; flowers medium-sized, in a variety of brilliant colors. Grows readily in most soils. Watch for mildew.

8. **Tropaeolum 'Jewel'**
   Nasturtium
   Annual
   Spring/Summer
   To 12 inches; leaves round; flowers in various colors. Likes sandy soil and moist conditions. Use buds and leaves in a salad.

1. Helianthus 'Piccolo'

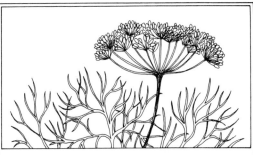
2. Anethum graveolens

3. Corn 'Golden Cross Bantam'

4. Tomato 'Patio'

5. Tagetes 'First Lady'

6. Radish 'Tendersweet'

7. Zinnia (Paint Brush type)

8. Tropaeolum 'Jewel'

26 / Country Garden

A white picket fence and an arched arbor make an old-fashioned garden plan come alive. The walkway stone paths in a flower motif are the accent. In the center, a mound of four-o'clocks; bushes and trees frame the plan; and mignonette and beebalm form a horizontal thrust of color. Polygonum flanked with campanulas frame the path.

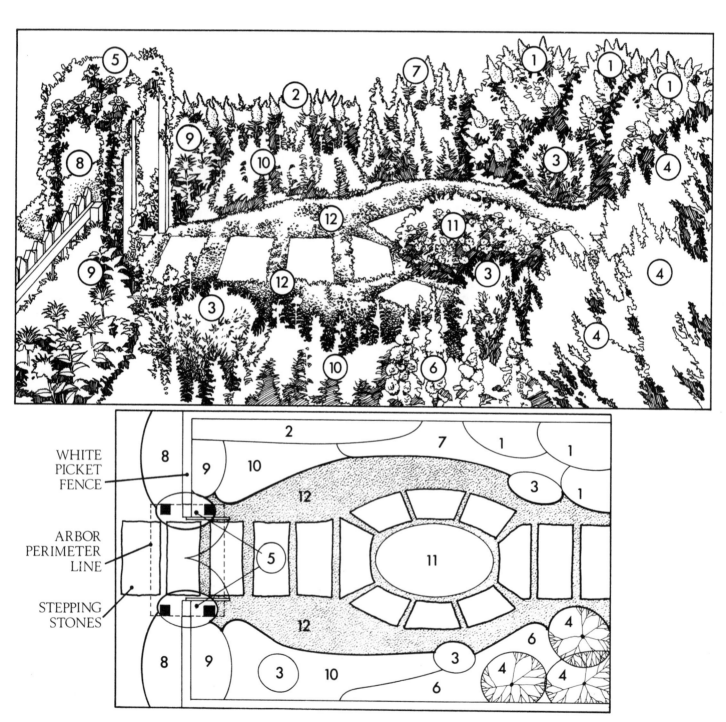

WHITE
PICKET
FENCE

ARBOR
PERIMETER
LINE

STEPPING
STONES

1. Syringa vulgaris 'Ludwig Spaeth'
Lilac
Shrub/Deciduous
Hardy to —35F
To 60 inches; leafy; plumes of lilac flowers in summer. Prefers limestone soil. Prune in early spring.

2. Spiraea prunifolia 'Plena'
Bridalwreath Spireae
Shrub/Deciduous
Hardy to —20F
To 48 inches; branching but vertical small white flowers. Vigorous, not particular about soil or light.

3. Daphne burkwoodii 'Somerset'
Shrub/Deciduous
Spring
Hardy to —10F
To 36 inches; gray-green spatulate leaves; masses of pink flowers. Elegant and airy.

4. Cercis chinensis 'Redbud'
Judas Tree
Tree/Deciduous
Hardy to —5F
To 15 feet; dense clusters of rosy-purple, long-lasting flowers. Grows in sun or shade.

5. Rosa 'Blossomtime'
Shrub/Deciduous
Hardy to —10F
Climbs to 20 feet; pink roses. Reblooming; resistant to rust.

6. Althaea 'Madcap'
Hollyhock
Perennial
Summer
To 60 inches; toothed leaves; large and unusual 4-inch flowers in many colors. Likes rich soil.

7. Digitalis purpurea
Foxglove
Biennial
Spring
To 60 inches; plumes of cup-shaped flowers.

8. Reseda odorata
Migonette
Annual
Summer
To 24 inches; gray-green leaves; white flowers.

9. Monarda didyma
Beebalm
Perennial
Summer/Fall
To 24 inches; downy and fragrant leaves; red flowers. Easily grown.

10. Campanula carpatica
Bellflower
Perennial
Summer/Fall
To 12 inches; small leaves; blue flowers in masses.

11. Mirabilis japonica
Four-o'clock
Perennial
Summer
To 36 inches; heart-shaped green leaves; red flowers.

12. Polygonum capitatum 'Magic Carpet'
Fleeceflower
Perennial
Spring
To 6 inches; reddish leaves; pink flowers. Easily grown. Excellent for ground cover. Invasive but easily controlled.

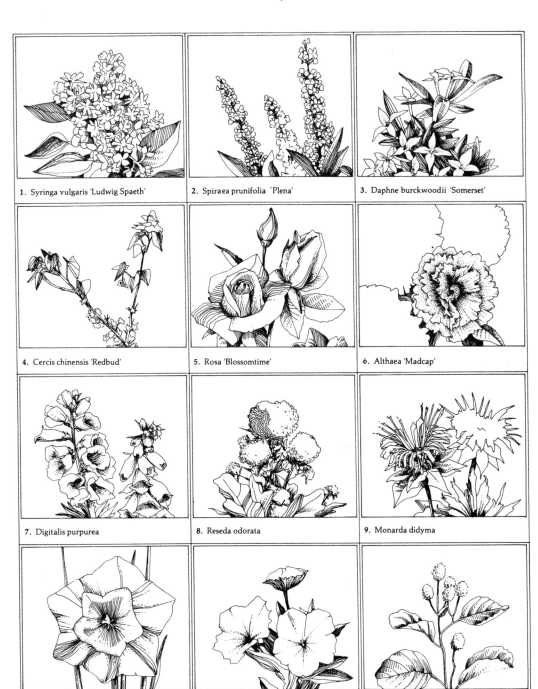

1. Syringa vulgaris 'Ludwig Spaeth'   2. Spiraea prunifolia 'Plena'   3. Daphne burckwoodii 'Somerset'

4. Cercis chinensis 'Redbud'   5. Rosa 'Blossomtime'   6. Althaea 'Madcap'

7. Digitalis purpurea   8. Reseda odorata   9. Monarda didyma

10. Campanula carpatica   11. Mirabilis japonica   12. Polygonum capitatum 'Magic Carpet'

27 / Courtyard Garden I

A red and blue frame is created for a courtyard garden with a border of intermingling begonias and plumbagos. A magnolia tree at the left rear is balanced with a malus at the right. Viburnum and picea bring the finishing touches to the rear of the plan and a pair of lovely hydrangeas frame the entrance to the house. The courtyard itself has a small lawn, brick floor, and ample space for seating furniture.

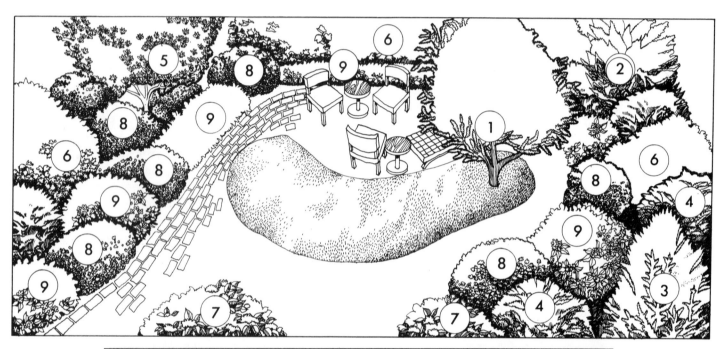

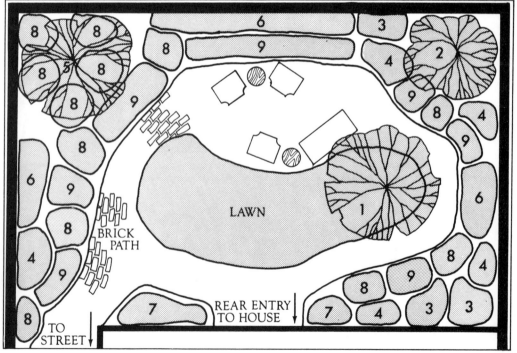

1. **Malus 'Van Eseltine'**
   Crab Apple
   Tree/Deciduous
   Hardy to −10F
   To 20 feet, leaves oblong;
   rose flowers in spring; ¾-inch
   yellow fruit with a trace of
   red. Needs sun and light
   feeding.

2. **Picea pungens 'Glauca'**
   Colorado Spruce
   Tree/Evergreen
   Hardy to −35F
   To 75 feet; leaves bluish and
   needlelike; cones 4 inches
   long. Tends to lose lower
   branches.

3. **Taxus media 'Hatfield'**
   Yew
   Shrub/Evergreen
   Hardy to −10F
   To 8 feet; leaves short and
   dark green. Tolerates neglect
   and poor soil.

4. **Taxus cuspidata**
   Japanese Yew
   Shrub/Evergreen
   Hardy to −10F
   To 50 feet; pointed leaves to 1
   inch long; red berry-like fruit
   in the fall. Will grow in poor
   soil.

5. **Magnolia stellata**
   'Dr. Merrill'
   Tree/Deciduous
   Hardy to −10F
   To 10 feet; leaves large and
   oblong; large white flowers
   bloom before leaves appear.

6. **Viburnum opulus**
   'Compacta'
   European Cranberry
   Bush
   Shrub/Deciduous
   Hardy to −35F
   To 48 inches; leaves small
   and three-lobed; red berries.
   Tolerant of practically any
   soil; dependable and rarely
   bothered by insects.

7. **Hydrangea petiolaris**
   Climbing Hydrangea
   Vine/Deciduous
   Perennial
   Summer
   Hardy to −10F
   To 50 feet; leaves heart-
   shaped; white flowers in 10-
   inch clusters. Needs sandy
   loamy soil and good drainage.
   A truly magnificent vine.

8. **Begonia 'Scarletta'**
   Wax Begonia
   Annual
   Summer
   To 12 inches; leaves succulent
   and round; brilliant red flow-
   ers. Let soil dry out between
   waterings.

9. **Plumbago larpentae**
   Shrub/Semievergreen
   Hardy to −10F
   To 12 inches; leaves small
   and oval; lovely blue flowers
   in dense panicles. Needs
   loose soil and responds well
   to light feeding.

1. Malus 'Van Eseltine'

2. Picea pungens 'Glauca'

3. Taxus media 'Hatfield'

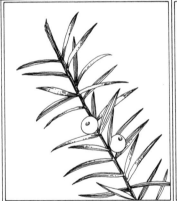

4. Taxus cuspidata

5. Magnolia stellata 'Dr. Merrill'

6. Viburnum opulus 'Compacta'

7. Hydrangea petiolaris

8. Begonia 'Scarletta'

9. Plumbago larpentae

28 / Courtyard Garden II

The herringbone brick pattern of the terrace floor is an important part of this courtyard plan for autumn. Small red cushion mums border pink chrysanthemums for a dramatic flair and the area around the terrace is filled with dazzling white begonias. Evergreen bittersweet flanks the walks; the trees are red maples.

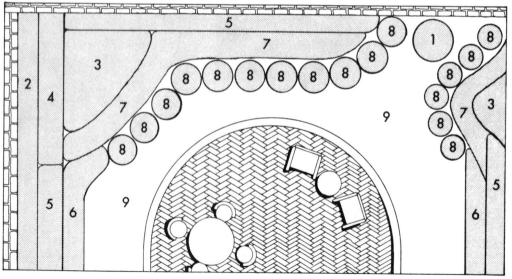

1. *Acer rubrum*
Red Maple
Tree/Deciduous
Hardy to −35F
To 100 feet; lobed leaves; bright red flowers in April before leaves appear. Grows in any good garden soil; not bothered by pests.

2. *Euonymus fortunei radicans*
Wintercreeper
Ground Cover/Evergreen
Hardy to −10F
To 60 inches; small 2-inch leaves; shrubby. Grows well in any good garden soil.

3. *Caryopteris clandonensis*
'Heavenly Blue'
Bluebeard
Shrub/Deciduous
Hardy to −10F
To 48 inches; opposite leaves; exquisite blue flowers in August or September. Prune in early spring. Likes sandy soil.

4. *Helianthus multiflorus*
Double Sunflower
Perennial
Summer
To 40 inches; coarse-grained leaves; gold double flowers.

5. **Chrysanthemum**
   (Hybrids)
Perennial
Spring/Summer
To 30 inches; large double gold flowers. 'Autumn Leaves,' 'Pumpkin,' 'Pink Chief,' and 'Golden Promise' are suggested; together these make a colorful display.

6. *Plumbago capensis*
Cape Plumbago
Shrub/Evergreen
Hardy to −10F
To 20 feet; small leaves; pale blue 1-inch flowers.

7. **Chrysanthemum**
'Clara Curtis'
Annual
Summer
To 24 inches; small leaves; pink flowers.

8. **Chrysanthemum 'Pancho'**
Perennial
Summer/Fall
To 20 inches; spatulate leaves; gold flowers. Cushion mum type.

9. *Begonia*
'White Tausendschuen'
Perennial
Summer
To 8 inches; green leaves; white flowers. Prolific bloomer, easily grown.

1. Acer rubrum

2. Euonymus fortunei radicans

3. Caryopteris clandonensis 'Heavenly Blue'

4. Helianthus multiflorus

5. Chrysanthemum (Hybrids)

6. Plumbago capensis

7. Chrysanthemum 'Clara Curtis'

8. Chrysanthemum 'Pancho'

9. Begonia 'White Tausendschuen'

29 / Cutting Garden

Easy to cultivate and reach, this cutting garden provides dozens of flowers. Black plastic is used under gravel to discourage weeds and high planter boxes allow hoses to be moved about without knocking down plants. Plants are selected for continuous bloom throughout summer.

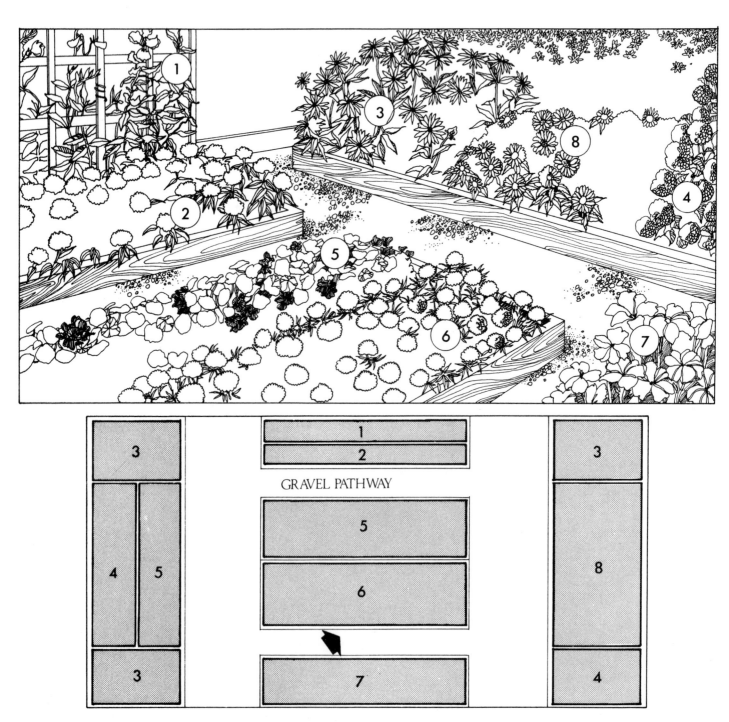

GRAVEL PATHWAY

1. **Lathyrus 'Spencer's Giant' Sweet Pea**
Annual
Summer
Climbs to 84 inches; round and opposite leaflets; flowers fragrant and of various colors. Plant very early. Water on the leaves causes mildew. Water the ground around the plant deeply, to avoid disease. Spectacular as cut flowers.

2. *Dianthus barbatus* **Sweet William**
Annual/Biennial
Summer/Fall
To 16 inches; leaves narrow; flowers in clusters, with reddish striped petals and red base. Will last for days after cutting.

3. *Rudbeckia gloriosa* **Gloriosa Daisy**
Perennial
Summer
To 48 inches; leaves oblong; flowers mahogany to clear yellow but usually golden yellow with brown center. Long-lasting cut flowers, mix well with marigolds.

4. **Dahlia (Pompom type)**
Bulb/Hardy
Summer/Fall
To 42 inches; leaves oblong; flowers round, with tightly quilted petals of various colors. Prepare soil with leaf mold and cottonseed meal. Water freely. Flowers best with bright morning sun. Feed lightly.

5. **Tropaeolum 'Glorious Gleam' Nasturtium**
Annual
Spring/Summer/Fall
To 12 inches; leaves round and regularly placed; flowers bright orange-red. Use soil of medium quality: poor soil results in short stems, sandy loam in less blooms but healthier and longer-stemmed plants.

6. **Tagetes 'Cream Puff' Marigold**
Annual
Summer
To 30 inches; leaves narrow; flowers yellow. Use one of the "odorless" varieties.

7. **Salpiglossis 'Splash'**
Annual
Spring
To 24 inches; leaves fleshy and light green; flowers large and of many colors. Long-lasting cut flowers.

8. **Chrysanthemum 'Thomas Killin' Shasta Daisy**
Perennial
Summer/Fall
To 24 inches; leaves long and narrow; flowers white with double petals. Easily grown. Responds magnificently when worked and lightly fertilized. Dislikes hot, dry climates.

1. Lathyrus 'Spencer's Giant'

2. Dianthus barbatus

3. Rudbeckia gloriosa

4. Dahlia (Pompom type)

5. Tropaeolum 'Glorious Gleam'

6. Tagetes 'Cream Puff'

7. Salpiglossis 'Splash'

8. Chrysanthemum 'Thomas Killin'

30 / Dahlia Garden

Though dahlias are used here, this plan of crossed stepping stones can be used for almost any special garden. No two islands are the same and thus there is interest and color throughout. This is a simple, informal working garden where one can putter and enjoy the flowers at will. It can be decreased or increased in size depending on the site.

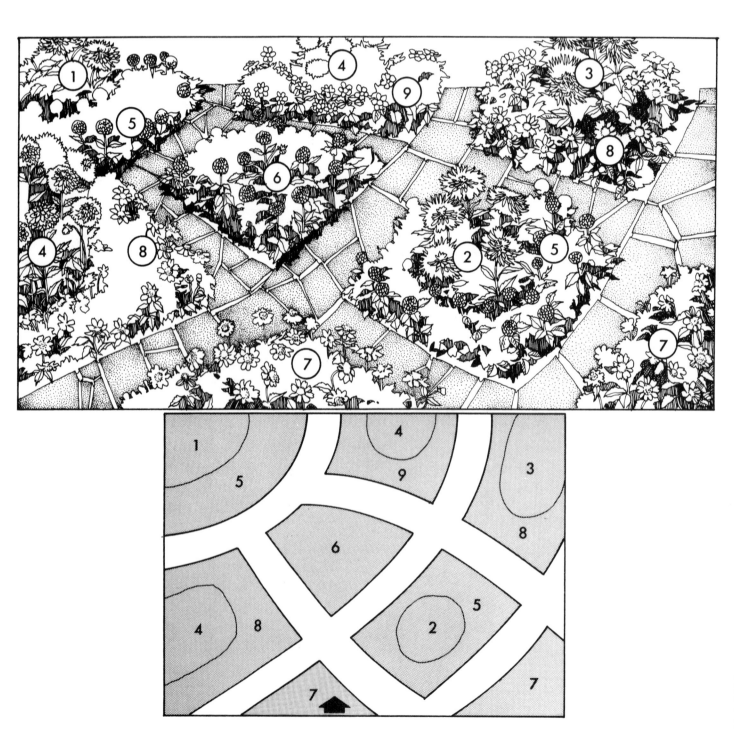

1. Dahlia 'Vicki Ann'
Bulb/Hardy
Summer
To 60 inches; leaves dark green; flowers lavender-rose. Giant water-lily type blooms 10 to 12 inches wide. Full bushy plant.

2. Dahlia 'Camelot'
Bulb/Hardy
Summer
To 60 inches; leaves green, flowers 10 inches wide and pink with glowing yellow center. Semicactus type; bushy plant.

3. Dahlia 'Sprite'
Bulb/Hardy
Summer
To 60 inches; flowers 10 inches wide, cherry-red with yellow center.

4. Dahlia 'Color Sketch'
Bulb/Hardy
Summer
To 60 inches; flowers 12 inches wide, lavender. Prolific and bushy.

5. Dahlia 'Alice'
Bulb/Hardy
Summer
To 36 inches; "pompom" flowers 2 inches wide, double, bright orange-red. Strong stems; good for cutting.

6. Dahlia 'Little Connecticut'
Bulb/Hardy
Summer
To 36 inches; "pompom" blossoms, very dense, red.

7. Dahlia 'Fabel and Roulette'
Bulb/Hardy
Summer
To 12 inches; flowers red and rose.

8. Dahlia 'Wiek'
Bulb/Hardy
Summer
To 12 inches; dwarf bedding type; flowers deep red with yellow button centers, single, to 4 inches wide.

9. Dahlia 'Siemon Doorents'
Bulb/Hardy
Summer
To 16 inches; leaves oval and toothed; flowers pink, single, and 4 inches wide.

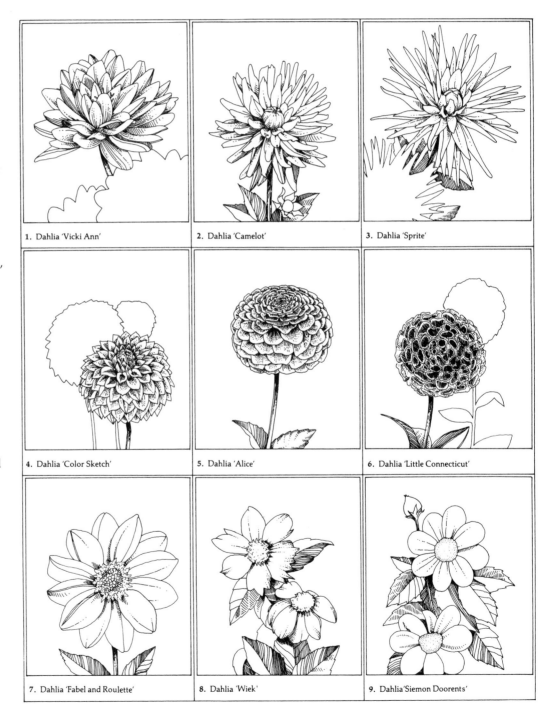

1. Dahlia 'Vicki Ann'

2. Dahlia 'Camelot'

3. Dahlia 'Sprite'

4. Dahlia 'Color Sketch'

5. Dahlia 'Alice'

6. Dahlia 'Little Connecticut'

7. Dahlia 'Fabel and Roulette'

8. Dahlia 'Wiek'

9. Dahlia 'Siemon Doorents'

31 / Deck Garden I

This deck garden relies on containers of perennials in wooden planters. There are cascading plants, with lots of color for midsummer bloom, but not so many plants to make it a garden laborious to care for.

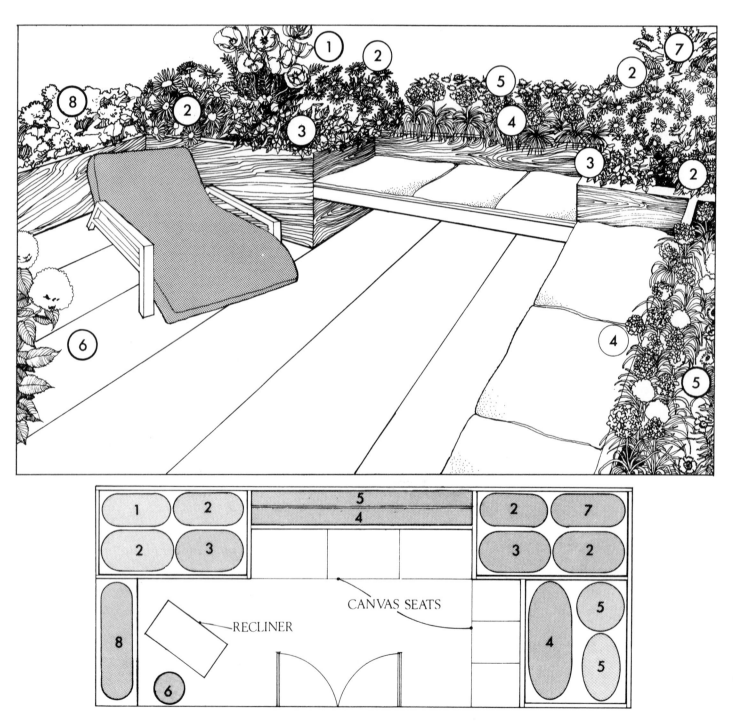

RECLINER

CANVAS SEATS

1. *Papaver nudicaule*
Iceland Poppy
Perennial
Summer
To 12 inches; long leaflets; flowers fragrant, solitary, and in various colors. Will tolerate almost any soil but must have good drainage.

2. **Chrysanthemum 'Little Miss Muffet' Shasta Daisy**
Perennial
Summer/Fall
To 16 inches; leaves lobed with abundant flowers. Needs ample sun and excellent drainage, but easy to grow.

3. *Convolvulus tricolor*
Dwarf Glorybind
Annual
Summer
To 12 inches; leaves semi-upright and oblong; flowers small and blue. Needs hot, dry conditions to prosper.

4. **Armeria 'Royal Rose'**
Perennial
Spring/Summer
To 15 inches; leaves linear and in tufts at base; flowers pink and globe-shaped. Best grown in slightly dry conditions, with minimal feeding.

5. **Dianthus 'Allwood's Delight'**
Biennial
Summer/Fall
To 18 inches; leaves green and linear; flowers white, pink or red, with darker central ring. Long season of bloom.

6. *Viburnum carlcephalum*
Snowball Bush
Shrub/Deciduous
Hardy to −10F
To 72 inches; leaves dull gray-green; flowers white and fragrant. Grows in almost any soil, resists insect attack, responds well to feeding.

7. *Clematis jackmanni*
Virgin's Bower
Vine/Deciduous
Perennial
Hardy to −20F
Summer
To 20 feet; leaves dark green; flowers large and purple. Needs rich, loose, fast-draining soil with lime added. Plant deep and feed moderately. Flowers produced on current year's growth.

8. **Geranium (Double-dip type)**
Perennial
Summer
To 16 inches; leaves round and dark green; flowers 5 inches wide, red and pink. Good yield.

1. Papaver nudicaule

2. Chrysanthemum 'Little Miss Muffet'

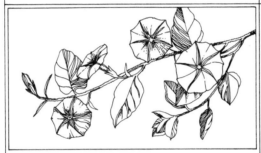
3. Convolvulus tricolor

4. Armeria 'Royal Rose'

5. Dianthus 'Allwood's Delight'

6. Viburnum carlcephalum

7. Clematis jackmanni

8. Geranium (Double-dip type)

32 / Deck Garden II (vegetables)

This totally utilitarian garden frames the deck with planter boxes constructed with benches. Eight vegetables can be easily grown in a relatively small area. A strawberry jar is used as an accent for favorite herbs. As lettuce and radishes are harvested, more should be planted.

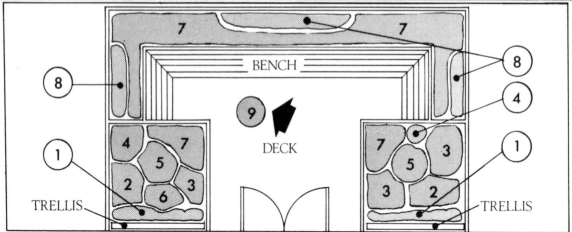

1. Cucumber 'Patio Pik'
Pick as soon as ready, otherwise new fruit will not set. Matures in 55 to 60 days. Space plants 10 inches apart.

2. Tomato 'Sugar Lump'
Likes plenty of water. Matures in 60 to 70 days. Space plants 18 to 28 inches apart and stake vertically.

3. Squash 'Aristocrat'
Needs lots of space. Matures in 48 days. Space plants 20 to 24 inches apart and grow vertically. Zucchini type.

4. Garden Cress 'Curlycress'
Matures in 25 to 45 days. Seeds sensitive to light. Space plants 10 to 12 inches apart.

5. Sweet Pepper 'Yolo Wonder'
Matures in 76 days. Use packaged manure in soil. Space plants 16 to 18 inches apart.

6. Onion 'Beltsville Bunching'
Matures in 95 to 120 days. Not as easy to grow as most produce. Space plants 2 to 3 inches apart.

7. Lettuce 'Oakleaf'
Excellent leaf lettuce; withstands heat. Matures in 50 days. Space plants 12 to 14 inches apart. 'Buttercrunch' and 'Ruby' also recommended.

8. Radish 'Scarlet Globe'
Easy to grow almost everywhere; matures in 24 days. Space plants 2 to 3 inches apart.

**9. *Ocimum basilicum*
Sweet Basil**
Herb/Annual
To 24 inches, leaves light green, flowers white and purple. Needs rich soil and lots of sun.

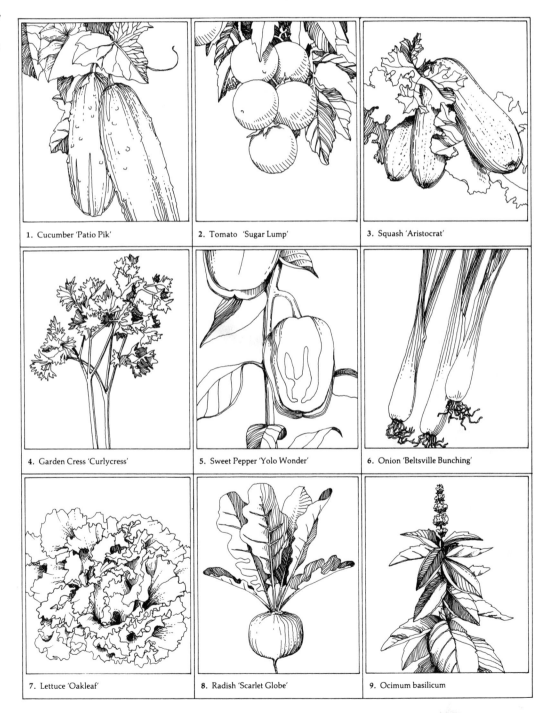

1. Cucumber 'Patio Pik'

2. Tomato 'Sugar Lump'

3. Squash 'Aristocrat'

4. Garden Cress 'Curlycress'

5. Sweet Pepper 'Yolo Wonder'

6. Onion 'Beltsville Bunching'

7. Lettuce 'Oakleaf'

8. Radish 'Scarlet Globe'

9. Ocimum basilicum

33 / Driveway Garden I

Based on an illusion of shapes and sizes of foliage to create depths, the driveway garden uses a fence as a background and two trees for vertical accent. Pink and red flowers provide a lot of color for a little effort.

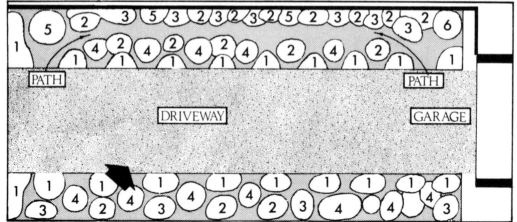

1. **Lobularia 'Rosie O'Day'**
   Sweet Alyssum
   Annual
   Summer/Fall
   To 3 inches high, 10 inches wide; leaves small and green; flowers rose-pink and abundant. Delightful aroma. Grows quickly. Keep well weeded. May reseed itself but easy to remove.

2. **Dahlia 'Fred Springer'**
   Bulb/Hardy
   Summer
   To 24 inches; leaves finely cut; flowers large and brilliant red with multiple petals. This dwarf has perfect-sized blossoms for the size of the plant. Water well and feed lightly.

3. **Dahlia 'Croydon Robin'**
   Bulb/Hardy
   Summer
   To 48 inches, leaves dissected and dark green; flowers showy, bright red and 10 inches wide. Good stock.

4. *Veronica rosea*
   Speedwell
   Perennial
   Summer
   To 18 inches; leaves long with toothed edges; flowers rose-pink. Needs loamy soil; several new varieties available.

5. *Euonymus radicans vegeta*
   Shrub/Evergreen
   Hardy to —5F
   To 48 inches; leaves small and round; berries bright orange-red; flowers inconspicuous. Remains compact and requires little pruning.

6. **Malus 'Strathmore'**
   Pyramidal Crab Apple
   Tree/Deciduous
   Hardy to —10F
   To 20 feet; leaves small; flowers pink. Beautiful pyramidal shape. Good yield.

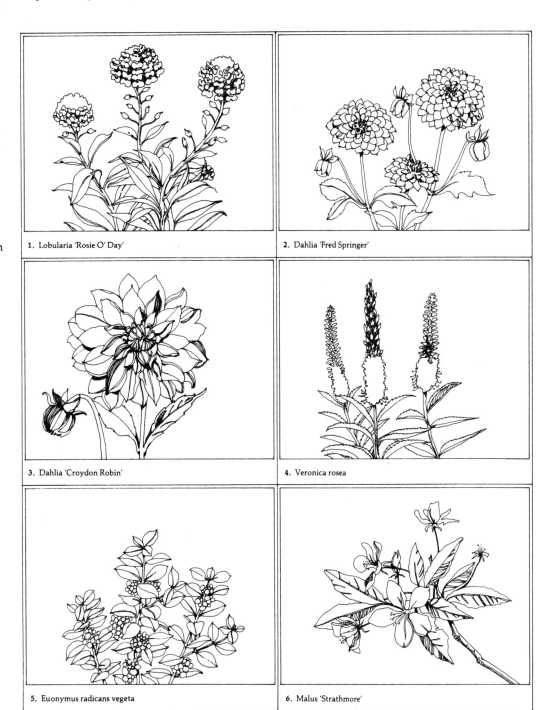

1. Lobularia 'Rosie O' Day'

2. Dahlia 'Fred Springer'

3. Dahlia 'Croydon Robin'

4. Veronica rosea

5. Euonymus radicans vegeta

6. Malus 'Strathmore'

34 / Driveway Garden II

Using a simple island plan, this easy-to-care-for driveway garden relies on colorful rhododendrons for accent. Nepeta is used as a ground cover in the foreground and there is a predominance of durable ferns strategically placed for green color. An existing tree at rear left completes the plan.

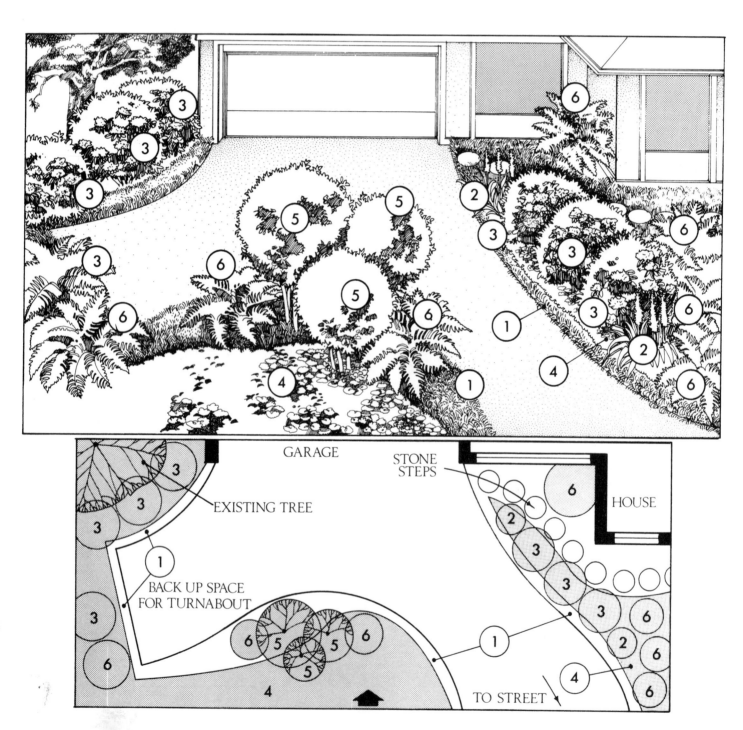

GARAGE

STONE STEPS

HOUSE

EXISTING TREE

BACK UP SPACE
FOR TURNABOUT

TO STREET

1. *Ophiopogon japonicus*
Dwarf Lilyturf
Ground Cover/Evergreen
Hardy to 5F
To 10 inches; leaves long and narrow; lilac flowers on short spikes. Grows in sun or shade.

2. *Liriope spicata*
Creeping Lilyturf
Ground Cover/Evergreen
Hardy to −10F
To 8 inches; grassy leaves that stay green in all but coldest months.

3. **Rhododendron 'David Gable'**
Shrub/Evergreen
Hardy to −10F
To 48 inches; fine pink flowering rhododendron. Acid loving. Must have good drainage; likes some sun.

4. *Nepeta hederacea*
Ground-Ivy
Ground Cover/Evergreen
Hardy to −35F
Creeping plant with mat-like growth; covers well. Easy to grow.

5. *Ilex vomitoria*
Yaupon
Shrub/Evergreen
Hardy to 10F
To 20 feet; leaves 1½ inches long; small red fruits. Fruits on previous year's growth. Drought resistant.

6. *Dennstaedtia punctilobula*
Hay-scented Fern
To 30 inches; sword-shaped fronds; finely cut edges.

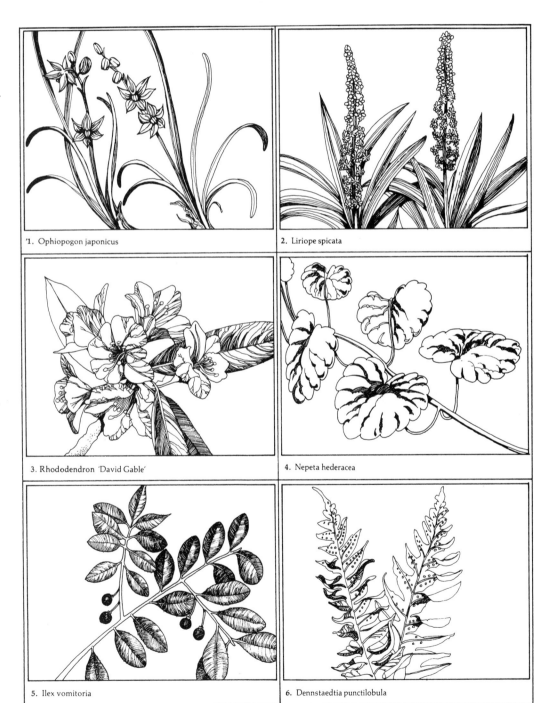

1. Ophiopogon japonicus

2. Liriope spicata

3. Rhododendron 'David Gable'

4. Nepeta hederacea

5. Ilex vomitoria

6. Dennstaedtia punctilobula

35 / Dwarf Plant Garden

In a ribbon pattern, the dwarf garden interspersed with rock walls uses red barberry as a dominant plant. The plantings are actually designed in levels running from high (barberry) to low (santolina) to create rhythm. There is a constant flow of color beautifully complemented by the amoeboid-shaped lawn. This garden needs a large area for maximum effect.

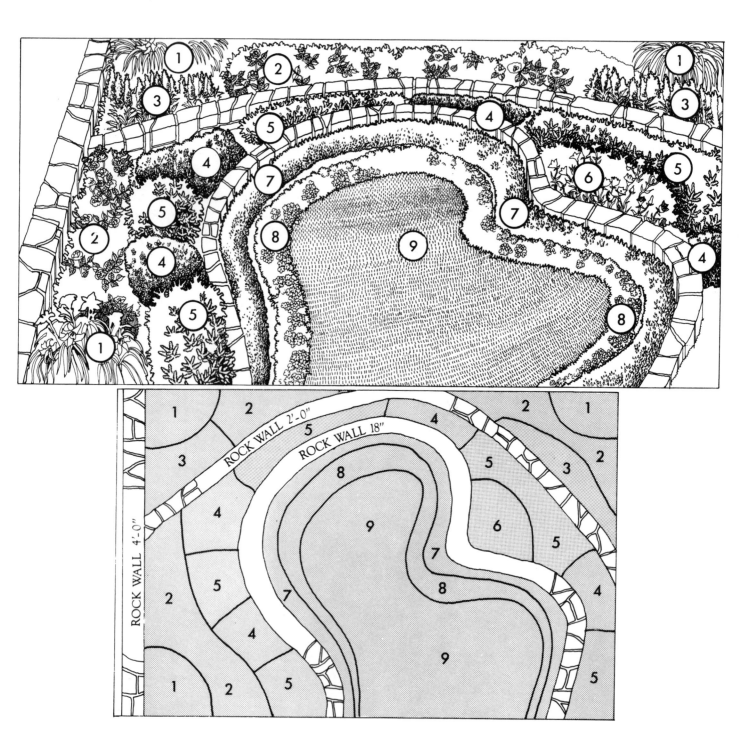

1. Hemerocallis 'Primrose Mascotte'
Bulb/Hardy
Summer
To 20 inches; leaves long and narrow; flowers yellow. Dwarf variety, prolific blooms. Responds well to good garden loam and feeding.

2. Rosa 'Perle d'Alconda'
Shrub/Deciduous
Hardy to 10F
To 20 inches; leaves oblong; flowers pale pink. Shape each winter to desirable height.

3. Veronica 'Crater Lake' Speedwell
Perennial
Spring/Summer
To 18 inches; leaves long and narrow; blue starlike flowers with white center. Needs full sun, well-drained soil.

4. Teucrium canadense Germander
Ground Cover/Semievergreen
Hardy to —10
To 12 inches; creeping, lanceolate leaves; purplish flowers. Likes moist soil, light shade. Dies back in cool regions.

5. Santolina chamaecyparissus 'Nana' Lavender Cotton
Ground Cover/Evergreen
Hardy to —5F
To 6 inches; foliage silvery, leaves divided; flowers yellow. Will grow in sandy or gravelly soil. Excellent edging plant.

6. Campanula 'Cobalt'
Perennial
Summer/Fall
To 10 inches; leaves small, round; bushy habit; vivid violet flowers. Likes coolness, good moisture.

7. Berberis thunbergii 'Crimson Pygmy' Japanese Barberry
Shrub/Evergreen
Hardy to —20F
To 12 inches; leaves bright red, small. A good low colorful hedge that requires no pruning. Thorny.

8. Phlox 'Pinafore Pink'
Perennial
Summer
To 6 inches; oval leaves 2 inches long; bright pink flowers in abundance.

9. Agrostis tenius Bent Grass
Very fine grass. Makes a luxuriant carpet. Needs full sun. If not suitable to your region use appropriate grass.

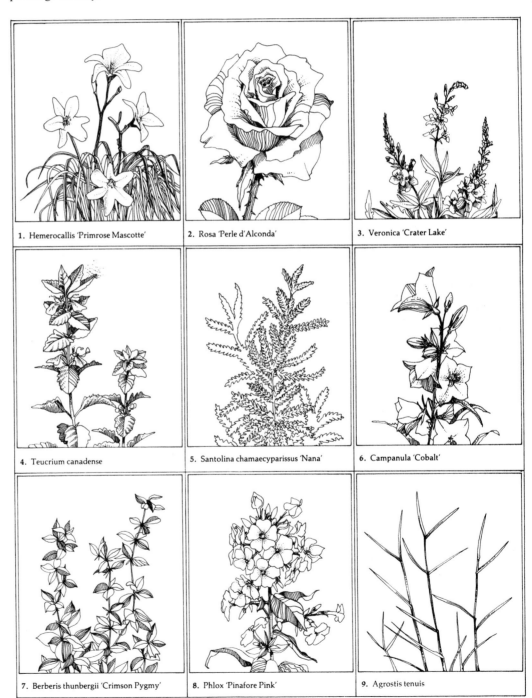

1. Hemerocallis 'Primrose Mascotte'   2. Rosa 'Perle d'Alconda'   3. Veronica 'Crater Lake'

4. Teucrium canadense   5. Santolina chamaecyparissus 'Nana'   6. Campanula 'Cobalt'

7. Berberis thunbergii 'Crimson Pygmy'   8. Phlox 'Pinafore Pink'   9. Agrostis tenuis

36 / Entrance Garden I

Predominantly blue and white, this intimate entrance garden uses a mound in its center filled with petunias and flanked by a luxurious green lawn. Colorful asters and anemones strike the eye immediately. Several trees give the garden stability and a hedge of euonymus is in the foreground.

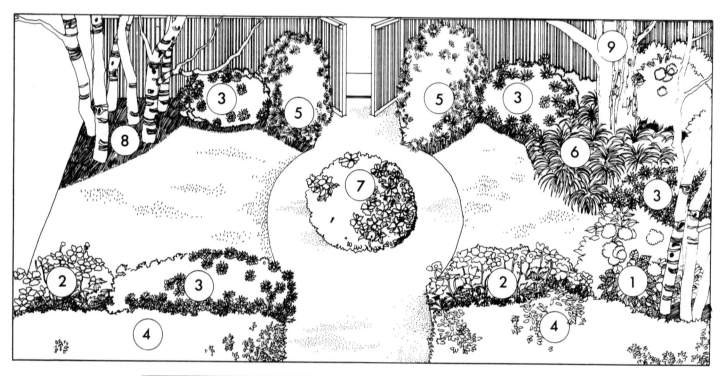

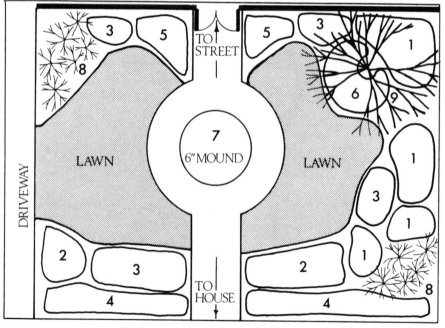

1. *Hydrangea macrophylla*
   'Blue Giant'
   Bigleaf Hydrangea
   Shrub/Deciduous
   Hardy to −10F
   To 72 inches; leaves oblong and ribbed; flowers blue or pink, in large globes. Acid in soil keeps flowers blue. Cut back in winter.

2. *Anemone japonica alba*
   Perennial
   Fall
   To 36 inches; three-toothed leaflets; white flowers, 3 inches wide. Very hardy.

3. **Aster 'Blue Radiance'**
   Michaelmas Daisy
   Perennial
   Summer/Fall
   To 36 inches; leaves ferny; flowers blue with yellow center. Grows in massed, rounded form.

4. **Euonymus 'Sarcoxie'**
   Wintercreeper
   Shrub/Evergreen
   Hardy to −10F
   To 60 inches; leaves dark green; flowers inconspicuous. Grows vigorously in any good garden soil.

5. *Pinus strobus* **'Nana'**
   Dwarf Eastern White
   Pine
   Tree/Evergreen
   Hardy to −20F
   To 60 inches; leaves needle-like in clusters of five; conical bush. Good and dependable pine.

6. *Ophiopogon japonicus*
   Dwarf Lilyturf
   Ground Cover/Evergreen
   Hardy to 5F
   To 10 inches; narrow leaves to 10 inches long; lilac flowers in short spikes. Grows in sun or shade.

7. **Petunia 'Fandango'**
   Annual
   Summer
   To 20 inches; flowers large and multiple, white and blue. These striking bicolors will bloom even more if you cut them.

8. *Betula pendula*
   European Birch
   Tree/Deciduous
   Hardy to −50F
   To 60 feet; white peeling bark; oblong leaves to 2½ inches; no flowers; pendant 1-inch catkins in summer and fall. Short-lived, but handsome.

9. *Acer griseum*
   Paperback Maple
   Tree/Deciduous
   Hardy to −10F
   To 25 feet; with three-toothed leaflets. Outstanding because of its ornamental bark.

1. Hydrangea macrophylla 'Blue Giant' 2. Anemone japonica alba 3. Aster 'Blue Radiance'

4. Euonymus 'Sarcoxie' 5. Pinus strobus 'Nana' 6. Ophiopogon japonicus

7. Petunia 'Fandango' 8. Betula pendula 9. Acer griseum

37 / Entrance Garden II

Using a narrow site at the front of the house, this small garden provides visual color and a cheerful greeting. Azaleas and chrysanthemums, the predominant plants, are used with hedges of buxus and barberry. Low ground cover euonymus borders the walk to provide a gradation of color and height in proportion to the other plants. This simple plan is easily maintained.

1. *Acer platanoides*
   'Crimson Sentry'
   Tree/Deciduous
   Hardy to −35F
   To 6 feet; lacy and lobed
   leaves turn fire red in fall.
   Columnar.

2. *Buxus microphylla koreana*
   Korean Box
   Shrub/Evergreen
   Hardy to −10F
   To 48 inches; leaves small
   and oval; tiny flowers. Loose
   and open in habit. Hardy.
   Keep pruned to fence height.

3. *Berberis thunbergii*
   'Knight Burgundy'
   Japanese Barberry
   Shrub/Evergreen
   Hardy to −10F
   To 48 inches; leaves small
   and burgundy. Thorny. Will
   grow in practically any soil.
   Prune to approximately 18
   inches.

4. **Azalea (Exbury hybrid)**
   'Fireball'
   Shrub/Deciduous
   Hardy to −10F
   To 60 inches; leaves oblong;
   flowers brilliant orange, and
   yellow. Needs cool, moist, humusy, acid soil. Dry out between watering.

5. *Forsythia intermedia*
   'Spring Glory'
   Shrub/Deciduous
   Hardy to −10F
   To 72 inches; yellow and
   abundant flowers appear before leaves. Robust. Prune
   only after flowering. Blooms
   on wood made the previous
   year.

6. **Chrysanthemum**
   'Thomas Killin'
   Shasta Daisy
   Perennial
   Summer/Fall
   To 24 inches; leaves long and
   narrow; flowers white with
   double petals. Does well on
   Pacific Coast and in the East.
   Dislikes hot and dry climates.

7. *Convallaria majalis*
   Lily-of-the-Valley
   Bulb/Hardy
   To 12 inches; leaves long and
   broad; flowers white and fra-
   grant. Needs lots of moisture.
   Likes to crowd. Use manure
   just before first snowfall.

8. *Euonymus fortunei*
   'Minima'
   Wintercreeper
   Shrub/Evergreen
   Hardy to −10F
   Creeps to 20 inches; leaves
   less than ½ inch long; no
   flowers. Will grow in most
   soils with little care. Slow
   growing.

1. Acer platanoides 'Crimson Sentry'

2. Buxus microphylla koreana

3. Berberis thunbergii 'Knight Burgundy'

4. Azalea (Exbury hybrid)

5. Forsythia intermedia 'Spring Glory'

6. Chrysanthemum 'Thomas Killin'

7. Convallaria majalis

8. Euonymus fortunei 'Minima'

38 / Entrance Garden III

Graceful retaining walls crammed with plants transform a barren upslope into a rainbow. The plants are set in ribbons at the rear and in drifts in the foreground for harmony. The masonry construction of walls and the concrete step up should be done by a professional.

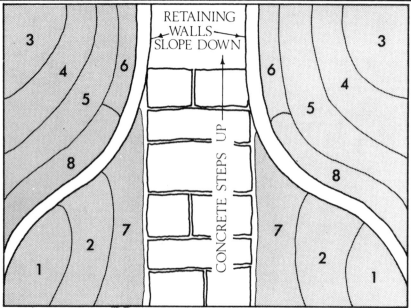

1. **Echinops 'Taplow Blue'**
Globe Thistle
Perennial
Summer/Fall
To 60 inches; leaves spiny; flowers blue-purple. Plants tolerate dry soil. Spectacular garden and excellent arrangement plant.

2. *Salvia pitcheri*
Pitcher's Sage
Perennial
Fall
To 42 inches; grassy foliage; vivid blue 1-inch flowers in dense racemes. Needs loamy, well-drained garden soil.

3. **Rudbeckia 'Goldsturm'**
Black-eyed Susan
Perennial
Summer
To 30 inches; oval leaves; large orange flowers with dark centers. Easy to grow in loamy garden soil; good for cutting.

4. *Platycodon grandiflorum*
Balloonflower
Perennial
Summer/Fall
To 30 inches; dark green leaves; single star-shaped blue flowers. Easily grown, good for cutting. Use loamy soil, needs good drainage.

5. *Oenothera tetragona*
Sundrops
Perennial
Fall
To 20 inches; narrow leaves; beautiful and profuse lemon-yellow flowers. Excellent for border color. Easily grown.

6. *Lithospermum diffusum*
'Heavenly Blue'
Gromwell
Shrub/Evergreen
Hardy to −10F
To 10 inches; tiny hairy leaves; masses of small, vivid blue flowers that will cascade. Also called Lithodora. Requires rich well-drained soil. Especially good for Southern gardens.

7. *Sedum spathufolium*
Goldmoss Stonecrop
Ground Cover/Semievergreen
Hardy to −20F
To 4 inches; bluish-green leaves; yellow flowers in spring. Likes sun and dryness. Good drainage is essential.

8. *Cotoneaster salicifolia*
'Autumn Fire'
Willow Leaf Cotoneaster
Shrub/Evergreen
Hardy to −5F
To 12 inches; cascading habit; narrow leaves; bright red berries in fall. Needs bright light, likes moisture.

3. Echinops 'Taplow Blue'

2. Salvia pitcheri

3. Rudbeckia 'Goldsturm'

4. Platycodon grandiflorum

5. Oenothera tetragona

6. Lithospermum diffusum 'Heavenly Blue'

7. Sedum spathulifolium

8. Cotoneaster salicifolia 'Autumn Fire'

39 / Entrance Garden IV

Using one major tree as a focal point, this entrance garden has island plantings on each side of the path. In the right foreground daisies predominate and the massive planting of epimedium around the trees furnishes low-maintenance ground cover. Notice that a stone wall purposely breaks the planting for a feeling of spaciousness—yet the garden is rather small. This two-level type of design works well in small entrance areas.

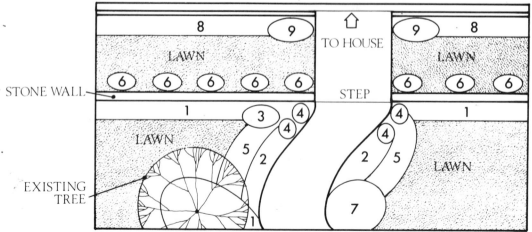

1. **Epimedium niveum**
   Snowy Epimedium
   Perennial
   Spring/Summer
   To 14 inches; heart-shaped leaflets light green in spring, glossy deep green in summer and bronze in fall. Generally violet flowers. Likes lots of moisture, humusy soil.

2. **Lobularia**
   'Carpet of Snow'
   Sweet Alyssum
   Annual
   Spring/Summer
   To 8 inches; leaves small; flowers white and heavily scented.

3. **Iris 'Gudrun'**
   Bulb/Hardy
   Spring
   To 36 inches; giant snowy white full blossom. Tall bearded type.

4. **Petunia 'Snow Cloud'**
   Annual
   Spring
   To 18 inches; white flowers, grandiflora type. Will bunch out if pruned. Many flowers.

5. **Polyanthus veris elatior**
   Primula
   Perennial
   Spring
   To 12 inches. Use Pacific Giant variety; white flowers only. Easily grown.

6. **Rosa 'Saratoga'**
   Shrub/Deciduous
   Hardy to −35F
   To 36 inches; gardenia-shaped, prolific white flowers. Easily grown.

7. **Chrysanthemum maximum**
   Perennial
   Summer
   To 24 inches; leaves long and narrow; flowers white with double petals. Dislikes hot, dry climates.

8. **Euonymus alatus**
   'Compacta'
   Winged Euonymus
   Shrub/Evergreen
   Hardy to −20F
   To 48 inches; dark green leaves turn scarlet in fall. Horizontal branching habit. Grows in any good soil.

9. **Juniperus chinensis aurea**
   Chinese Juniper
   Shrub/Evergreen
   Hardy to −10F
   To 40 feet; silver-green foliage, somewhat pyramidal. Prefers alkaline soil.

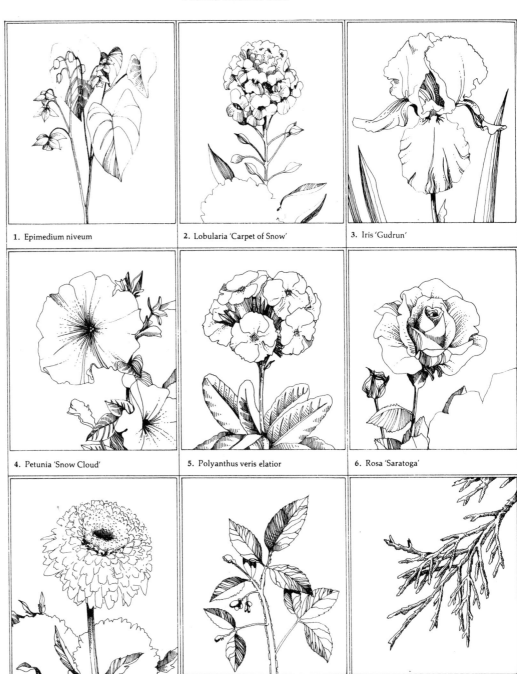

1. Epimedium niveum

2. Lobularia 'Carpet of Snow'

3. Iris 'Gudrun'

4. Petunia 'Snow Cloud'

5. Polyanthus veris elatior

6. Rosa 'Saratoga'

7. Chrysanthemum maximum

8. Euonymus alatus 'Compacta'

9. Juniperus chinensis aurea

40 / Everlasting Garden

A formal design contained by a six foot concrete wall, this handsome garden is pleasant to walk through and has a pretty seating place. Statice and echinops are colorful and also can be dried for winter use. This plan needs a long area with a width of at least 20 feet. A mound in the center island creates the focal point.

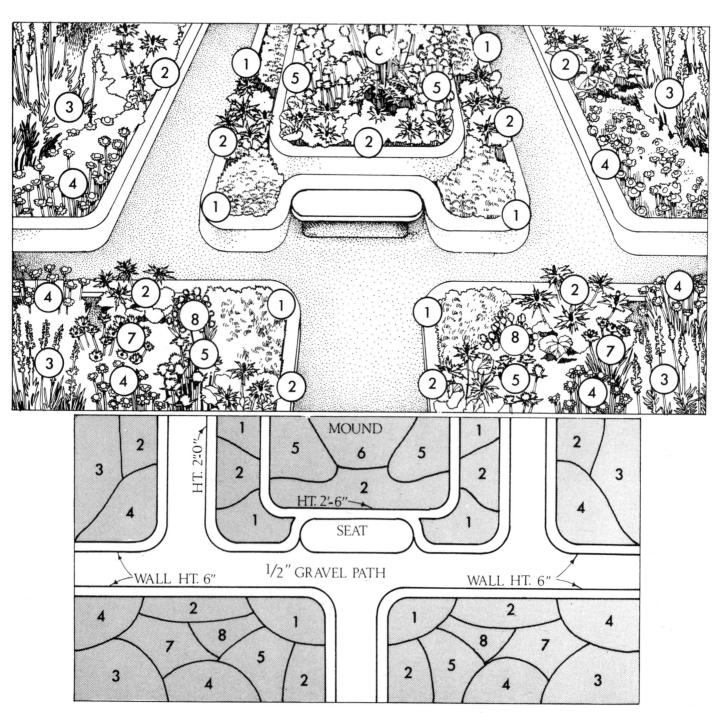

**1. *Statice latifolia*
Sea Lavender**
Annual
Summer
To 12 inches; dense foliage; showy pink flowers. Needs well-drained soil. Sometimes called Limonium. Responds well to feeding. Must have sun.

**2. *Eryngium amethystinum*
Sea Holly**
Perennial
Summer
To 24 inches; broad green leaves; fluffy purple flowers. Does best in full sun and sandy soil.

**3. Lavandula 'Hidcote'
Lavender**
Perennial
Summer
To 12 inches; fine-cut fragrant leaves; deep purple flowers. A compact dwarf. Likes warm, dry spot.

**4. *Ammobium alatum*
Winged Everlasting**
Annual
Summer
To 36 inches; winged branches, white flowers with yellow centers. Needs full sun and sandy soil.

**5. *Xeranthemum annuum*
Common Immortal**
Annual
Summer/Fall
To 36 inches; tomentose leaves; purple flower heads. Difficult to transplant. Grow in a very porous soil in full sun.

**6. Echinops 'Taplow Blue'
Globe Thistle**
Perennial
Summer/Fall
To 60 inches; deeply lobed leaves; tall stems with round purple flower heads. Plants tolerate dry soil.

**7. Catananche 'Blue Giant'
Cupid's Dart**
Perennial
Summer/Fall
To 36 inches; grassy foliage; large layered violet flowers. Succeeds in most soil, but needs almost perfect drainage. Responds to feeding.

**8. *Gomphrena globosa*
Globe Amaranth**
Annual
Summer
To 16 inches; small flower heads, usually purple or white. Needs sun and well-drained soil. Likes hot weather.

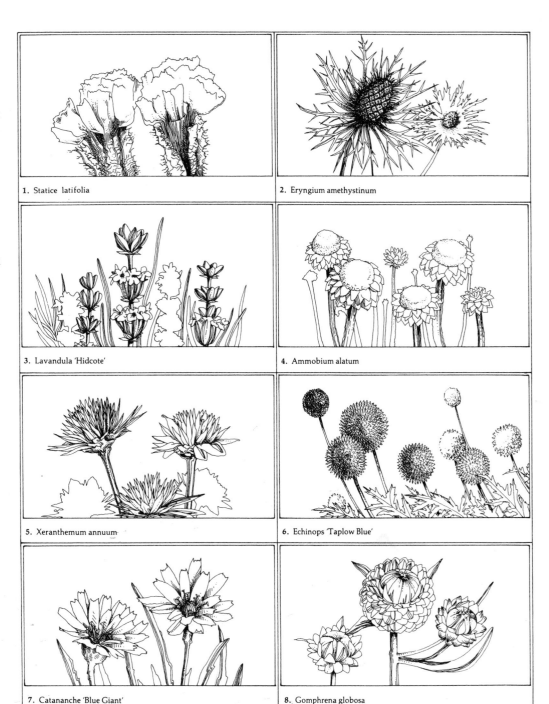

1. Statice latifolia

2. Eryngium amethystinum

3. Lavandula 'Hidcote'

4. Ammobium alatum

5. Xeranthemum annuum

6. Echinops 'Taplow Blue'

7. Catananche 'Blue Giant'

8. Gomphrena globosa

41 / Fern Garden

This fern garden is a desirable choice for a shady site. Planned around an existing tree and embellished with a stone path, a combination of frilly species and bold-leaved species are repeated to create a lush look. This plan can be used in a small or large site.

STONE PATH

**1. *Osmunda regalis*
Royal Fern**
Fronds to 48 inches, full and dense, tall and branching. Requires a very acid soil and good moisture.

**2. *Osmunda cinnamomea*
Cinnamon Fern**
Fronds to 36 inches, turn cinnamon-brown as spores mature.

**3. *Camptosorus rhizophyllus*
Walking Fern**
Fronds to 9 inches long, heart-shaped at base, tapering at tip; frond may root its tip. Likes lime in soil and a moist, shaded location.

**4. *Adiantum pedatum*
Maidenhair Fern**
Fronds to 18 inches long, nearly round and forked. Needs a cool moist soil and shade.

**5. *Dryopteris marginalis*
Leatherwood Fern**
To 30 inches; rather stiff dark green fronds. Likes humusy soil.

**6. *Pellea rotundifolia*
Button Fern**
To 28 inches; small button-shaped leaves on pendent stems. Pretty and unusual, nice dark green accent. Likes moisture and coolness.

**7. *Osmunda claytoniana*
Interrupted Fern**
To 36 inches; rather upright habit; fronds lush green. Likes moisture and shade.

**8. *Asplenium nidus*
Bird's Nest Fern**
To 24 inches, bright green spatulate leaves. Unusual. Keep in shade.

**9. *Pteris argyraea*
Brake Fern**
To 36 inches, fronds with white bands. Give it shaded, moist conditions.

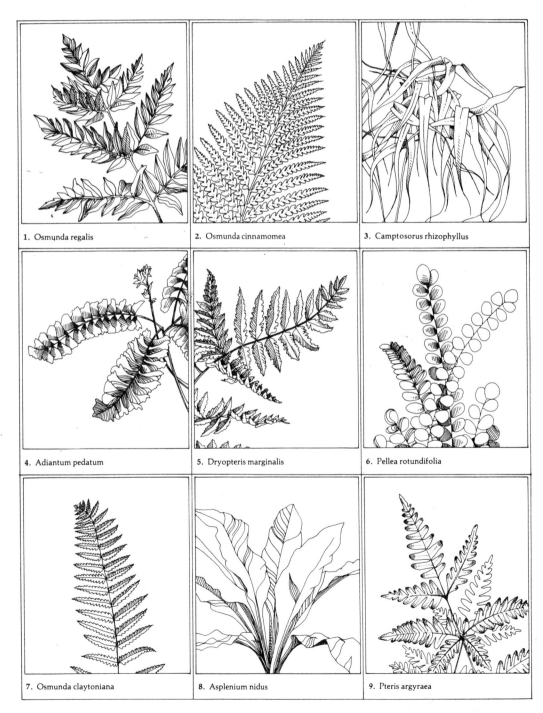

1. Osmunda regalis

2. Osmunda cinnamomea

3. Camptosorus rhizophyllus

4. Adiantum pedatum

5. Dryopteris marginalis

6. Pellea rotundifolia

7. Osmunda claytoniana

8. Asplenium nidus

9. Pteris argyraea

42 / Flowering Shrub Garden

This garden has a serpentine lawn and serpentine drifts of flowers. A hedge of English hawthorn at the side provides dimension and throughout there is a free flow of plant material. The garden uses only six plants repeated in specific areas.

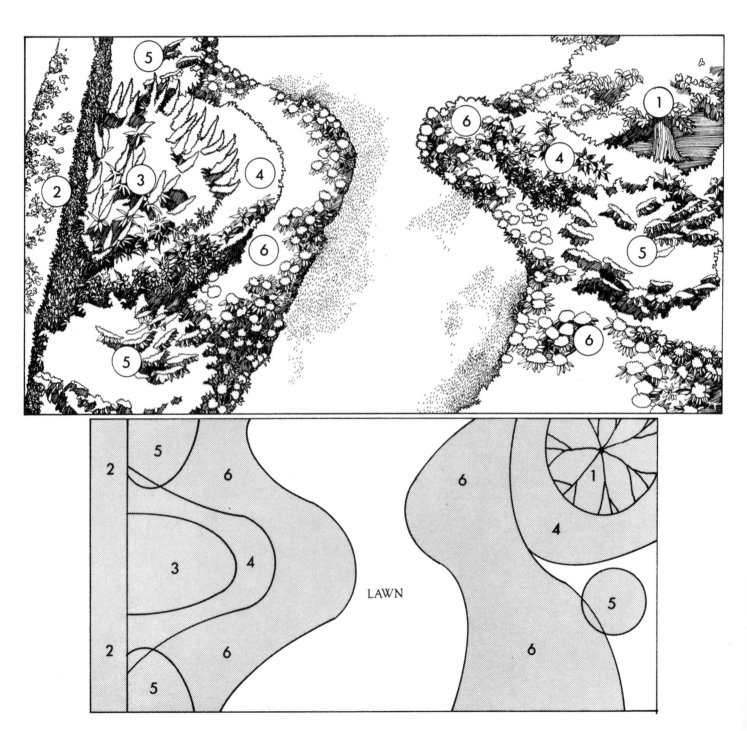

LAWN

1. *Cornus florida* 'Rainbow'
   Dogwood
   Tree/Deciduous
   Hardy to −10F
To 20 feet; leaves green and yellow in summer, changing in autumn; white flowers.

2. *Crataegus oxyacantha*
   English Hawthorn
   Tree/Deciduous
   Hardy to −10F
To 15 feet; with 1-inch spines; lobed leaves 2 inches wide; flowers white; berries red. Slow growing; tolerates poor soils.

3. *Vitex agnus-castus*
   'Silver Spire'
   Chaste Tree
   Shrub/Deciduous
   Hardy to 5F
To 72 inches; hand-like fragrant leaves; flowers white. Dies back in some regions but recovers quickly.

4. *Weigela florida*
   'Bristol Ruby'
   Shrub/Deciduous
   Hardy to −10F
To 72 inches; leaves oblong; red flowers abundant in spring. Needs plenty of water and sun, good drainage.

5. *Viburnum plicatum*
   'Mariesii'
   Japanese Snowball
   Shrub/Deciduous
   Hardy to −10F
To 72 inches; leaves oval and ribbed; flowers white; berries red. Grows in almost any soil; tolerates light shade.

6. *Daphne cneorum*
   Rose Daphne
   Shrub/Evergreen
   Hardy to −20F
To 12 inches; leaves to 1 inch long; flowers in rose-red clusters. Needs cool moist conditions.

1. Cornus florida 'Rainbow'

2. Crataegus oxyacantha

3. Vitex agnus-castus 'Silver Spire'

4. Weigela florida 'Bristol Ruby'

5. Viburnum plicatum 'Mariesii'

6. Daphne cneorum

43 / Formal Garden

This handsome garden has a symmetrical elegance in what is almost a mirror-image plan. The hedges are neatly trimmed, the plantings sparse, the total plan is in clean straight lines. There is brick surfacing and a charming center bird bath.

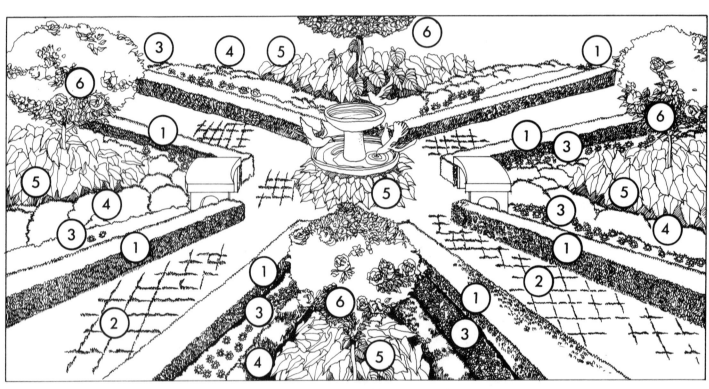

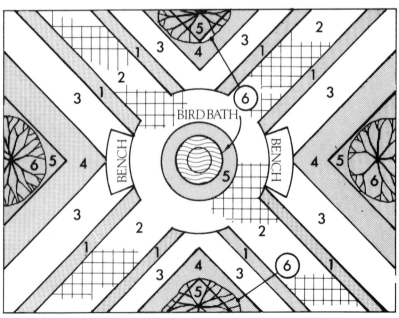

1. *Teucrium chamaedrys*
   Germander
   Ground Cover/Semievergreen
   Hardy to −10F
   To 12 inches; leaves toothed,
   hairy and oblong; flowers ¾
   inch long, red and on spikes.
   Good carpet plant. Grows
   readily in most soils.

2. *Thymus serpyllum*
   Woolly Thyme
   Ground Cover/Evergreen
   Hardy to −35F
   To 3 inches; leaves prostrate,
   grayish and oblong; flowers
   purplish. An excellent ground
   cover plant with good color.
   Likes sandy loam.

3. *Anthemis nobilis*
   Roman Camomile
   Ground Cover/Semievergreen
   Hardy to −20F
   To 3 inches; leaves fernlike;
   flowers usually yellow and
   daisylike. Clip this back peri-
   odically and use the dried
   clippings for tea.

4. *Artemisia schmidtiana*
   Satiny Wormwood
   Ground Cover/Deciduous
   Hardy to −20F
   To 24 inches; covered with
   silvery hairs; leaves greatly
   dissected; flowers in small
   heads. Likes poor somewhat
   dry soil. Dies down in winter.

5. **Caladium**
   'White Christmas'
   Bulb/Tender
   To 24 inches; leaves large,
   heart-shaped, green with
   white vein. A favorite foliage
   plant. Needs loamy soil and
   lots of water. Keep out of sun.

6. **Rosa 'Pascoli'**
   Shrub/Deciduous
   Hardy to −10F
   To 60 inches; treeform, leafy;
   flowers large and white.
   Watch for sprouts from the
   roots and remove any you
   see.

1. Teucrium chamaedrys

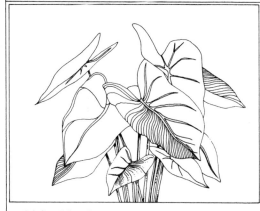

2. Thymus serpyllum

3. Anthemis nobilis

4. Artemisia schmidtiana

5. Caladium 'White Christmas'

6. Rosa 'Pascoli'

44 / Fragrant Garden

This garden, which can be built on a deck or patio or in the backyard, is resplendent with fragrant plants. To avoid monotony, plantings are in 12-inch concrete terraces at three levels. Plants have been selected for height as well as fragrance.

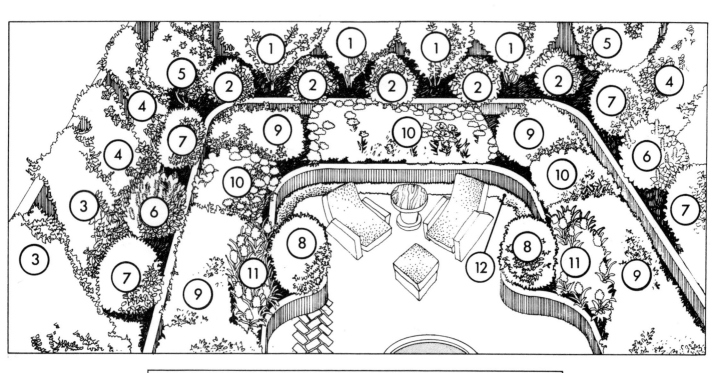

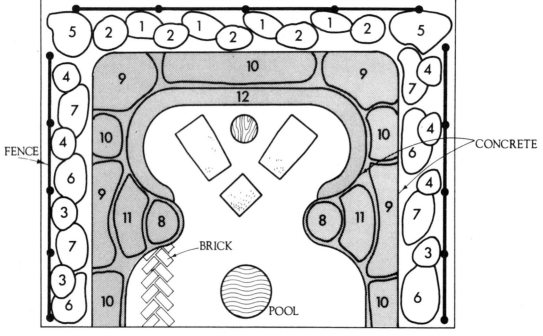

FENCE

CONCRETE

BRICK

POOL

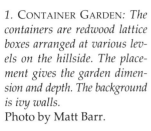

1. CONTAINER GARDEN: The containers are redwood lattice boxes arranged at various levels on the hillside. The placement gives the garden dimension and depth. The background is ivy walls.
Photo by Matt Barr.

2. WATER GARDEN: Peace and serenity are part of any water garden, and here water lilies are the central focus. Note the brick wall, a perfect compliment for the water garden.
Photo by Jack Kramer.

3. GRAVEL GARDEN: Known as a gravel garden or textured garden, this simple arrangement of paths and walls makes a handsome picture.
Photo by Matt Barr.

4. WALL GARDEN: *Various ground-cover plants adorn the rise in the ground, creating a somewhat walled landscape.*
Photo by George Taloumis.

5. BULB GARDEN: *An assortment of bulbs and some white azaleas make this San Francisco garden a colorful, peaceful place. Design elements—stone wall and paved, block floor—have been carefully selected. The total effect is harmonious.*
Photo by Jack Kramer.

6. PATIO GARDEN: *Garden-goers enter this lovely garden through a beautiful picket fence. Inside, a secluded patio landscape awaits them.*
Photo by Jack Kramer.

7. GEOMETRIC GARDEN: *A rare but handsome design, this garden arrangement is based on geometics (blocks of plantings.) Note the traditional bench in the background against a brick wall.*
Photo by Andrew Addkison.

8. CUTTING GARDEN: *A fine cutting garden is an asset to any garden montage. A stone wall provides the background.*
Photo by Andrew Addkison.

9. CITY GARDEN: *This fine city garden in Boston relies on the natural beauty of brick and wrought-iron fencing—a pleasing combination.*
Photo by George Taloumis.

10. IRIS GARDEN: *A speciality garden—whether roses or irises—is always a pleasure to view. This one is in full glory.* Photo by Molly Adams.

11. ENTRANCE GARDEN: *An entrance garden welcomes any visitor; in this scene azaleas and roses grow profusely. The garden is styled as a midwest garden.* Photo by George Taloumis.

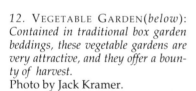

12. VEGETABLE GARDEN(*below*): *Contained in traditional box garden beddings, these vegetable gardens are very attractive, and they offer a bounty of harvest.* Photo by Jack Kramer.

13. CITY GARDEN: *Nestled below looming buildings, this small city retreat is amass with flowers.*
Photo by George Taloumis.

14. SHADE GARDEN: *A serene garden provides a peaceful place to sit, meditate, and enjoy nature.*

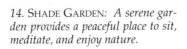

15. PERENNIAL GARDEN: *A perennial garden can be many things; this one boasts an assortment of flowers.*
Photo by George Taloumis.

16. HERB GARDEN: *All sorts of herbs are grown in this border garden, which is both attractive and useful.* Photo by C. Gilberg.

17. COURTYARD GARDEN(*below*): *Around a small pond, this courtyard garden in Georgia is a lovely green scene. The formal landscape has both vertical and horizontal accents, and the circular pond acts as mass to unite the other elements.* Photo by Andrew Addkison.

18. ROCK GARDEN(*above*): *Green plants dominate this rock garden which borders a path.* Photo by George Taloumis.

19. BALCONY GARDEN: *Located in the Northeast, this small balcony garden with a wooden floor is a delightfully handsome—and useful—retreat.*
Photo by George Taloumis.

20. PERENNIAL GARDEN: *Masses of color accent this border garden.*
Photo by George Taloumis.

21. PATIO GARDEN: *This quiet patio garden contains soothing tones of green, which predominate over the scene.*
Photo by Jack Kramer.

22. ENTRANCE GARDEN: *Random stonework leads the way to this California home.* Photo by George Taloumis.

23.ENTRANCE GARDEN*(below): An island of green is the welcome in this country entrance garden.* Photo by Jack Kramer.

24. WOODLAND GARDEN: *Hostas and astilbes create a woodland scene that is both beautiful and serene.* Photo by C. Gilberg.

1. **Rosa 'Dream Girl'**
Shrub / Deciduous
Hardy to −10F
Climbs to 72 inches; leaves compound; flowers fragrant, pink and multipetaled. Train in arching pattern on trellis for better blooms.

2. *Viburnum carlcephalum*
Snowball Bush
Shrub / Deciduous
Hardy to −10F
To 72 inches; leaves gray-green and oblong; flowers white in large spherical clusters. Prune to 4 feet. Robust grower. Excellent in spring for flowers, in summer for foliage, and in autumn for brightly colored berries. Watch for aphids. Responds to feeding.

3. *Lonicera japonica*
'Halliana'
Hall's Honeysuckle
Vine / Semievergreen
Perennial
Hardy to −20F
Spring / Summer
To 20 feet; leaves to 3 inches long; flowers buff yellow. Likes acid soil. Tends to grow rampant.

4. *Ipomoea noctiflora*
Moon Vine
Vine
Annual
Summer
To 15 feet; leaves large and heart-shaped; flowers fragrant, 6 inches long and white, often with green bands. Grows in any soil.

5. *Magnolia stellata*
'Dr. Merrill'
Star Magnolia
Tree / Deciduous
Hardy to −10F
To 15 feet; leaves large, oblong, and glossy; flowers small, star-shaped, and white. Delightful fragrance.

6. *Clethra alnifolia rosea*
Summersweet
Shrub / Evergreen
Hardy to −35F
To 60 inches; toothed leaves to 4 inches long; pink flowers on erect spikes. Loves water and a slightly acid soil.

7. *Philadelphus coronarius*
'Enchantment'
Mock Orange
Shrub / Deciduous
Hardy to −10F
To 84 inches; leaves narrow; fragrant, double white flowers in clusters. Keep about 60 inches tall. Prune.

8. **Azalea (Rothschild type)**
Shrub / Deciduous
Hardy to −20F
To 60 inches; leaves oblong; flowers large and pink, with five petals each in huge globelike clusters. Very fragrant.

9. *Nicotiana alata*
Nicotine Plant
Annual
Summer
To 30 inches; leaves greenish yellow; tubular flowers white, pink, yellow, or scarlet. One of the most fragrant of all summer annuals. Easy to grow.

10. *Dianthus barbatus*
Sweet William
Annual / Biennial
Summer / Fall
To 16 inches; leaves narrow; red flowers in clusters. Easy to grow. Good as cut flowers.

11. *Matthiola bicornus*
Stock
Annual
Summer
To 18 inches; leaves 3 inches long and lance-shaped; lilac flowers fragrant.

12. *Thymus serpyllum*
Woolly thyme
Ground Cover / Evergreen
Hardy to −35F
To 3 inches; leaves ½ inch long and oblong; flowers ¼ inch wide and purplish. this crushes underfoot as you walk, lending a fresh aroma. Likes sandy loam.

1. Rosa 'Dream Girl'

2. Viburnum carlcephalum

3. Lonicera japonica 'Halliana'

4. Ipomoea noctiflora

5. Magnolia stellata 'Dr. Merrill'

6. Clethra alnifolia rosea

7. Philadelphus coronarius 'Enchantment'

8. Azalea (Rothschild type)

9. Nicotiana alata

10. Dianthus barbatus

11. Matthiola bicornus

12. Thymus serpyllum

45 / Garden Around a Fountain

This plan features a circular fountain surrounded with a lush planting of flowers. The circular island which predominates is placed to create ample walkways. Iris and lilacs are the basic plantings, with eremurus used at the two far corners; ornamental pears complete the plan.

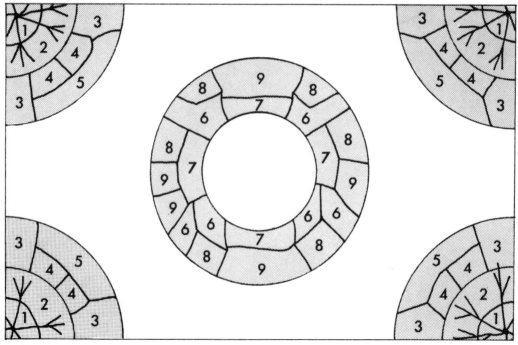

1. *Pyrus calleryana* **'Bradford'** **Bradford Pear**
Tree/Deciduous
Hardy to —25F
To 30 feet; white flowers; foliage turns red in winter. Bears fruit in late summer.

2. *Clethra alnifolia rosea* **Summersweet**
Shrub/Evergreen
Hardy to —35F
To 60 inches; leaves to 4 inches and toothed; flowers pink. Needs somewhat acid soil and good light.

3. **Eremurus (Shelford hybrid)** **Foxtail Lily**
Bulb/Hardy
To 60 inches; leaves narrow and basal; flowers small, close set on tall spike, in several colors.

4. **Iris 'China Maid'**
Bulb/Hardy
Spring
To 36 inches; leaves long and narrow; flowers pink with some yellow. Elegant color. Likes loose loamy soil. Feed heavily *after* bloom. A Bearded Iris type.

5. **Hemerocallis 'Primrose Mascotte'**
Bulb/Hardy
Summer
To 20 inches; dwarf; leaves long and narrow; flowers yellow and fragrant. Likes loose loam. Responds well to feeding.

6. *Zantedeschia rehmanni* **Pink Calla**
Bulb/Tender
Summer
To 36 inches; leaves large, long and thick, arising from base of stem; flowers pink. Likes moisture. Good cut flower.

7. **Campanula 'Joan Elliot'**
Perennial
Spring
To 15 inches; oblong leaves; purple flowers in clusters on tips of stalks. Good drainage necessary. Water often.

8. *Haemanthus coccineus* **Blood Lily**
Bulb/Tender
Fall
To 12 inches; leaves basal; flowers coral-red on long stem. Cannot survive cold. Allow to rest during fall and winter in barely moist soil.

9. *Armeria maritima laucheana* **Thrift**
Perennial
Spring/Summer
To 6 inches; leaves narrow, to 6 inches long; flowers pink in hemispherical heads. Likes sandy soil, minimal feeding.

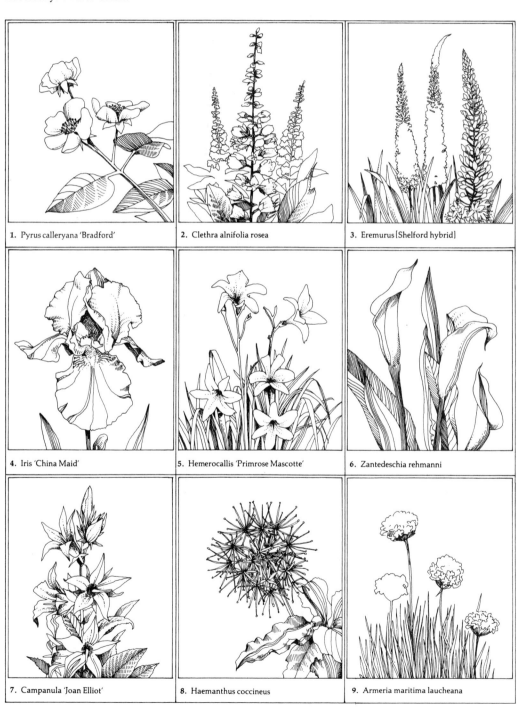

1. Pyrus calleryana 'Bradford'

2. Clethra alnifolia rosea

3. Eremurus [Shelford hybrid]

4. Iris 'China Maid'

5. Hemerocallis 'Primrose Mascotte'

6. Zantedeschia rehmanni

7. Campanula 'Joan Elliot'

8. Haemanthus coccineus

9. Armeria maritima laucheana

46 / Garden by a Brook

A bridge over a brook connects two paths in a magnificent colorful garden. Trees and shrubs predominate with brilliant gerbera foiled by purple violas. Russell Hybrid lupines furnish additional color. For all the plants, the garden still has a delicate character but a great deal of trimming and pruning is necessary to keep things in bounds.

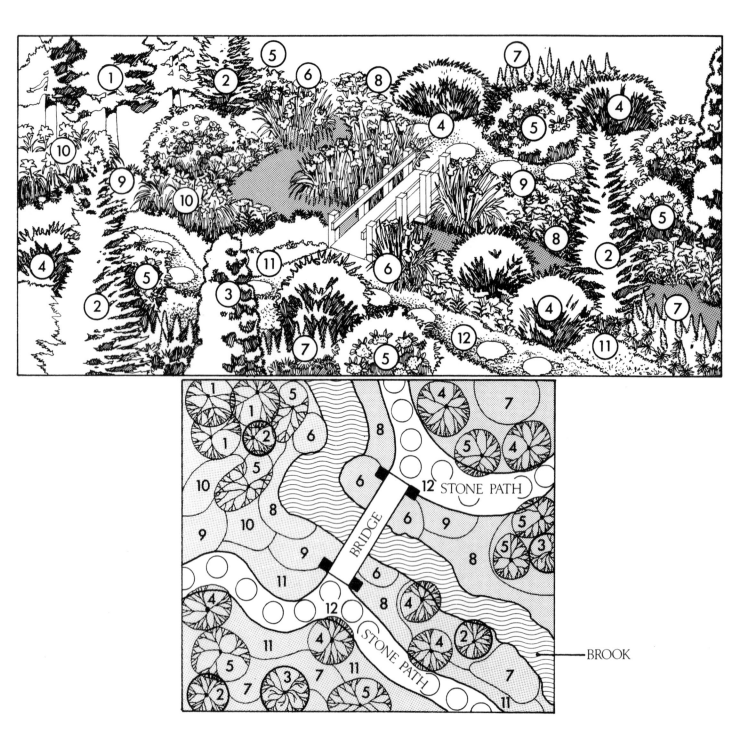

1. **Pinus aristata**
   Bristlecone Pine
   Tree/Evergreen
   Hardy to −5F
   To 25 feet; shrubby; long dark green leaves. Grows slowly; generally dwarf and picturesque.

2. **Abies concolor**
   White Fir
   Tree/Deciduous
   Hardy to −20F
   To 120 feet; narrow and pyramidal; bluish-green needles. Withstands heat and drought. One of the best firs for northern gardens.

3. **Cryptomeria japonica**
   Tree/Evergreen
   Hardy to −10F
   To 150 feet; splendid evergreen with small needles. Pyramidal, symmetrical when young and easy to grow.

4. **Abelia grandiflora**
   Glossy Abelia
   Shrub/Evergreen
   Hardy to −10F
   To 60 inches; glossy leaves turn bronze in autumn. Dense, most free-flowering of abelias. Makes good hedge.

5. **Camellia japonica**
   Shrub/Evergreen
   Hardy to 5F
   To 15 feet; broad leaves; white or red flowers. Easy to grow.

6. **Iris kaempferi**
   Japanese Iris
   Bulb/Hardy
   To 48 inches; handsome large blue flowers on tall stems in summer. Likes moisture. Use acid fertilizer.

7. **Lupinus**
   'Russell's hybrids'
   Lupine
   Perennial
   Summer/Fall
   To 48 inches; tall spikes; close-set, handsome blue, pink and yellow flowers. Avoid water on the leaves. Does not tolerate wind.

8. **Filipendula 'Flore Pleno'**
   Meadowsweet
   Perennial
   Summer
   To 18 inches; ferny foliage; clusters of white flowers. Grows compactly. Prefers a moist location. Good cutting flowers.

9. **Gerbera (hybrid)**
   Transvaal Daisy
   Perennial
   Summer
   To 18 inches; aster type; giant pink, red, and orange flowers. Elegant and stately.

10. **Hemerocallis**
    'Magic Dawn'
    Bulb/Hardy
    Summer
    To 36 inches; large red lily. Easily grown, responds to watering, needs good drainage.

11. **Viola 'Royal Robe'**
    Violet
    Perennial
    Spring
    To 6 inches; dark green cup-shaped leaves; brilliant blue flowers.

12. **Helxine soleirolii**
    Baby's-tears
    Ground Cover/
    Semievergreen
    Hardy to −10F
    To 4 inches; dense mat; bright green.

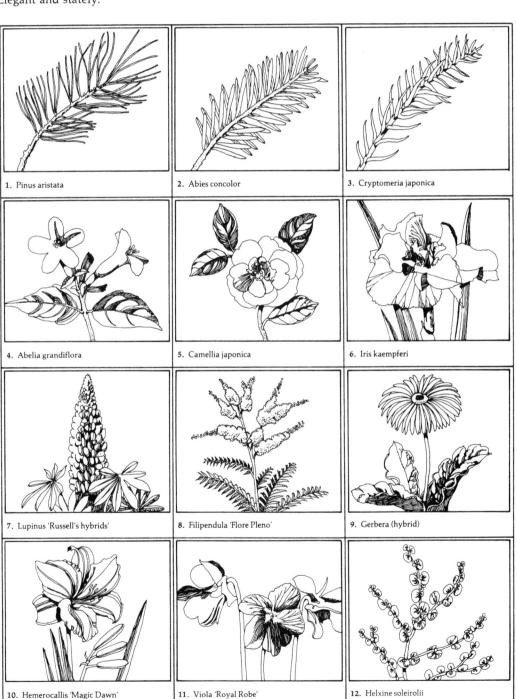

1. Pinus aristata

2. Abies concolor

3. Cryptomeria japonica

4. Abelia grandiflora

5. Camellia japonica

6. Iris kaempferi

7. Lupinus 'Russell's hybrids'

8. Filipendula 'Flore Pleno'

9. Gerbera (hybrid)

10. Hemerocallis 'Magic Dawn'

11. Viola 'Royal Robe'

12. Helxine soleirolii

47 / Garden for the Elderly

This simple garden, relying on raised planting containers, has a wide aisle for easy movement of traffic. Fruits and vegetables are complemented with colorful flowers good for cutting. Fruit trees frame the garden and the grape arbor is a peaceful place to sit in shade. Steps are provided throughout to make gardening and harvesting easy. This garden can be created in a 25-foot lot.

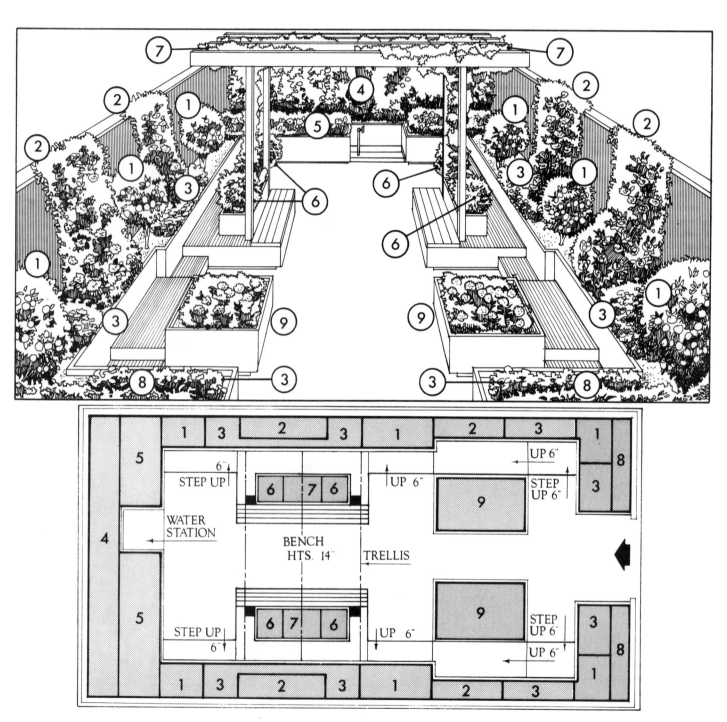

1. *Prunus armeniaca*
   'Chinese Golden'
   Apricot
   Tree/Deciduous
   Hardy to −5F
   To 10 feet; large smooth-skinned fruit. Ripens in mid-August. Plant two different varieties for cross-pollination.

2. **Rosa 'Thor'**
   Shrub/Deciduous
   Hardy to −20F
   Climbs to 10 feet; profuse blazing red roses. Resists most rose maladies.

3. **Tropaeolum**
   'Glorious Gleam'
   Nasturtium
   Annual
   Spring/Summer/Fall
   To 12 inches; leaves dense and round; flowers bright orange-red. The more flowers picked the more the bloom. Sandy loam best; yields less flowers but more vigorous growth.

4. **Pole Bean**
   'Kentucky Wonder'
   Space 6 to 8 inches apart and 18 inches between rows. Stake with trellis. Germination takes 65 days.

5. **Petunia 'Red Cascade'**
   Annual
   Spring
   To 12 inches; flowers red. Needs rich soil and plenty of water. Spectacular cut flowers; buds open in house.

6. **Tomato 'Pixie'**
   Space plants 10 to 12 inches apart. Stake on small trellis. One of best small tomatoes. Germination takes 52 days.

7. **Grape 'Seedless Concord'**
   Exceptionally sweet, easy-to-grow seedless grape. Needs loamy soil.

8. **Peas 'Alaska'**
   Space plants 2 to 3 inches apart and stake. Germination takes 55 days. Likes coolness.

9. **Zinnia 'Zipasee'**
   Annual
   Summer/Fall
   To 18 inches; flowers large and multicolored. Easy to grow. Outstanding cut flowers.

1. Prunus armeniaca 'Chinese Golden'   2. Rosa 'Thor'   3. Tropaeolum 'Glorious Gleam'

4. Pole Bean 'Kentucky Wonder'   5. Petunia 'Red Cascade'   6. Tomato 'Pixie'

7. Grape 'Seedless Concord'   8. Peas 'Alaska'   9. Zinnia 'Zipasee'

48 / Garden for a Triangular Lot

This garden is arranged so that there is a gradual pyramid of flowers to relate to the triangular shape of the site. Starting with a mound of lilies and followed by a brick walk and patio, a pyramidal lawn area frames this section. Bordering this pyramid is a triangle pattern of colorful hydrangeas, delphiniums, azaleas, and dogwood trees. The plan is capped with a magnificent weeping willow tree.

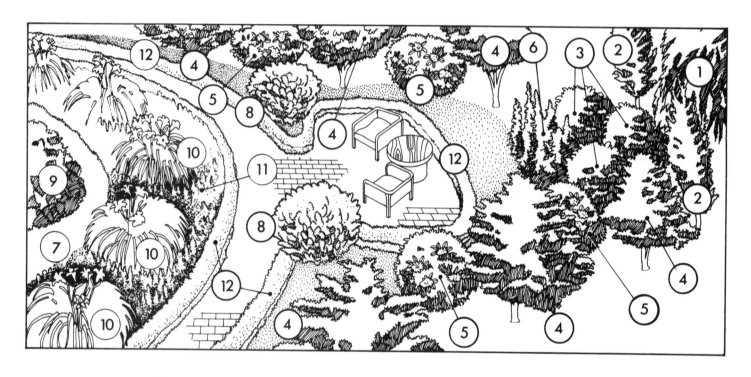

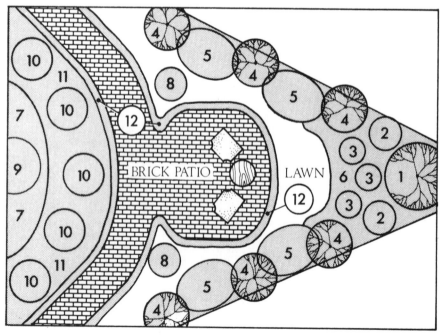

1. **Salix babylonica 'Salmonii' Weeping Willow**
Tree/Deciduous
Hardy to −35F
To 20 feet; small leaves; dense foliage; weeping habit. *S. babylonica* okay as substitute. Likes moisture and porous soil.

2. **Malus 'Strathmore' Pyramidal Crab Apple**
Tree/Deciduous
Hardy to −10F
To 20 feet; pyramidal habit; lovely pink flowers.

3. **Hydrangea macrophylla 'Blue Giant' Bigleaf Hydrangea**
Shrub/Deciduous
Hardy to −10F
To 72 inches; dense, oval, dark green leaves; clusters of blue or pink flowers. Can be cut back in winter. Use acid soil to get blue flowers.

4. **Cornus florida 'Rubra' Dogwood**
Tree/Deciduous
Hardy to −10F
To 20 feet; branching habit; lovely pink flowers. An attractive tree for garden use.

5. **Azalea (Exbury hybrids)**
Shrub/Deciduous
Hardy to −10F
To 60 inches; oval, dark green leaves; masses of white and pink flowers. Use cool, moist, acid soil.

6. **Delphinium (Giant Pacific hybrids) Larkspur**
Perennial/Biennial
Summer
To 72 inches; lobed leaves; tall spikes of vivid blue flowers. Use 'King Arthur,' 'Galahad,' 'Summer Skies.'

7. **Ageratum 'Summer Snow' Flossflower**
Annual
Summer
To 6 inches; dense carpet topped with mounds of white flowers.

8. **Syringa decaisne Lilac**
Shrub/Deciduous
Hardy to −10F
To 60 inches; full, bushy and low-growing; light blue or purplish flowers.

9. **Phlox 'Balmoral' Summer Phlox**
Perennial
To 60 inches; elliptical leaves; pink flowers. Also use 'Lilactime' (lavender), 'Russian violet' (purple), and 'Charles van Delft' (rose).

10. **Lilium 'Pink Glory Strain' Lily**
Bulb/Hardy
To 60 inches; grassy foliage, tall stems with huge pink flowers.

11. **Veronica 'Crater Lake' Speedwell**
Perennial
Spring/Summer
To 18 inches; lovely spikes of deep blue flowers. Prolific. Responds well to feeding. Needs full sun, well-drained soil.

12. **Aubrieta 'Red Cascade' Rockcress**
Perennial
Summer
To 6 inches; dense cascading mound of tiny purple-red flowers.

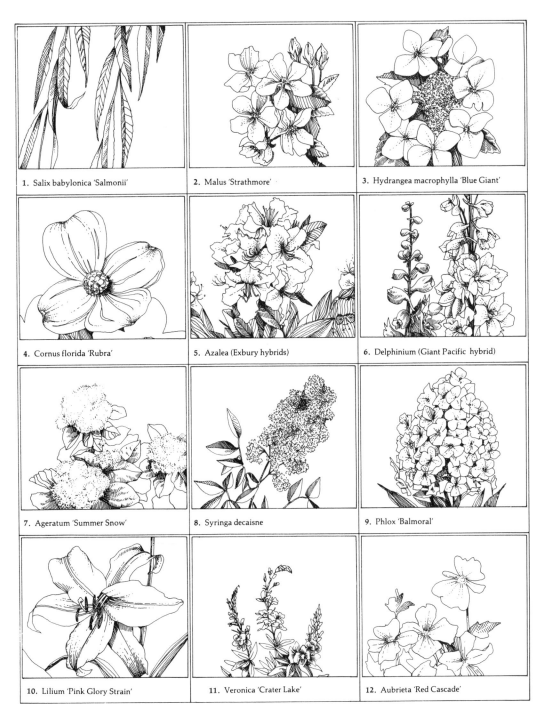

1. Salix babylonica 'Salmonii'
2. Malus 'Strathmore'
3. Hydrangea macrophylla 'Blue Giant'
4. Cornus florida 'Rubra'
5. Azalea (Exbury hybrids)
6. Delphinium (Giant Pacific hybrid)
7. Ageratum 'Summer Snow'
8. Syringa decaisne
9. Phlox 'Balmoral'
10. Lilium 'Pink Glory Strain'
11. Veronica 'Crater Lake'
12. Aubrieta 'Red Cascade'

49 / Gazebo Garden

Though it has flower-show impact, this small gazebo garden is not a difficult project because the plants which have been selected are easy to grow. There is an inner frame of colorful hanging begonias and four planting islands which cascade with color. The hanging achimenes and tuberous begonias furnish vertical beauty.

Gazebos can be purchased in kits or you can make your own from plans available from several lumber manufacturers.

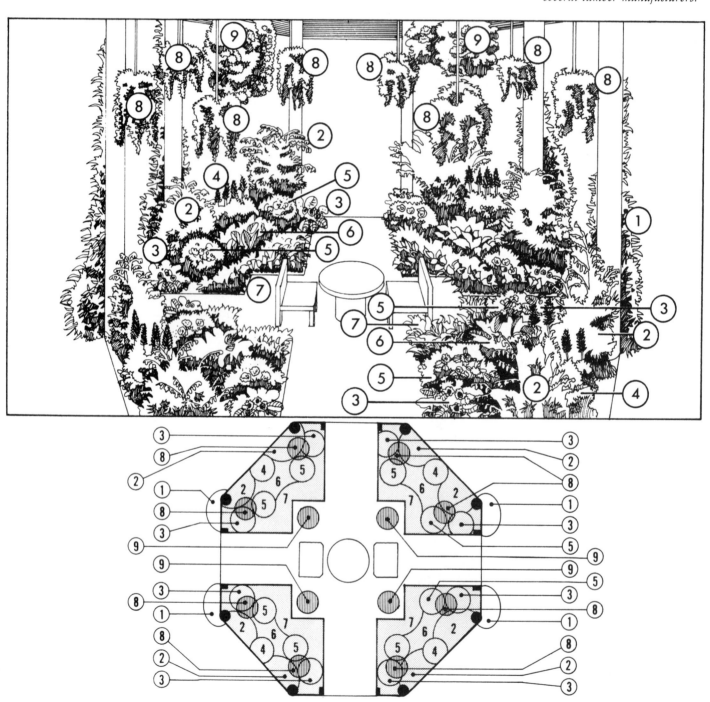

1. **Clematis patens
   'Nelly Moser'**
   *Vine/Deciduous
   Perennial
   Hardy to −35F
   Summer*
   Climbs to 20 feet; dark green leaves; large pinkish-blue flowers. Needs alkaline or limestone soil. Tolerates shade but likes morning sun.

2. **Dicentra spectabilis
   Common Bleeding-Heart**
   *Perennial
   Spring*
   To 24 inches; lobed leaves; pendent pink-red flowers.

3. **Gloxinia 'Emperor'**
   *Bulb/Tender
   Summer*
   To 16 inches; large crinkly leaves; mammoth scarlet flowers with white heads. Water often but avoid wetting leaves. Avoid direct sunlight.

4. **Spiraea 'Red Sentinel'**
   *Shrub/Deciduous
   Summer
   Hardy to −10F*
   To 6 inches; handsome lobed foliage; plumes of red flowers. Vigorous, not demanding about soil or light.

5. **Begonia tuberhybrida
   Tuberous Begonia**
   *Bulb/Tender
   Summer*
   To 30 inches; upright type; pink or red flowers. Many varieties. Needs some sun. Start in February.

6. **Hosta sieboldi
   Siebold's Plantain Lily**
   *Perennial
   Hardy to −10F*
   To 24 inches; dark blue broad leaves in dense rosette. Valued for foliage. Does best in light shade, humusy soil.

7. **Hosta lancifolia
   albomarginata
   Plantain Lily**
   Perennial
   To 10 inches; large broad green leaves marked with white.

8. **Achimenes
   'Cascade Violet Night'
   Rainbow Flower**
   *Bulb/Tender
   Summer*
   To 12 inches; heart-shaped leaves; flat-faced violet flowers. Difficult to start. Needs warmth and plenty of water.

9. **Begonia pendula**
   *Bulb/Tender
   Summer*
   Cascades to 60 inches; masses of pink or orange flowers. Needs loamy porous soil and perfect drainage. Plant in leaf mold mix and feed lightly with 15–30–15.

1. Clematis patens 'Nelly Moser'
2. Dicentra spectabilis
3. Gloxinia 'Emperor'
4. Spiraea 'Red Sentinel'
5. Begonia tuberhybrida
6. Hosta sieboldi
7. Hosta lancifolia albomarginata
8. Achimenes 'Cascade Violet Night'
9. Begonia pendula

50 / Geometric Garden

This lovely, formal diamond-shape plan has yews and lavender cotton as the key plants. The crosswalk complements the plan and while plants are sparse, they are also colorful. Hypericum is used as the ground cover to further emphasize the diamond designs.

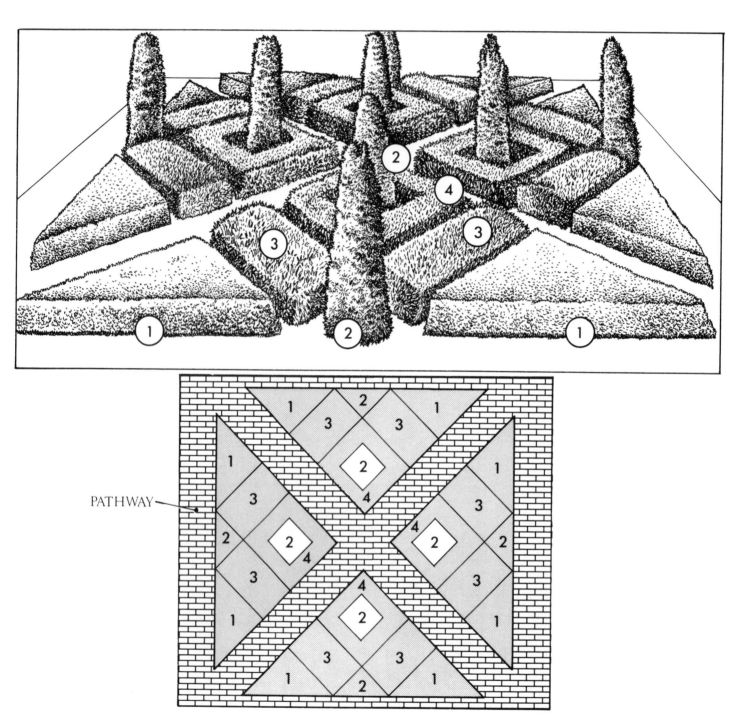

PATHWAY

1. *Ribes alpinum*
   Alpine Currant
   Shrub/Deciduous
   Hardy to −35F
   To 84 inches; leaves small
   and bushy; berries red. Dense
   and compact, and ideal hedge.
   Prune to 30 inches.

2. *Taxus baccata 'Stricta'*
   English Yew
   Tree/Evergreen
   Hardy to −5F
   To 45 feet; narrow leaves
   upright habit. Can take ne-
   glect.

3. *Santolina chamaecyparissus*
   Lavender Cotton
   Ground Cover/Evergreen
   Hardy to −5F
   To 24 inches; shrubby; silver-
   gray woolly leaves; yellow
   flowers.

4. *Hypericum patulum*
   'Sungold'
   Shrub/Evergreen
   Hardy to −10F
   To 16 inches; bright yellow
   flowers. Use as a ground
   cover. Invasive, easily grown.

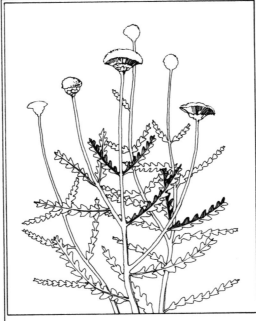

1. Ribes alpinum

2. Taxus baccata 'Stricta'

3. Santolina chamaecyparissus

4. Hypericum patulum 'Sungold'

51 / Gravel Garden

This small garden relies on low-maintenance plants as its attraction. The gravel beds are installed over black plastic to eliminate weeds and the flowers are easy to care for. Masses of bloom are framed with tritoma at the right and buddleia at left for a circular effect. Gravel is also used as a path through the garden.

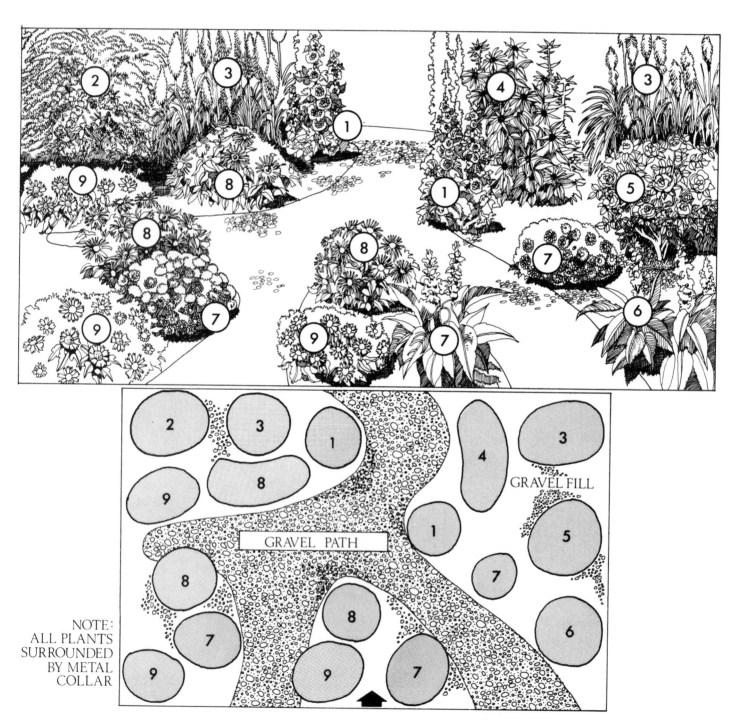

GRAVEL FILL

GRAVEL PATH

NOTE:
ALL PLANTS
SURROUNDED
BY METAL
COLLAR

1. *Althaea rosea*
   Hollyhock
   Biennial
   Summer
   To 72 inches; broad leaves; tall and stately stems; pink flowers. Requires rich loam.

2. *Buddleia davidii 'Sungold'*
   Butterfly Bush
   Shrub/Deciduous
   Hardy to −10F
   To 48 inches; dense foliage; free-blooming, bright orange-saffron flowers. Ball-shaped and spectacular in the garden. Easily grown.

3. **Kniphofia 'Earliest of All'**
   Summer
   To 48 inches; grassy foliage; tall spikes of rust-colored flowers. Also called Tritoma.

4. **Rudbeckia 'Goldsturm'**
   Black-eyed Susan
   Perennial
   Summer
   To 30 inches; broad oval leaves; large star-shaped orange flowers. Easy to grow in loamy garden soil; good for cutting.

5. **Rosa 'Medallion'**
   Hybrid Tea
   Shrub/Deciduous
   Summer
   To 36 inches; buff-orange iridescent flowers, large plant.

6. **Canna 'Stadt Fellbach'**
   Bulb/Hardy
   Summer
   To 30 inches; tall, full spikes of beautiful golden-orange flowers.

7. **Chrysanthemum 'Mini Autumn'**
   Perennial
   Summer
   To 18 inches; rust-gold blooms; cushion type. Use rich loam. Pinch back regularly to make it branch as much as possible.

8. *Inula orientalis*
   Caucasian Inula
   Perennial
   Summer
   To 16 inches; bushy green leaves with small gold flowers. Needs average garden soil, good sun.

9. *Gaillardia aristata*
   Blanketflower
   Perennial
   Summer
   To 36 inches; wide-lobed leaves; bright red flowers, tipped yellow.

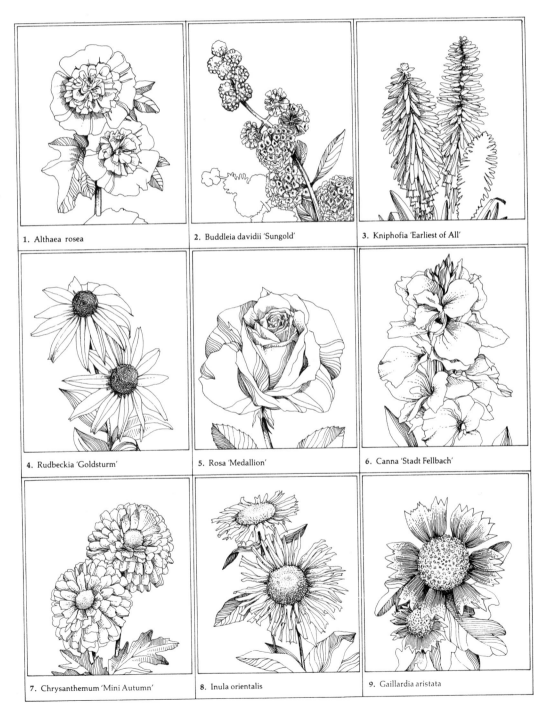

1. Althaea rosea

2. Buddleia davidii 'Sungold'

3. Kniphofia 'Earliest of All'

4. Rudbeckia 'Goldsturm'

5. Rosa 'Medallion'

6. Canna 'Stadt Fellbach'

7. Chrysanthemum 'Mini Autumn'

8. Inula orientalis

9. Gaillardia aristata

52 / Ground Cover Garden I

This low-maintenance carpet garden of ground covers and lawn is becoming increasingly popular. The lawn area dominates the plan and serves as a break between flowering ground covers. The stepping stones are placed at random. The garden can be widened by repeating the border plants or it can be decreased to accommodate a small site.

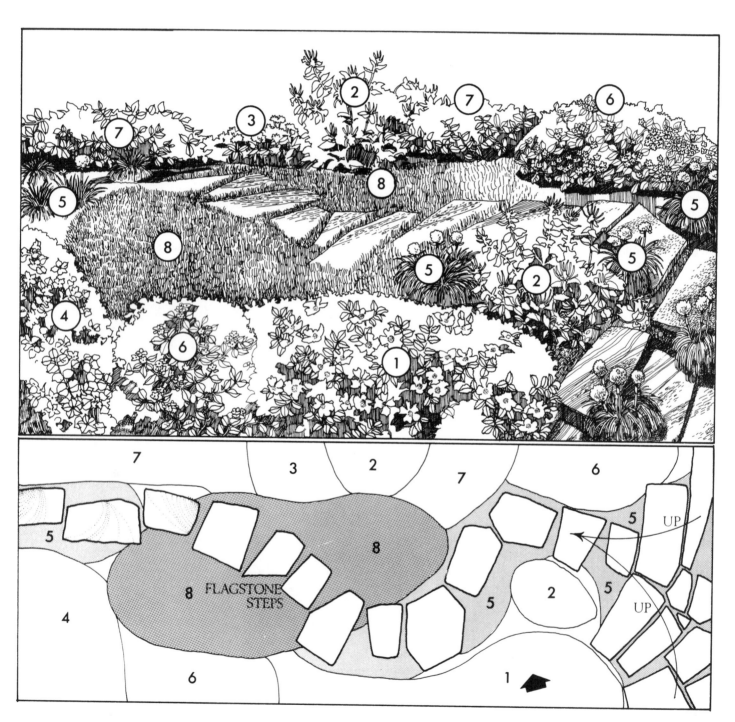

1. **Rosa Wichuriana**
   Shrub/Deciduous
   Hardy to −10F
   To 12 inches; lovely trailing habit; white flowers in abundance.

2. **Lonicera heckrottii**
   Everblooming
   Honeysuckle
   Vine/Evergreen
   Perennial
   Summer
   Hardy to −10F
   To 20 inches; dwarf; purple and yellow flowers; red fruits. Orderly, contained habit: won't take over your garden. Used to be called 'Winchester.'

3. **Asperula odorata**
   Sweet Woodruff
   Ground Cover/Deciduous
   Hardy to −10F
   To 8 inches; lovely white flowers in spring. Dies to ground in fall.

4. **Lysimachia nummularia**
   Creeping Jenny
   Ground Cover/Semievergreen
   Hardy to −35F
   To 4 inches; 1-inch leaves; masses of tiny yellow flowers.

5. **Armeria maritima**
   laucheana
   Thrift
   Perennial
   Spring/Summer
   To 6 inches; grassy leaves; deep rose-pink flowers. Does best in light sandy soil with minimal feeding.

6. **Plumbago larpentiae**
   Shrub/Semievergreen
   Hardy to −10F
   To 12 inches; a fine carpet of bright green leaves; can be used as ground cover. Vivid blue flowers. Needs loose soil, light feeding. Also called *Ceratostigma plumbaginoides*.

7. **Euonymus obovatus**
   Running Euonymus
   Shrub/Deciduous
   Hardy to −35F
   To 6 inches; leafy and fast-growing; red in autumn.

8. **Festuca ovina glauca**
   Blue Fescue
   Grass
   Durable lawn; blue-green in color. Substitute suitable grass variety for your region.

1. Rosa Wichuriana

2. Lonicera heckrottii

3. Asperula odorata

4. Lysimachia nummularia

5. Armeria maritima laucheana

6. Plumbago larpentiae

7. Euonymus obovatus

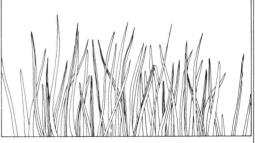

8. Festuca ovina glauca

53 / Ground Cover Garden II

This garden depends on mounds of plants—a dazzling array of phlox—to bring it to life. The winding path follows the contour of the mounds. There is a variety of ground covers, each chosen for texture and color.

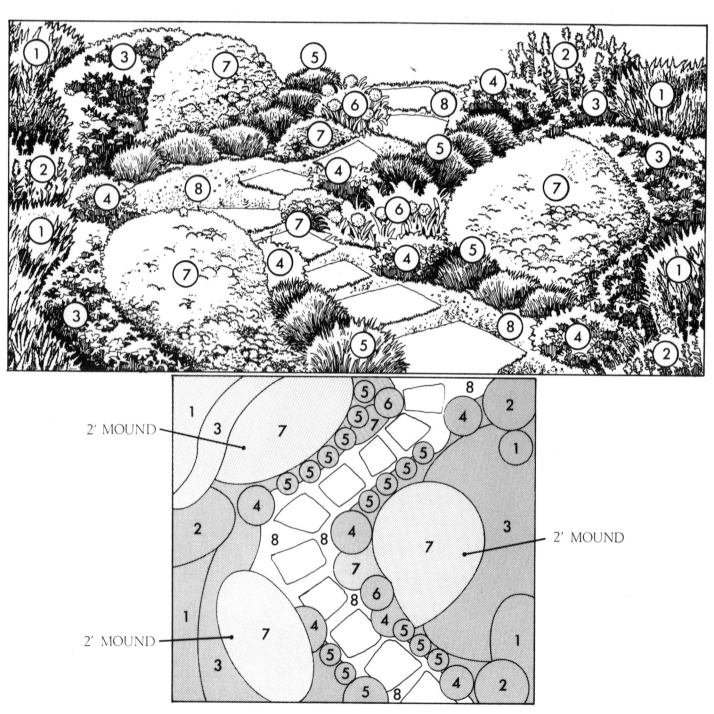

2' MOUND

2' MOUND

2' MOUND

1. *Calluna vulgaris*
   Heather
   Shrub/Evergreen
   Hardy to −10F
   To 18 inches; frilly foliage; pink or red flower spikes in summer. Dense. Needs sun for flowers; in shade plants make good ground covers.

2. **Lavandula 'Gray Lady'**
   Lavender
   Perennial
   Summer
   To 24 inches; usually evergreen; purple flowers in clusters on spikes.

3. *Hypericum calycinum*
   Aaron's Beard
   Ground Cover/Semievergreen
   Hardy to 10F
   To 12 inches; 3- to 4-inch leaves; bright yellow flowers. Excellent for sandy soil and semishaded locations.

4. *Polygonum reynoutria*
   Fleeceflower
   Perennial
   Summer
   To 12 inches; alternate green leaves turn red in fall; flowers red. Prune back in early spring to encourage fresh growth. Somewhat invasive.

5. *Festuca ovina glauca*
   Blue Fescue
   Grass
   Tufted, blue-green grass. Substitute suitable grass variety for your region.

6. *Armeria maritima*
   laucheana
   Thrift
   Perennial
   Spring/Summer
   To 6 inches; grasslike evergreen leaves; deep rose flowers. Needs sandy soil. Makes good ground cover.

7. **Phlox 'Eventide'**
   Moss Pink
   Perennial
   Summer
   To 8 inches; small foliage; dense masses of pink flowers; cascading habit. Easily grown.

8. *Arenaria verna caespitosa*
   Moss Sandwort
   Perennial
   Spring
   Mosslike 3-inch evergreen leaves. Foliage forms dense green mat. Likes sandy soil that has some leaf mold. A good creeping plant.

1. Calluna vulgaris

2. Lavandula 'Gray Lady'

3. Hypericum calycinum

4. Polygonum reynoutria

5. Festuca ovina glauca

6. Armeria maritima laucheana

7. Phlox 'Eventide'

8. Arenaria verna caespitosa

54 / Hanging Garden

This garden takes work but it is extremely beautiful. Hanging pots are suspended in tandem for an effect of columns of color throughout the garden. Four-by-four posts are used as the skeleton of the garden with two-by-four members creating the framework. Because of the diamond-and-square design, this garden requires a 25- by 50-foot site, but you could make only half the garden, as suggested in the drawing.

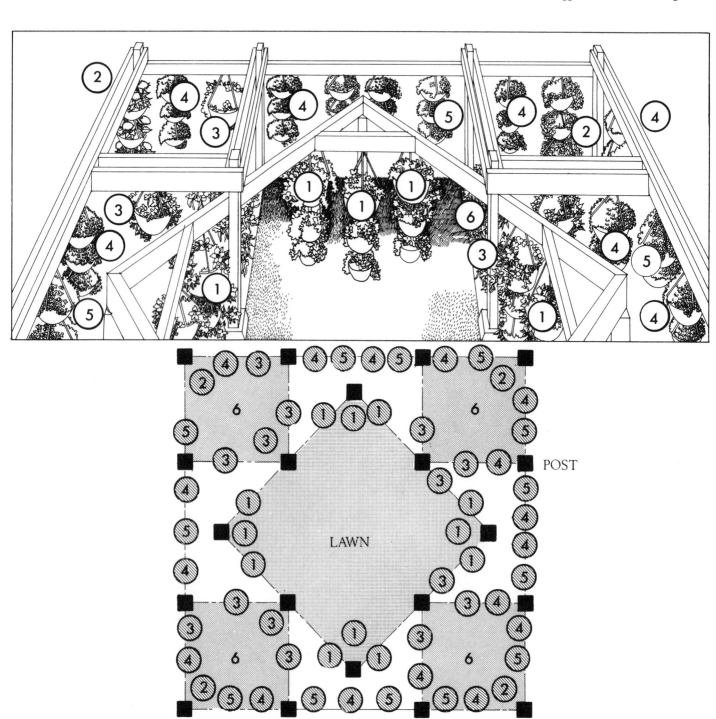

POST

LAWN

1. **Petunia 'Cascade Sky'**
   Annual
   Summer
   To 18 inches; leaves broad, light green; flowers funnel-shaped, blue. Needs ample water, sun. Hang in tandem in tiers of three.

2. **Chrysanthemum 'King's Ransom'**
   Perennial
   Fall
   To 24 inches; leaves lobed; flowers double, golden-yellow. Good cascading variety. Hang in tandem in groups of three.

3. **Impatiens 'A-Go-Go'**
   Annual
   Summer/Fall
   To 10 inches; leaves dark green, slightly toothed; red-and-white bicolor flowers. Needs coolness and good moisture.

4. **Lobelia 'Bluestone'**
   Annual
   Summer
   To 4 inches; leaves narrow; flowers small, abundant, clear blue. Will cascade in time.

5. **Aubrieta 'Purple Cascade'**
   Perennial
   Spring
   To 4 inches; flowers purple. Good low-spreading hanging plant. Use in tandem.

6. **Aquilegia 'Fairyland' Columbine**
   Perennial
   Spring
   To 18 inches; bushy bright green foliage; blue flowers with four spurs. Effective ground cover.

1. Petunia 'Cascade Sky'

2. Chrysanthemum 'King's Ransom'

3. Impatiens 'A-Go-Go'

4. Lobelia 'Bluestone'

5. Aubrieta 'Purple Cascade'

6. Aquilegia 'Fairyland'

55 / Herb Garden

Using an octagonal plan, this useful herb garden is easy to tend. The wide aisles around the hexagon create visual beauty and the alternating diamond shapes allow you to gather herbs easily. This garden can be planned on a small or large scale by reducing or adding to the suggested herbs.

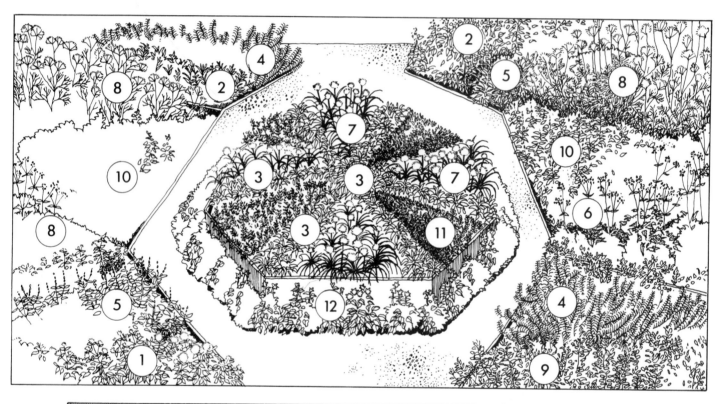

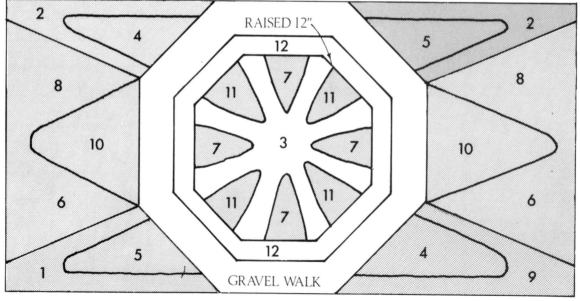

RAISED 12"

GRAVEL WALK

1. *Mentha spicata*
Spearmint
Herb/Perennial
To 16 inches; dark green crinkly leaves. Pinch back occasionally to encourage branching.

2. *Artemisia dracunculus*
Tarragon
Herb/Perennial
To 24 inches; leaves dark green with pointed tips. Needs good, rich, well-drained soil.

3. *Salvia officinalis*
Garden Sage
Herb/Perennial
To 24 inches; grayish green leaves, oblong and heavily veined; pungent flowers white, blue, or purple. Easy to grow.

4. *Rosmarinus officinalis*
Rosemary
Herb/Perennial
To 48 inches; leaves gray-green; flowers violet-blue. Likes heat and well-drained soil. Dwarf form available.

5. *Marjorana hortensis*
Marjorum
Herb/Perennial
To 30 inches; leaves green with purple stems.

6. *Levisticum officinalis*
Lovage
Herb/Perennial
To 36 inches; leaves celery-like. Needs a slightly alkaline soil.

7. *Allium schoenoprasum*
Chives
Herb/Perennial
To 12 inches; leaves grassy green and needlelike; flowers rose-purple. Needs plenty of sun and water.

8. *Anethum graveolens*
Dill
Herb/Annual
To 48 inches; leaves lacy light green. Do not overwater.

9. *Origanum vulgare*
Oregano
Herb/Perennial
To 30 inches; broad and oval-shaped leaves with oval tips; flowers purple. Needs plenty of sun.

10. *Ocimum basilicum*
Sweet Basil
Herb/Annual
To 24 inches; leafy leaves light green; flowers white to purple. Needs rich soil and lots of sun.

11. *Thymus vulgaris*
Thyme
Herb/Perennial
To 12 inches; leaves tiny and gray-green; flowers lilac to purple. Must have excellent drainage. Prune.

12. *Borago officinalis*
Common Borage
Herb/Annual
To 36 inches; leaves gray-green and large; flowers blue, purple, or white. Let soil dry out between waterings.

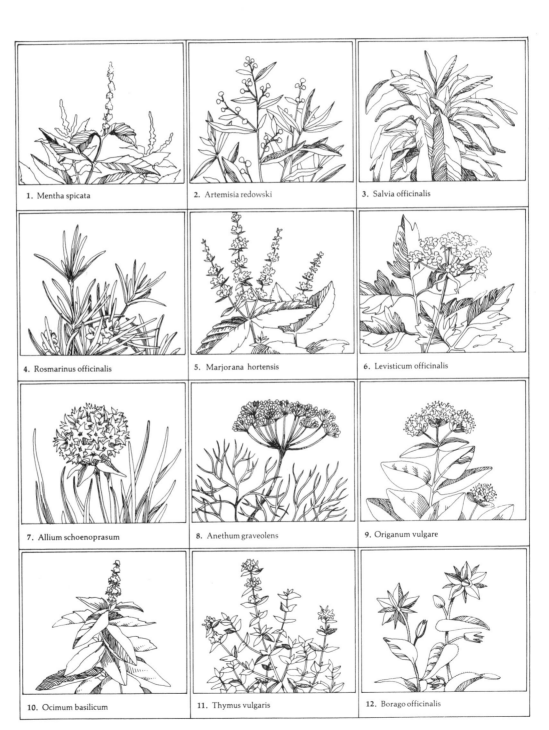

1. Mentha spicata
2. Artemisia redowski
3. Salvia officinalis
4. Rosmarinus officinalis
5. Marjorana hortensis
6. Levisticum officinalis
7. Allium schoenoprasum
8. Anethum graveolens
9. Origanum vulgare
10. Ocimum basilicum
11. Thymus vulgaris
12. Borago officinalis

56 / Hillside Garden (shade)

Made with redwood rounds, this plan takes you up through a shady garden. White and green caladiums in foreground are highlighted with brilliant red and pink impatiens above. Impatiens and hydrangeas are planted around a tree. Ferns tucked here and there add accent.

RETAINING WALL

1. **Caladium
'White Christmas'**
Bulb/Tender
To 24 inches; leaves large, heart-shaped and silvery with various patterns; flowers inconspicuous. Likes a loamy soil. Keep out of sun. Mix with "June Bird" for a pleasant effect.

2. **Impatiens 'Shady Lady'**
Annual
Summer/Fall
To 18 inches; leaves oblong; flowers abundant and in a variety of red or pink tones. Use rich and loamy soil. Impatiens respond remarkably to 15–30–15 fertilizer. Does not like hot sun.

3. *Hydrangea macrophylla*
'Blue Giant'
Bigleaf Hydrangea
Shrub/Deciduous
Hardy to −10F
To 72 inches; leaves oblong and ribbed; flowers blue or pink, large, and globe-shaped. Grows differently in various soils and atmospheric conditions. Use acid in soil to get blue flowers. Cut back in winter to desired shape.

4. **Azalea 'Hino Red'**
Shrub/Evergreen
Hardy to −10F
To 20 inches; leaves oblong; large flowers in shades of red. Use pinks in this garden. Acid- and mulch-loving. Check your local nursery for species to suit your area.

5. *Polystichum acrostichiodes*
Christmas Fern
To 30 inches; fronds to 24 inches long, 5 inches wide, divided into linear sections. Needs evenly moist soil. Easily grown.

6. *Cyclamen europaeum*
Bulb/Hardy
Summer
To 12 inches; leaves heart-shaped and green with silvery marbling; flowers pink and fragrant. Likes rich loam and frequent watering.

7. *Thymus vulgaris*
Thyme
Perennial
Spring
To 12 inches; leaves gray-green, short and oblong; flowers small and lilac to purple. Use as a ground cover. Keep under control or it will grow rampant. Needs good drainage.

8. *Gentiana septemfida*
Gentian
Perennial
Summer
To 10 inches; leaves oblong; flowers dark blue. Rich loam is essential. Grow in large drifts for best effect. Easy to grow.

1. Caladium 'White Christmas'
2. Impatiens 'Shady Lady'

3. Hydrangea macrophylla 'Blue Giant'
4. Azalea 'Hino Red'

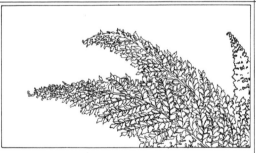

5. Polystichum acrostichiodes
6. Cyclamen europaeum

7. Thymus vulgaris
8. Gentiana septemfida

143

57 / Hillside Garden (spring, bulbs)

Drifts of daffodils, tulips and crocus dominate the center of this plan. Stepping stones define this area; tulips and daffodils are massed at a higher level. Frittillarias make a solid wall of color at the left, helping to define the basic shape of the plan. The total effect is a garden ablaze with color.

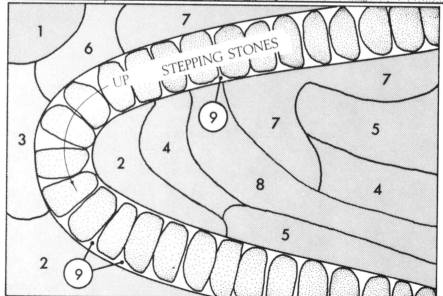

1. **Eremurus (Shelford hybrids)**
   Foxtail Lily
   Bulb/Hardy
   Spring/Summer
   To 60 inches; long, thin leaves; tall spikes of yellow flowers in many colors.

2. **Tulipa 'Apricot Beauty'**
   Bulb/Hardy
   Spring
   To 24 inches; foliage grassy; flowers large, Darwin-type and apricot. Mix with 'King's Ransom' (pastel gold), 'Cream Jewel' (cream), or 'Queen of Bartigour' (pink). Plant 5 inches deep.

3. *Fritillaria imperialis*
   Crown Imperial
   Bulb/Hardy
   Spring
   To 36 inches; leaf rosettes; flowers yellow and bell-shaped. Can be left undisturbed for years. Plant bulb on its side 7 inches deep.

4. **Daffodil 'Pink Supreme'**
   Bulb/Hardy
   Spring
   To 20 inches; pastel pink flowers. Plant 6 inches deep.

5. **Daffodil 'Bridal Crown'**
   Bulb/Hardy
   Spring
   To 8 inches; lovely white double-flowering daffodil. Plant 6 inches deep.

6. *Tulipa kaufmanniana*
   Bulb/Hardy
   Spring
   To 14 inches; flowers long, open, creamy white or yellow. Plant 1 inch deep.

7. *Crocus chrysanthus*
   'Cream Beauty'
   Early Crocus
   Bulb/Hardy
   Spring
   To 6 inches; short stems; cupped and brilliant yellow flowers. Plant 2 inches deep.

8. *Calochortus uniflora*
   Mariposa Lily
   Bulb/Semihardy
   Spring
   To 8 inches; grasslike foliage; pink flowers.

9. *Anemone blanda*
   Greek Anemone
   Bulb/Hardy
   Spring
   To 4 inches; small and deeply cut leaves; blue flowers, 2 inches wide. Plant 2 inches deep. Very bright and early blooming.

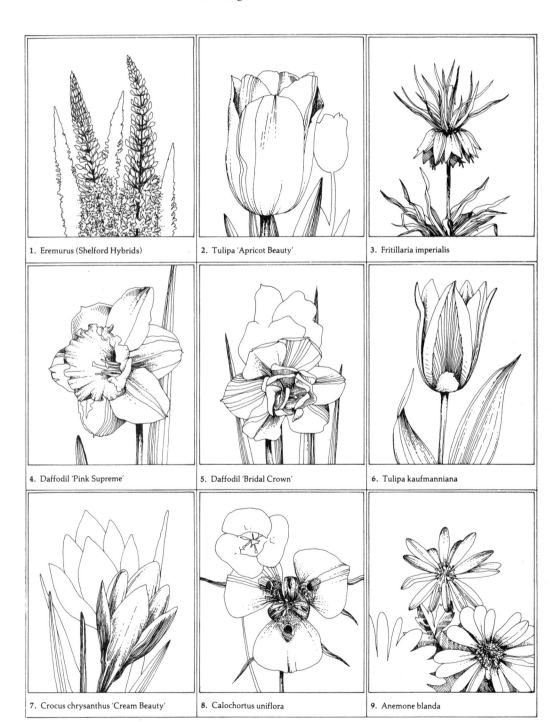

1. Eremurus (Shelford Hybrids)   2. Tulipa 'Apricot Beauty'   3. Fritillaria imperialis
4. Daffodil 'Pink Supreme'   5. Daffodil 'Bridal Crown'   6. Tulipa kaufmanniana
7. Crocus chrysanthus 'Cream Beauty'   8. Calochortus uniflora   9. Anemone blanda

58 / Hillside Garden (summer)

This design is based on a background planting of red and yellow gaillardias and sedum interspersed with vertical thrust of tritoma, achillea, lavendula, and artemisia. All plants are drought-resistant and give a brilliant display of colors. A graduation of heights is balanced with a fountain-shape of tritoma.

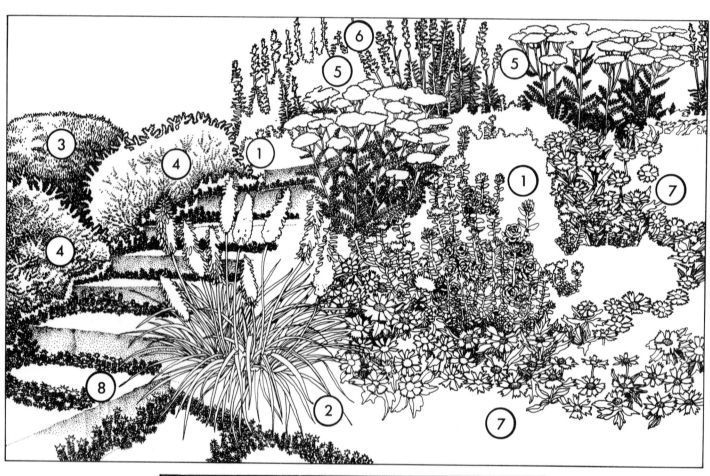

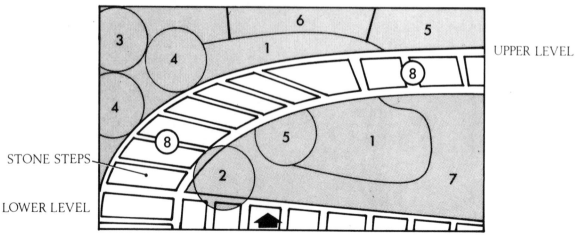

UPPER LEVEL

STONE STEPS

LOWER LEVEL

1. *Sedum spathulifolium*
Goldmoss Stonecrop
Ground Cover/Semievergreen
Hardy to —20F
To 4 inches; blue-green leaves in rosettes; bright yellow flowers in spring. Likes sun and dryness. Good drainage essential.

2. Kniphofia
'Vanilla'
Red-Hot-Poker
Perennial
Summer
To 24 inches; leaves grasslike; flowers profuse and pale yellow. Sun-loving. In warm climate can be invasive. Good cut flower. Also called Tritoma.

3. Artemisia 'Silver Mound'
Satiny Wormwood
Ground Cover/Semideciduous
Hardy to —35F
To 8 inches; leaves gray and fernlike; flowers small and yellow. Likes dryness, sun. Dies down in winter.

4. *Santolina chamaecyparissus*
Lavender Cotton
Ground Cover/Evergreen
Hardy to —5F
To 24 inches; leaves green, narrow and crowded; flowers yellow and dainty. Use 'Ericoides' variety to give a green contrast to the artemisia. Can be pruned to keep in shape.

5. Achillea 'Moonshine'
Yarrow
Perennial
Summer
To 18 inches; leaves silvery-gray and fernlike; flowers profuse and yellow. Prefers sun and dryness. Cut for bouquets. Very hardy.

6. Lavandula 'Gray Lady'
Lavender
Perennial
Summer
To 24 inches; leaves gray and aromatic; flowers purple, fragrant and abundant. Indestructible. A natural home potpourri.

7. Gaillardia 'Sun Dance'
Blanketflower
Perennial
Summer
To 12 inches; leaves wide and lobed; flowers bright orange with red edges. Add lots of leaf mold and some sand to soil. Likes a little more water than other plants in this garden.

8. *Sedum acre*
Goldmoss Stonecrop
Ground Cover/Semievergreen
Hardy to —20F
Prostrate, to 5 inches; leaves fleshy and short; flowers bright yellow. Grows slowly but surely. Can be trimmed toward end of season to shape.

1. Sedum spathulifolium

2. Kniphofia 'Vanilla'

3. Artemisia 'Silver Mound'

4. Santolina chamaecyparissus

5. Achillea 'Moonshine'

6. Lavandula 'Gray Lady'

7. Gaillardia 'Sun Dance'

8. Sedum acre

59 / Iris Garden

Built in a low ravine this colorful spring garden for the collector is accented with water and with walkways. Appropriate species of iris are selected for different soil conditions.

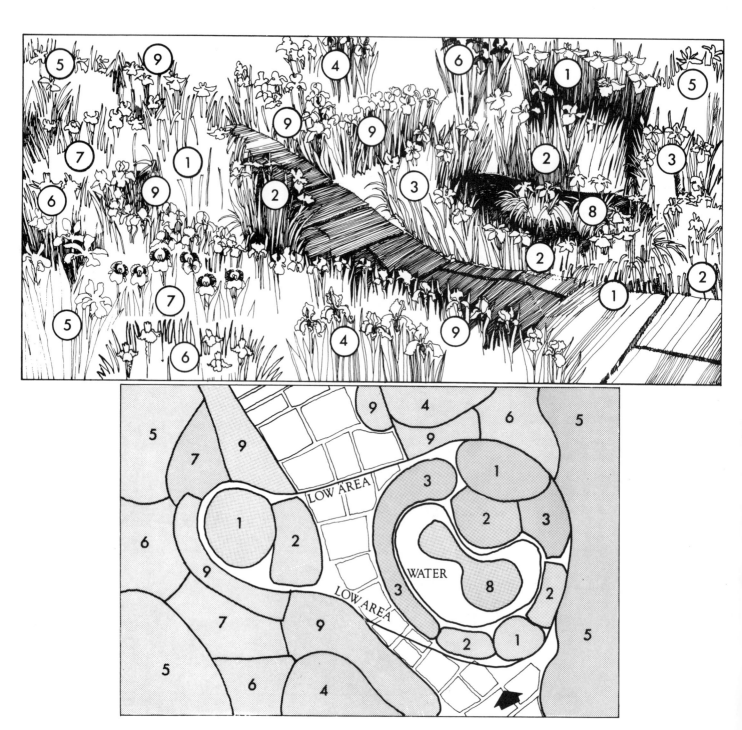

1. **Iris 'Leave Me Sighing'**
   Bulb/Hardy
   Spring
   To 48 inches; large, pink-yellow flowers. Needs wet acid soil. Lovely Japanese variety.

2. **Iris 'Vi Luihn'**
   Bulb/Hardy
   Spring
   To 36 inches; vivid colbalt-blue flowers on erect stems. Siberian type. Likes wet, acid conditions.

3. **Iris 'This I Love'**
   Bulb/Hardy
   Spring
   To 26 inches; rose-yellow flowers. Wet, acid soil conditions necessary. Louisiana type.

4. **Iris 'Rare Wine'**
   Bulb/Hardy
   Spring
   To 30 inches; large, tall, bearded, rose-wine flowers. Allow soil to dry out between waterings.

5. **Iris 'Golden Nugget'**
   Bulb/Hardy
   Spring
   To 60 inches; small bright yellow flowers. Spuria type. Needs well-drained, acid soil.

6. **Iris 'Opening Night'**
   Bulb/Hardy
   Spring
   To 38 inches; tall, bearded violet-black flowers.

7. **Iris 'Sheik'**
   Bulb/Hardy
   Spring
   To 36 inches; violet flowers. Arilbred type. Easily grown.

8. *Iris pseudocorus*
   Bulb/Hardy
   Spring
   To 28 inches; lemon-yellow flowers. Needs wet, acid soil. May grow in water.

9. **Iris 'Brassie'**
   Bulb/Hardy
   Spring
   To 18 inches; small, handsome, yellow flowers. Semi-dwarf type.

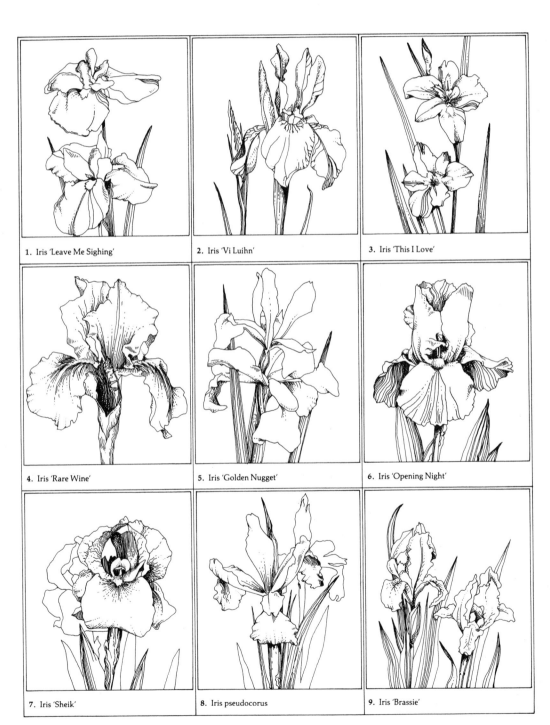

1. Iris 'Leave Me Sighing' 2. Iris 'Vi Luihn' 3. Iris 'This I Love'
4. Iris 'Rare Wine' 5. Iris 'Golden Nugget' 6. Iris 'Opening Night'
7. Iris 'Sheik' 8. Iris pseudocorus 9. Iris 'Brassie'

60 / Meditation Garden

An arbor and bench carefully placed create a garden where one can sit in serenity. The garden is a soothing green with white, blue, and red overtones. A graceful weeping willow tree is at one side of the lawn; a handsome flowering cherry at the other side. Plants are kept to a minimum.

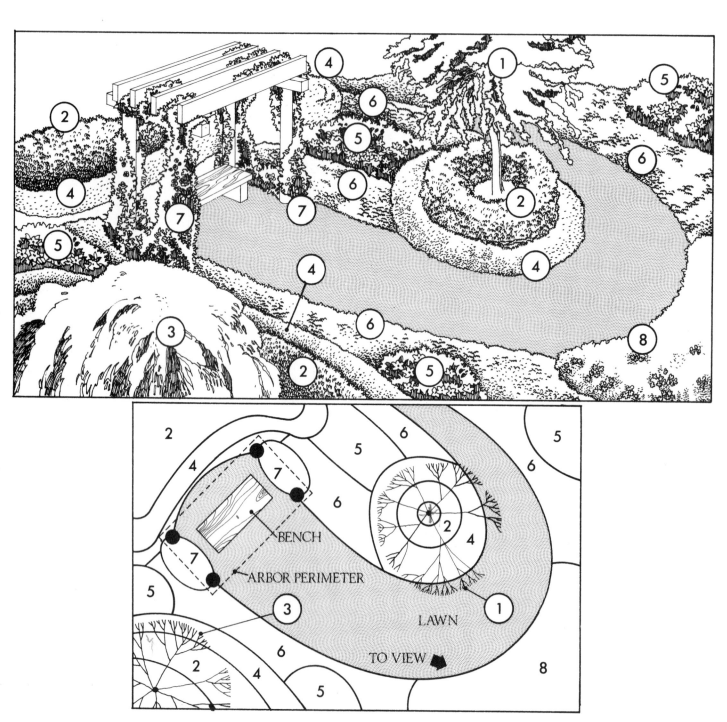

1. *Prunus subhirtella*
Weeping Cherry
Tree/Deciduous
Hardy to −10F
To 18 feet, pale pink flowers in spring; orange leaves in fall.

2. *Berberis thunbergii*
'Knight Burgundy'
Japanese Barberry
Shrub/Evergreen
Hardy to −10F
To 48 inches; dense and thorny, with small burgundy leaves. Will grow almost anywhere. Prune to approximately 18 inches.

3. *Salix babylonica*
'Salmonii'
Weeping Willow
Tree/Deciduous
Hardy to −20F
To 20 feet; weeping habit; pale green tiny leaves. More erect and vigorous than *S. babylonica*. Likes moisture and porous soil.

4. *Teucrium chamaedrys*
Germander
Ground Cover/Semievergreen
Hardy to −10F
To 12 inches; small dense leaves; red flowers on spikes. Good carpet plant, easily trimmed. Grows readily in most soils. Dies down in winter.

5. **Petunia 'Malibu'**
Annual
Summer
To 24 inches; frilly leaves; dark violet flowers. Prolific. Grandiflora type.

6. **Lobularia**
'Carpet of Snow'
Sweet Alyssum
Annual
Spring/Summer
To 8 inches; mounds of tiny white flowers.

7. **Ipomoea 'Pearly Gates'**
Morning Glory
Vine/Annual
Summer
To 20 feet; lobed leaves; funnel-shaped, white flowers. The white form of 'Heavenly Blue.'

8. **Phlox 'Eventide'**
Moss Pink
Perennial
Summer
To 8 inches; dense foliage; masses of blue flowers, cascading habit. Easily grown.

1. Prunus subhirtella

2. Berberis thunbergii 'Knight Burgundy'

3. Salix babylonica 'Salmonii'

4. Teucrium chamaedrys

5. Petunia 'Malibu'

6. Lobularia 'Carpet of Snow'

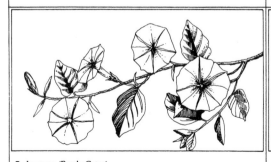

7. Ipomoea 'Pearly Gates'

8. Phlox 'Eventide'

61 / Midsummer Garden

Four mounds of orange, yellow, and gold flowers frame flagstone walks in this cheerful midsummer garden. The flowers are arranged in a layered pattern to repeat the mounds harmoniously.

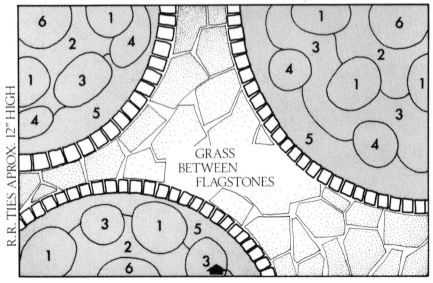

R.R. TIES APROX. 12" HIGH

GRASS BETWEEN FLAGSTONES

1. *Santolina chamaecyparissus*
   Lavender Cotton
   Ground Cover/Evergreen
   Hardy to −10F
   To 18 inches; silver gray foliage; small yellow flowers. Flourishes in dry conditions.

2. **Rudbeckia**
   'Orange Bedder'
   Black-eyed Susan
   Perennial
   To 20 inches; paperlike green foliage; large yellow-orange flowers. Hardy. Responds to very light feeding.

3. *Eschscholzia californica*
   California Poppy
   Perennial
   Spring
   To 12 inches; profuse open-faced orange flowers. Will grow in very poor soil.

4. *Portulaca grandiflora aurea*
   Common Portulaca
   Annual
   Summer
   To 8 inches; small fleshy leaves; large flowers. (Use only yellow here.)

5. *Calliopsis grandiflora*
   Tickseed
   Annual
   Summer
   To 8 inches; golden-yellow flowers with red center. Bright and cheerful, easy to grow.

6. **Kniphofia**
   'Primrose Beauty'
   Red-Hot-Poker
   Perennial
   Summer/Fall
   To 36 inches; grassy foliage; tall spikes of yellow flowers. Also called Tritoma.

1. Santolina chamaecyparissus

2. Rudbeckia 'Orange Bedder'

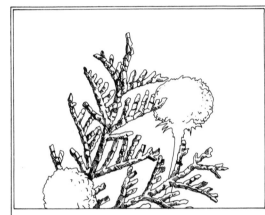

3. Eschscholzia californica

4. Portulaca grandiflora aurea

5. Calliopsis grandiflora

6. Kniphofia 'Primrose Beauty'

153

62 / Mobile Home Garden

The aesthetic problem of mobile homes is the bareness of the surrounding site. Yet most people do not want to install elaborate plantings in case they move away. This plan creates a handsome landscape with little work. Most of the plants are quick and colorful easy-to-grow annuals and perennials.

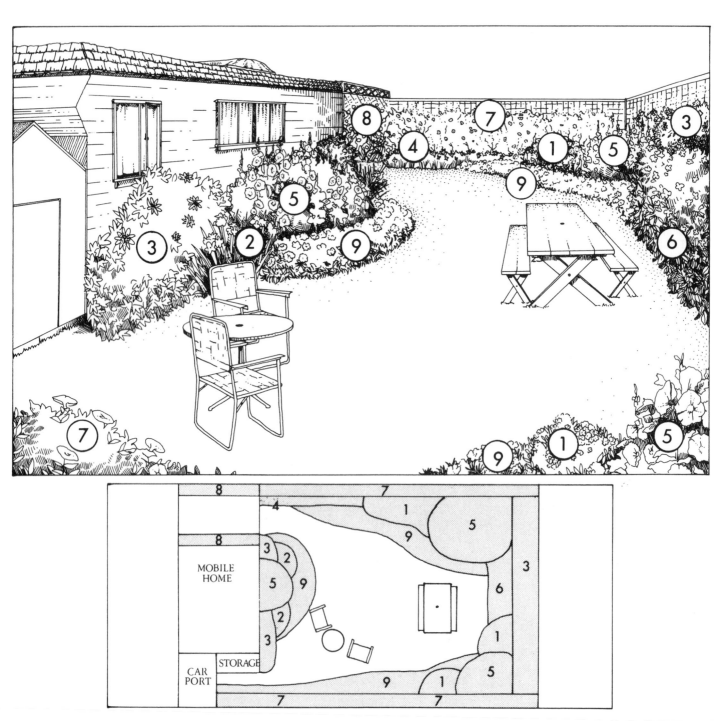

1. Phlox 'Progress'
Perennial
Spring/Summer
To 36 inches; leaves oblong and small; flowers blue. Also use 'Prince Charming' (coral pink) and 'Olive Wells Durant' (salmon).

2. Salpiglossis 'Splash'
Annual
Summer
To 24 inches; leaves fleshy; flowers large, showy and in many colors.

**3. *Passiflora caerulea*
Passion Flower**
Vine
To 20 feet; leaves with five lance-shaped lobes; flowers large, purple and white.

**4. *Nicotiana affinis*
Nicotine**
Annual
Summer
To 60 inches; leaves oblong; large flowers with narrow tubes, which close at night.

**5. *Althaea rosea*
Hollyhock**
Biennial
Summer
To 72 inches; leaves toothed, hairy and lobed; rose flowers on tall spikes.

6. *Pentapetes phoenicea*
Annual
Summer/Fall
To 48 inches; leaves toothed and dark green; scarlet flowers appear all along the stems.

**7. Ipomoea 'Early Call Rose'
Morning Glory**
Vine
Annual
Summer
To 84 inches; leaves oblong; flowers 4 inches wide and rose with white throat.

**8. *Ipomoea noctiflora*
Moon Vine**
Vine
Annual
Summer
To 15 feet; leaves oblong; flowers white, fragrant, and open rapidly in early morning. Grows in any soil.

**9. Portulaca
(Double Prize Strain)**
Annual
Summer
To 12 inches; leaves very divided; flowers open in sun. Many colors available.

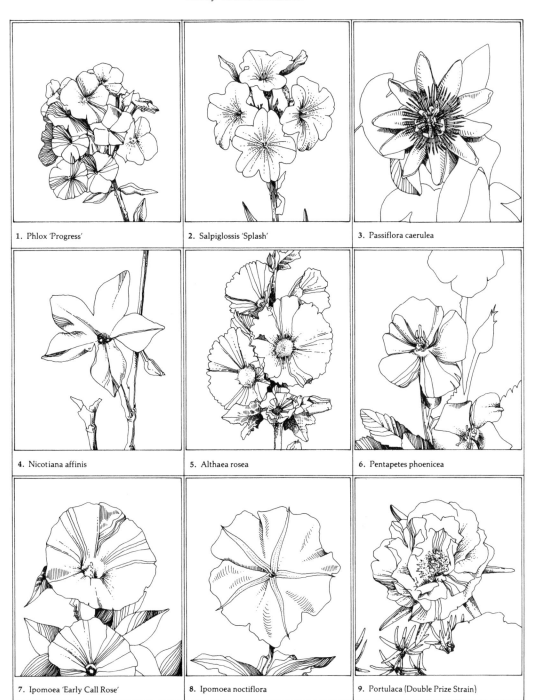

1. Phlox 'Progress'   2. Salpiglossis 'Splash'   3. Passiflora caerulea

4. Nicotiana affinis   5. Althaea rosea   6. Pentapetes phoenicea

7. Ipomoea 'Early Call Rose'   8. Ipomoea noctiflora   9. Portulaca (Double Prize Strain)

63 / Modular Garden

This formal garden uses a square modular unit. Raised planters are filled with lavender coneflowers carefully delineated with white ageratums, begonias and periwinkle.

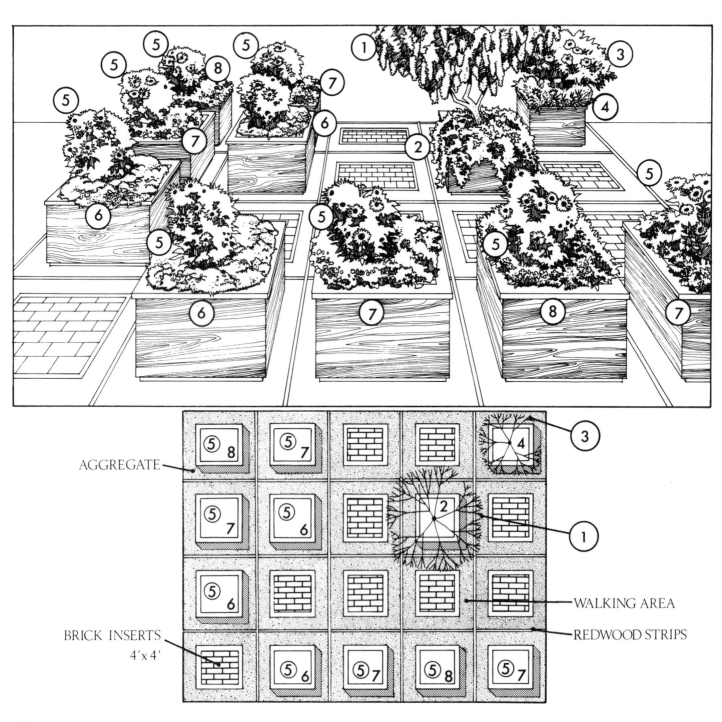

AGGREGATE

BRICK INSERTS
4' x 4'

WALKING AREA

REDWOOD STRIPS

1. *Wisteria floribunda*
   Tree Wisteria
   Vine/Deciduous
   Perennial
   Hardy to −10F
   Spring
   To 96 inches; lacy leaves; plumes of violet flowers.

2. *Hedera helix*
   'Manda's Crested Crinkled Ivy'
   Ivy
   Vine/Evergreen
   Perennial
   Hardy to −10F
   To 24 feet; crinkled leaves catch light and give lacy effect.

3. **Paeonia 'Yachiyot Subaki' Japanese Tree Peony**
   Shrub/Deciduous
   Summer
   Hardy to −10F
   To 36 inches; bright green dense foliage; large pink flowers.

4. **Dianthus 'Snowflake'**
   Annual
   Summer
   To 10 inches; grasslike leaves; lovely white open-faced flowers.

5. **Echinacea 'The King' Coneflower**
   Perennial
   Summer
   To 36 inches; paperlike green foliage; large lavender flowers. Likes sun and sandy soil; tolerates wind.

6. **Ageratum 'Summer Snow' Flossflower**
   Annual
   Summer
   To 6 inches; dense foliage topped with mounds of white flowers.

7. **Begonia 'White Christmas'**
   Annual
   Summer
   To 6 inches; cup-like green leaves; masses of tiny white blooms.

8. **Vinca 'Little Blanche' Periwinkle**
   Annual
   Summer
   To 6 inches; handsome oval leaves; prolific white flowers. Compact dwarf.

1. Wisteria floribunda

2. Hedera helix 'Manda's Crested Crinkled Ivy'

3. Paeonia 'Yachiyot Subaki'

4. Dianthus 'Snowflake'

5. Echinacea 'The King'

6. Ageratum 'Summer Snow'

7. Begonia 'White Christmas'

8. Vinca 'Little Blanche'

64 / Office Court Garden

White birches at the rear set the stage for a simple but beautiful office court garden. Complemented by a frilly maple in the foreground, two islands of heath and dianthus provide pink color. A four-island arrangement, the landscape is completed with borders of ophiopogon. Ample seating space is provided on an exposed area which may be concrete, lawn or any attractive surface.

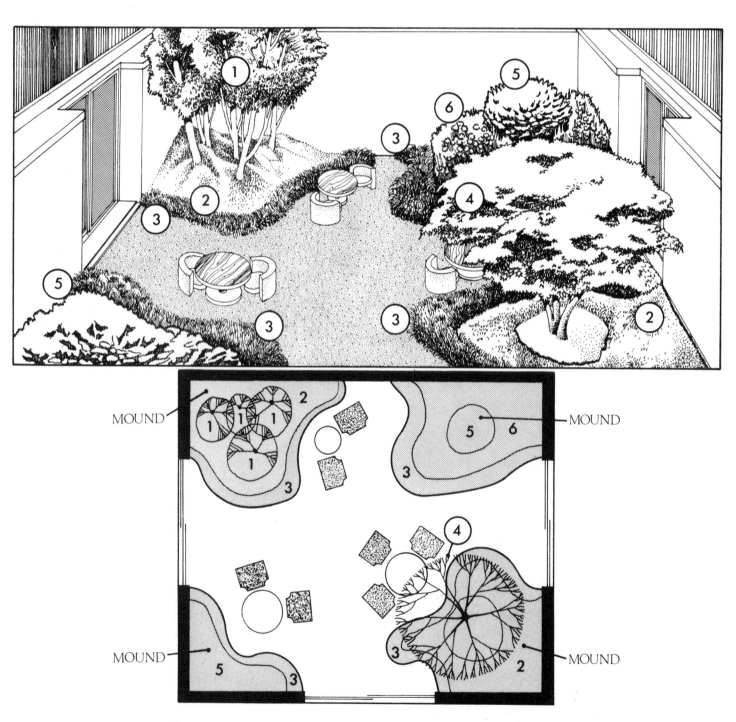

1. *Betula papyrifera*
Canoe Birch
Tree/Deciduous
Hardy to −35F
To 90 feet; graceful, heart-shaped scalloped leaves. Thrives in wet or dry soils. Good autumn color.

2. *Arenaria verna caespitosa*
Moss Sandwort
Perennial
Hardy to −35F
To 3 inches; mosslike evergreen leaves; flowers tiny and white. Prostrate. Needs slightly sandy soil.

3. *Ophiopogon japonicus*
Dwarf Lily Turf
Ground Cover/Evergreen
Hardy to 5F
To 10 inches; grassy foliage; tiny lilac flowers. Grows in sun or shade.

4. *Acer palmatum*
'Atropurpureum'
Bloodleaf Japanese Maple
Tree/Deciduous
Hardy to −20F
To 20 feet; dark red, lacy leaves throughout growing season. Compact, bushy.

5. *Erica carnea*
Spring Heath
Shrub/Evergreen
Hardy to −10F
To 12 inches; bright green leaves; myriad small rosy flowers. Likes poor acid soil.

6. **Dianthus 'Tiny Rubies'**
Perennial
Summer
To 20 inches; profuse, fragrant blooms. Make a carpet of bright pink. Good cut flowers. Water frequently.

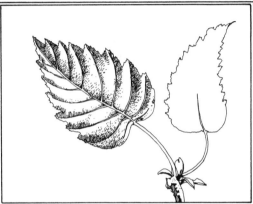

1. Betula papyrifera

2. Arenaria verna caespitosa

3. Ophiopogon japonicus

4. Acer palmatum 'Atropurpureum'

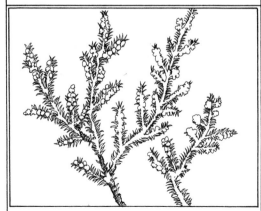

5. Erica carnea

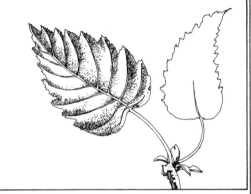

6. Dianthus 'Tiny Rubies'

65 / Patio Garden I

Planter boxes are the main element of this simple plan. The two center boxes contain colorful blooms and the garden is defined with hedges to create privacy. There is ample seating space and though there are enough plants there are not so many that gardening becomes a chore.

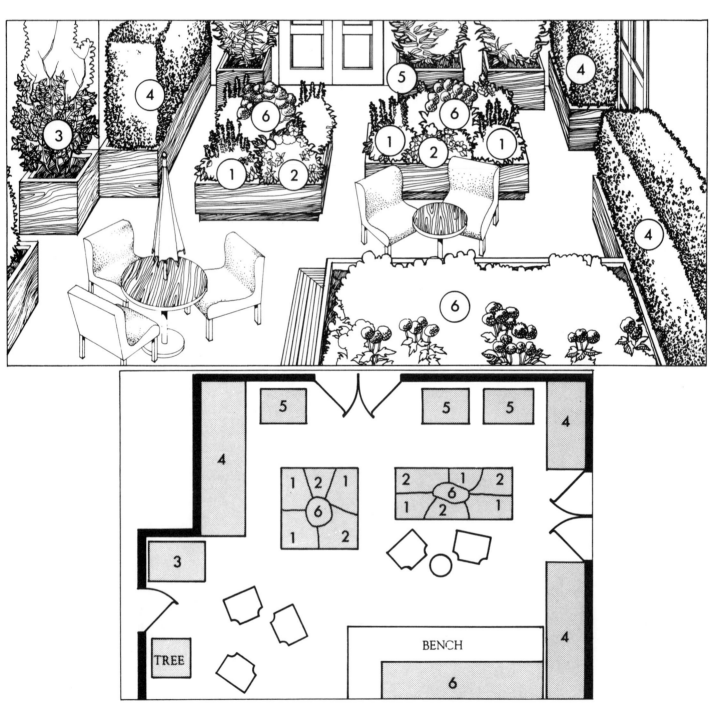

1. **Salvia splendens**
   Scarlet Sage
   Annual
   Summer
To 36 inches; leaves fragrant;
flowers small and red on
spikes. Needs loamy soil and
good drainage.

2. **Petunia 'Cascade'**
   Annual
   Summer
To 12 inches; leaves fleshy
and hairy, funnel-shaped
flowers in a variety of colors.
Needs a great deal of water
and sun.

3. **Rosa 'Doubloons'**
   Shrub/Deciduous
   Hardy to −10F
To 10 feet; leaves small and
oblong; flowers yellow. Needs
routine rose care. Long
blooming season.

4. **Deutzia gracilis**
   Shrub/Deciduous
   Summer
   Hardy to −20F
To 72 inches; leaves serrated;
flowers white to purple and
abundant. Prune in spring.

5. **Clematis lanuginosa**
   'Ramona'
   Vine/Deciduous
   Perennial
   Hardy to −20F
   Summer
To 30 feet; leaves oblong and
toothed or smooth; flowers
abundant and pink. Needs
rich, fast-draining soil with
some lime added.

6. **Dahlia**
   'Little Connecticut'
   Bulb
   Summer
To 24 inches; flowers red and
abundant. Good color for lit-
tle effort.

1. Salvia splendens

2. Petunia 'Cascade'

3. Rosa 'Doubloons'

4. Deutzia gracilis

5. Clematis lanuginosa 'Ramona'

6. Dahlia 'Little Connecticut'

66 / Patio Garden II (for dining)

This plan uses a few plants imaginatively and requires little maintenance. Marigolds or other midsummer blooming annuals deck the patio and small plantings of buckthorn and lantana are repeated in corners. Red salvia is used for accent. Wrought iron lamps are placed around the tables.

1. **Zinnia 'Peter Pan'**
   Annual
   Fall
   To 16 inches; leafy green foliage; red flowers.

2. *Rhamnus frangula* **'Columnaris' Alder Buckthorn**
   Shrub/Deciduous
   Hardy to −50F
   To 15 feet; hedgelike, glossy green leaves. Hardiest and easiest to grow of the columnar hedges. Prune occasionally.

3. *Lantana nana compacta*
   Shrub/Evergreen
   Summer
   Hardy to −10F
   To 24 inches; floriferous with red and yellow flowers. Likes loamy soil.

4. **Rosa 'Don Juan'**
   Shrub/Deciduous
   Hardy to −10F
   Climbs to 20 feet; fiery roses bloom all summer. Great grower.

5. **Tagetes 'Triple Gold' Marigold**
   Annual
   Summer
   To 15 inches; large orange and gold blossom frilled and ruffled. Stellar variety.

6. **Salvia 'St. John's Fire' Scarlet Sage**
   Annual
   Summer
   To 16 inches; green glossy leaves; red blooms on spines.

1. Zinnia 'Peter Pan'

2. Rhamnus frangula 'Columnaris'

3. Lantana nana compacta

4. Rosa 'Don Juan'

5. Tagetes 'Triple Gold'

6. Salvia 'St. John's Fire'

67 / Patio Garden III (evergreen)

A retaining wall gives this garden a strong horizontal dimension and helps make it a pleasant place to sit. The low-maintenance planting is sparse but attractive, with the accent on evergreens and spring flowering azaleas.

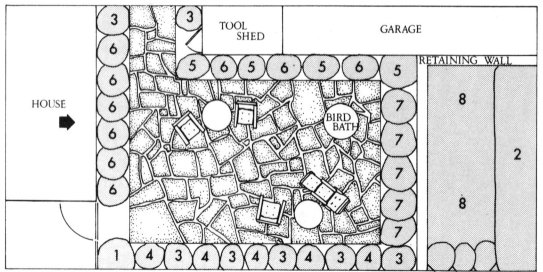

1. **Cupressus sempervirens 'Stricta'**
   Italian Cypress
   Tree/Evergreen
   Hardy to 10F
   To 80 feet; upright habit; scalelike, dark green leaves. Excellent pyramidal form. A true cypress.

2. **Ilex opaca**
   American Holly
   Tree/Evergreen
   Hardy to −10F
   To 45 feet; leaves lobed and stiff. Need good drainage. Slow growing.

3. **Taxus baccata 'Stricta'**
   English Yew
   Tree/Evergreen
   Hardy to −5F
   To 45 feet; upright in habit; leaves needlelike and narrow. Can tolerate neglect.

4. **Taxus baccata 'Repandens'**
   Spreading Irish Yew
   Tree/Evergreen
   Hardy to −20F
   To 40 feet; leaves narrow, yellow-green and needlelike. Very graceful. Hardiest of the yews.

5. **Rhododendron smirnowii**
   Smirnow Rhododendron
   Shrub/Evergreen
   Hardy to −10F
   To 12 feet; downy leaves; white to rose-red flowers. Easier to maintain than most rhododendrons. Not troubled with lace bug.

6. **Rhododendron 'Fedora'**
   Shrub/Evergreen
   Hardy to −10F
   To 18 inches; pink flowers. If not available, substitute a full pink type which grows well in your area.

7. **Arctostaphylos uva-ursi**
   Bearberry
   Ground Cover/Evergreen
   Hardy to −35F
   To 8 inches; foliage turns bronze in fall. Once established, needs little attention.

8. **Kalmia latifolia**
   Mountain Laurel
   Shrub/Evergreen
   Hardy to −20F
   To 30 feet; dark green leaves; handsome pink and white flowers. Requires an acid soil.

1. Cupressus sempervirens 'Stricta'

2. Ilex opaca

3. Taxus baccata 'Stricta'

4. Taxus baccata 'Repandens'

5. Rhododendron smirnowii

6. Rhododendron 'Fedora'

7. Arctostaphylos uva-ursi

8. Kalmia latifolia

68 / Patio Garden IV (multileveled)

This flower-packed garden surrounds an arc-shaped brick patio. Tall red flowering heucheras dominate the plan, with boxes of red impatiens near the house wall to create a total ring of flowers. This shaded garden provides color all year but it takes work.

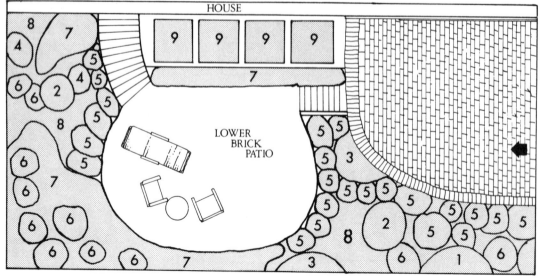

1. *Ginko biloba*
   Maidenhair Tree
   Tree/Deciduous
   Hardy to —20F
   To 100 feet; fan-shaped alternate leaves. Robust.

2. *Pinus strobus*
   Eastern White Pine
   Tree/Evergreen
   Hardy to —35F
   To 100 feet; needled. Many varieties.

3. *Viburnum rhytidophyllum*
   Shrub/Deciduous
   Hardy to —10F
   To 10 feet; handsome crinkled leaves; red to black fruits.

4. *Cornus florida*
   'White Cloud'
   Tree/Deciduous
   Hardy to —20F
   To 20 feet; leafy, dense branching; white flowers.

5. *Heuchera bressingham*
   Perennial
   Spring
   To 18 inches; heart-shaped lobed leaves; tall spikes of red flowers. Needs leaf mold and responds to feeding.

6. *Dennstaedtia punctilobula*
   Hay-scented Fern
   To 30 inches; sword-shaped fronds; finely cut edges.

7. *Doronicum caucasicum*
   Leopard's-bane
   Perennial
   Spring
   To 15 inches; green lobed foliage; bright orange 3-inch flowers. Flowers fade quickly in summer, but easy to grow.

8. *Epimedium pinnatum sulphureum*
   Persian Epimedium
   Ground Cover/Evergreen
   Hardy to —10F
   To 9 inches; lance-shaped leaves; yellow blooms. A good ground cover that stays green all year.

9. **Impatiens 'Imp'**
   Annual
   Summer
   To 16 inches; dark green leaves; flowers fiery red and profuse. Responds to feeding of 15–30–15 fertilizer. Good drainage essential, water frequently.

1. Gingko biloba

2. Pinus strobus

3. Viburnum rhytidophyllum

4. Cornus florida 'White Cloud'

5. Heuchera bressingham

6. Dennstaedtia punctilobula

7. Doronicum caucasicum

8. Epimedium pinnatum sulphureum

9. Impatiens 'Imp'

69 / Perennial Garden

A brick walk defines the corner of this garden banked with plants that bloom from early summer to frost. The background delphiniums bloom early and create a foil for the lilies and lupine. Phlox is the workhorse of this garden, with dianthus to border the area neatly. This plan requires little work once established and can be tucked into any sunny corner area.

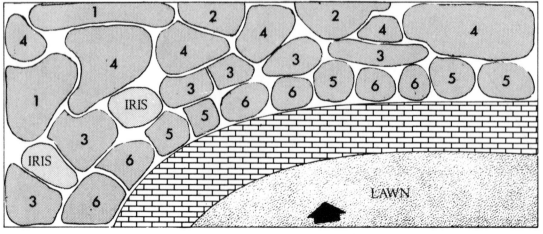

168

1. **Delphinium 'Bellamosa'**
    Garland Larkspur
    Perennial
    Summer/Fall
    To 72 inches; leaves palmate;
    flowers blue. Needs loamy
    soil. Prepare bed well before
    planting so as not to disturb
    later. Stake plants. Feed regu-
    larly after the first year.

2. **Lilium (Aurelian hybrids)**
    Bulb/Hardy
    Summer
    To 36 inches; leaves thin;
    white, yellow, pink, orange,
    and apricot flowers with pas-
    tel trumpets.

3. **Lupinus (Russell's**
        hybrids)
    Lupine
    Perennial
    Summer/Fall
    To 48 inches; leaves palmate;
    flowers of all colors. Out-
    standing variety. Does not
    like wind. Water well but
    avoid water on leaves, which
    causes mildew. Spectacular
    cut flowers.

4. *Phlox paniculata*
    Garden Phlox
    Perennial
    Spring/Summer
    To 30 inches; leaves green
    and narrow; flowers dark pink
    and red. Often needs to be
    staked. Subject to mildew.

5. *Nepeta mussinii*
    Persian Ground Ivy
    Ground Cover/Deciduous
    Hardy to —10F
    To 12 inches; leaves silver-
    gray; flowers pale lavender.
    Hardy and useful foil for
    more colorful plants.

6. **Dianthus 'Zing'**
    Maiden Pinks
    Perennial
    Summer
    To 12 inches; leaves green
    and narrow; vivid mass of
    long-blooming pink flowers.
    In warmer climate these are
    often biannuals. Mulch well
    in winter.

1. Delphinium 'Bellamosa'

2. Lilium (Aurelian hybrid)

3. Lupinus (Russell's hybrid)

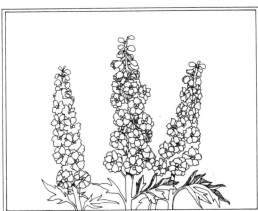
4. Phlox paniculata

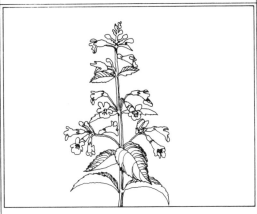
5. Nepeta mussinii

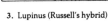
6. Dianthus 'Zing'

This is a basic perennial garden for a lot of color all year. It requires low maintenance and relies on a massive drift of Exbury azaleas to make its spring statement. Will require little replanting through the years.

PATHWAY

FENCE

1. *Robinia freisia*
Golden Locust
Tree/Deciduous
Hardy to −20F
To 70 feet; leaves compound and golden-yellow; flowers white. Hardy, easily grown.

2. *Epimedium pinnatum*
   sulphureum
Persian Epimedium
Ground Cover/Evergreen
Hardy to −10F
To 9 inches; leaves heart-shaped; flowers yellow and spurred. Stellar type. Likes loose loam. Do not feed until well-established.

3. *Campsis radicans flava*
Trumpet Vine
Vine/Semievergreen
Perennial
Hardy to −10F
Summer/Fall
To 30 feet; leaves dark green; flowers yellow and trumpet-shaped.

4. *Ligustrum vicaryi*
Golden Privet
Shrub/Semievergreen
Hardy to −10F
To 60 inches; leaves small and yellow; flowers inconspicuous. Slow-growing. Needs full sun to turn golden.

5. *Forsythia intermedia*
'Lynwood Gold'
Shrub/Deciduous
Hardy to −10F
To 60 inches; leaves simple; flowers abundant and golden-yellow. Blooms on old wood.

6. **Azalea (Exbury hybrids)**
Shrub/Deciduous
Hardy to −10F
To 60 inches; leaves oblong; flowers large, yellow, pink and in sphere-shaped clusters. Use cool, moist, acid soil.

7. **Kniphofia**
'Primrose Beauty'
Perennial
Summer
To 30 inches; leaves basal, long, and narrow; flowers yellow and tubular in spikes. This is the accent in this garden. Also called Tritoma.

8. *Paeonia moutan*
Peony
Shrub/Deciduous
Hardy to −10F
To 48 inches; leaves oblong; flowers large, pink fully double and spectacular. One of the great tree peonies. Needs good humusy soil and full sun.

9. *Lobularia saxatile*
Alyssum
Perennial
Spring
To 6 inches; leaves grayish, narrow and mostly basal; flowers yellow. Likes sandy loam. Watch for mildew if watering overhead.

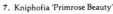

1. Robinia freisia

2. Epimedium pinnatum sulphureum

3. Campsis radicans flava

4. Ligustrum vicaryi

5. Forsythia intermedia 'Lynwood Gold'

6. Azalea (Exbury hybrids)

7. Kniphofia 'Primrose Beauty'

8. Paeonia moutan

9. Lobularia saxatile

71 / Perennial Garden III (summer)

Designed for an entrance or step area, this garden uses dwarf asters to provide a colorful carpet that cascades down the edges of the steps. To balance the horizontal line and busy character of the plan, lilies, heliopsis and lythrum provide vertical accent. Gypsophila give background color.

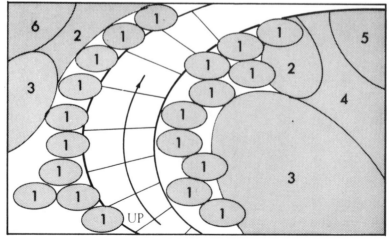

1. *Callistephus alpinus*
   Dwarf Aster
   Perennial
   Summer/Fall
   To 18 inches; leaves green and narrow; flowers white to red to blue and cascading.

2. *Platycodon grandiflorum*
   Balloonflower
   Perennial
   Summer/Fall
   To 30 inches; leaves oblong; flowers star-shaped and blue. Use light loamy soil which drains well. Needs full sun. Use all blue here to create a mass of one color.

3. Heliopsis 'Incompatabilis'
   Orange Sunflower
   Perennial
   Summer/Fall
   To 36 inches; leaves oblong; flowers showy and bright gold. A favorite. Hardy; likes sun.

4. Lythrum 'Morden's Pink'
   Loosestrife
   Perennial
   Summer
   To 36 inches; leaves small and lance-shaped; flowers deep pink. Likes sun and moist soil. Creates large clump of bright pink.

5. Lilium
   'Royal Gold Strain'
   Bulb/Hardy
   Summer
   To 60 inches; leaves long and narrow; flowers large and gold. Elegant, demanding Oriental hybrid cross. Mix well-decayed leaf mold into soil.

6. Gypsophila 'Perfect'
   Baby's-breath
   Perennial
   Summer
   To 36 inches; leaves airy; flowers white. Great background plant. Likes some lime in soil. Excellent cut flower.

1. Callistephus alpinus

2. Platycodon grandiflorum

3. Heliopsis 'Incompatibilis'

4. Lythrum 'Morden's Pink'

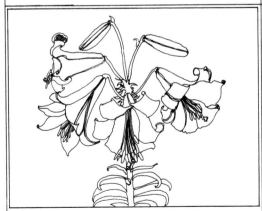

5. Lilium 'Royal Gold Strain'

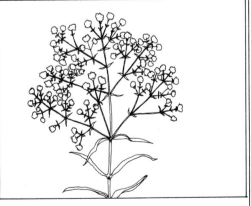

6. Gypsophila 'Perfect'

72 / Porch Garden I

With colorful old favorite plants such as lilacs and hollyhocks, this is a simple garden. Prolific blooms create a cheerful welcome. In close proximity to the house, the gardener can gather flowers for the breakfast table or a sprig of mint for iced tea. The plants are relatively easy to grow.

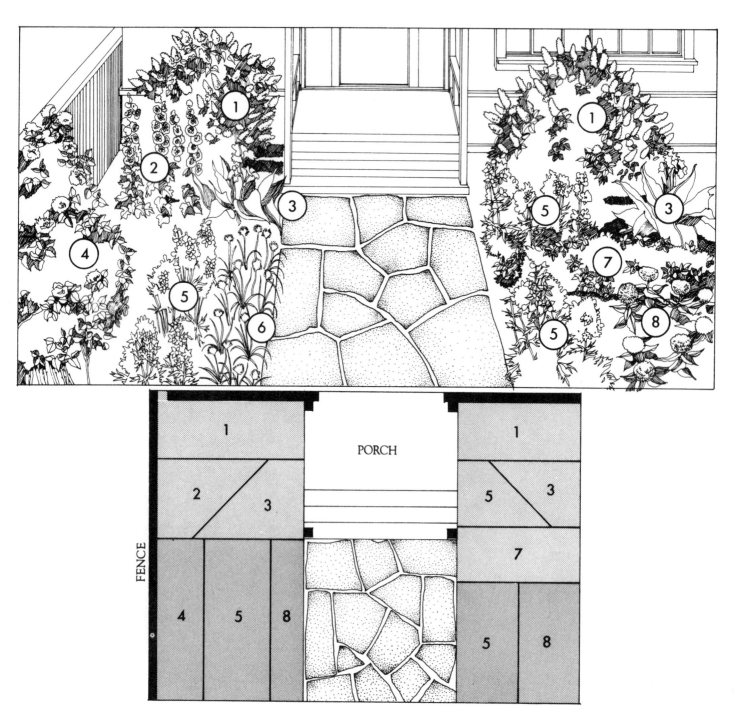

1. ***Syringa vulgaris***
'Ludwig Spaeth'
Lilac
Shrub/Deciduous
Hardy to −20F
To 60 inches; leaves oval, lilac flowers in large clusters in summer. Prefers lime in soil. Prune in early spring.

2. **Althaea 'Pompadour'**
Hollyhock
Biennial
Summer
To 72 inches; leaves lobed; flowers large and apricot on tall stems. Grows in most soil; likes sun.

3. **Canna 'Porcelain Rose'**
Perennial
Summer
To 36 inches; leaves broad and bold green; flowers pink. Likes moisture, sun, rich soil.

4. **Rosa 'Columbia'**
Shrub/Deciduous
Hardy to −10F
To 72 inches; leaves dense; flowers rose-pink and scented. Robust.

5. **Delphinium**
'Connecticut Yankee'
Perennial
Summer
To 30 inches; leaves ferny, lobed; flowers bright blue. Outstanding.

6. ***Allium schoenoprasum***
Chives
Perennial
Summer
To 12 inches; leaves grassy green and needlelike; flowers rose-pink. Needs plenty of sun and water.

7. ***Mentha spicata***
Spearmint
To 16 inches; small crinkly leaves; branching habit. Prune occasionally.

8. **Zinnia 'Thumbelina'**
Annual
Summer
To 6 inches; leaves green; flowers pink. Needs ample sun and water. Use 'Mini-Salmon.'

1. Syringa vulgaris 'Ludwig Spaeth'

2. Althaea 'Pompadour'

3. Canna 'Porcelain Rose'

4. Rosa 'Columbia'

5. Delphinium 'Connecticut Yankee'

6. Allium schoenoprasum

7. Mentha spicata

8. Zinnia 'Thumbelina'

73 / Porch Garden II

Placing planter boxes and containers on a porch transforms it into a gardener's dream. Benches are part of the planter design and the garden mixes flowers, vegetables and strawberries to create an almost ideal retreat.

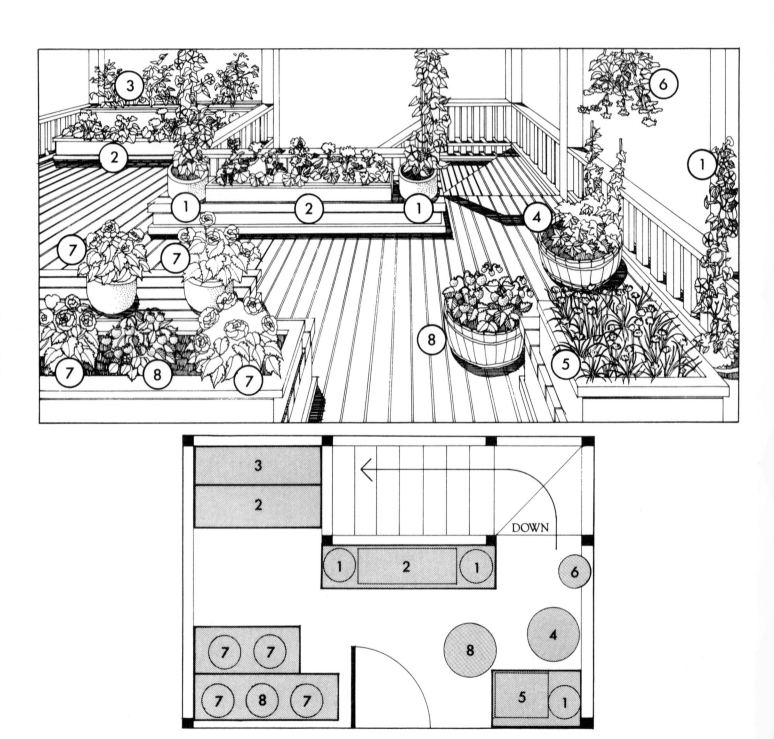

1. *Ipomoea purpurea*
   'Heavenly Blue'
   Morning Glory
   Vine
   Annual
   Summer
   To 20 feet; leaves oval; flowers blue. Too rich soil will produce more foliage than flowers. Use a lot of leaf mold. Water freely.

2. **Geranium (Double-dip type)**
   Perennial
   Summer
   To 16 inches; leaves round and centered on stem; flowers double and pink. Good yield and easy to grow.

3. **Tomato 'Small Fry'**
   To 24 inches; red, cherry-type tomatoes. Matures in 65 days. Needs staking. Water heavily.

4. **Squash 'Diplomat'**
   (Zucchini type)
   Climbs to 60 inches; 7-inch zucchini. Matures in 55 days. Needs no staking. Space plants 18 to 24 inches apart. Three plants will produce enough squash for a family of four.

5. *Allium schoenopraesum*
   Chives
   Perennial
   Summer
   To 12 inches; leaves grassy green and needlelike; flowers rose-purple. Needs plenty of sun and water.

6. *Begonia pendula*
   Bulb / Tender
   Summer
   Cascades to 60 inches; leaves hanging and oblong; flowers pink or orange. Many varieties. Needs loamy porous soil and perfect drainage. Plant in leaf mold and soil mix; feed lightly with 15-30-15.

7. *Begonia tuberhybrida*
   Bulb / Tender
   Summer
   To 24 inches; leaves broad; flowers large and red. Many varieties. Needs perfect drainage. Plant in pure leaf mold, feed lightly and regularly with 15-30-15.

8. *Fragaria vesca*
   'Baron Solemacher'
   Alpine Strawberry
   Summer
   To 12 inches; leaves divided into three leaflets; flowers white; fruit bright red and small. An everbearing type. Remove first blooms so plant will send out runners. Feed often.

1. Ipomoea purpurea 'Heavenly Blue'

2. Geranium (Double-dip type)

3. Tomato 'Small Fry'

4. Squash 'Diplomat'

5. Allium schoenopraesum

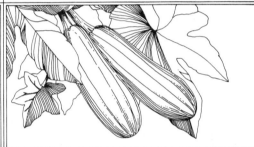

6. Begonia pendula

7. Begonia tuberhybrida

8. Fragaria vesca 'Baron Solemacher'

74 / Porch Garden III (evergreen)

A simple front-porch garden, this plan relies on nandina for grace and charm and evergreen mugo pine for year-long greenery. The curving brick path echoes the form of the fir tree that is the accent of the garden. The path is bordered with hedge yew.

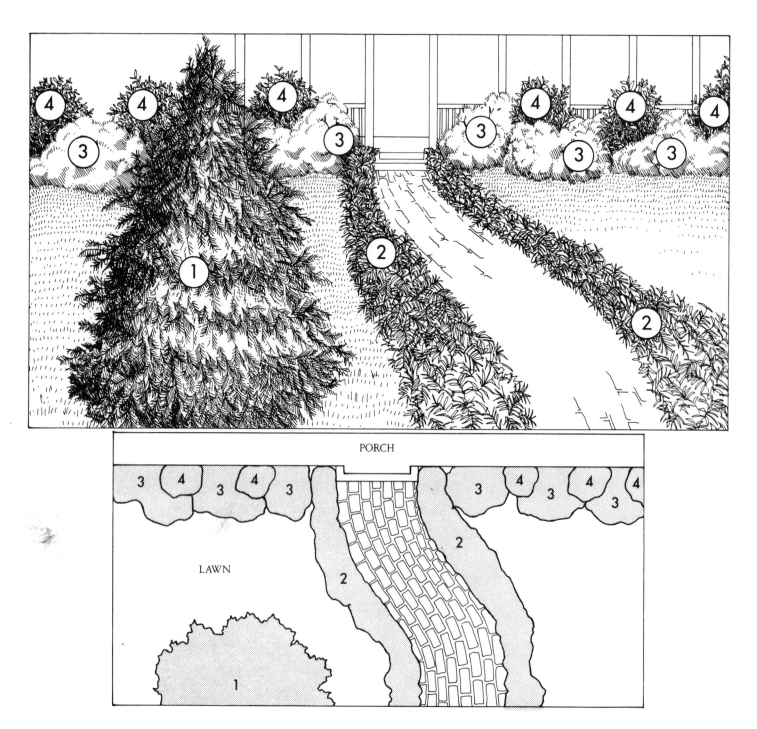

1. **Picea pungens**
   Blue Spruce
   Tree/Evergreen
   Hardy to −35F
   To 100 feet; whorled and stiff
   branches in layers.

2. **Taxus baccata 'Repandens'**
   Spreading English Yew
   Shrub/Evergreen
   Hardy to −20F
   To 40 feet; low flat-top shrub;
   yellow-green needles. Very
   graceful.

3. **Pinus mugo**
   Swiss Mountain Pine
   Shrub/Evergreen
   Hardy to −35F
   To 25 feet; dense, bright
   green needles. Easy to train
   and shape.

4. **Nandina domestica**
   Shrub/Evergreen
   Hardy to 10F
   To 60 inches; lacy bright
   green leaves; red berries;
   upright habit.

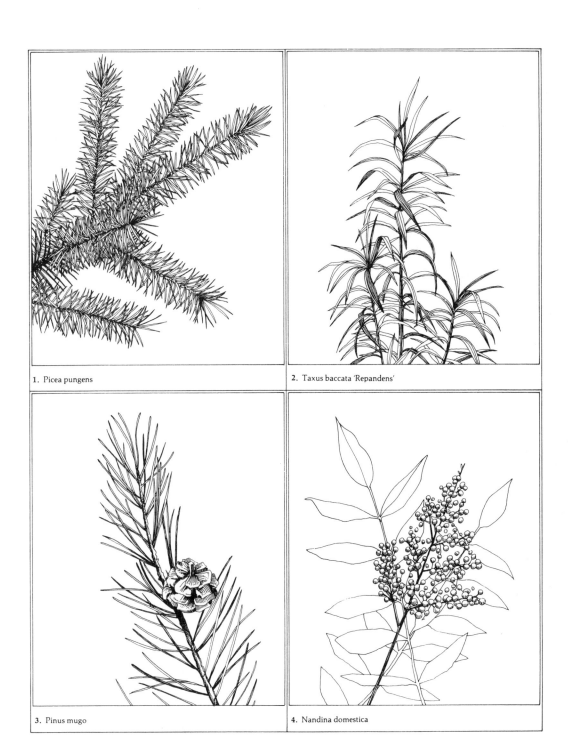

1. Picea pungens

2. Taxus baccata 'Repandens'

3. Pinus mugo

4. Nandina domestica

75 / Portable Garden

Salmon and pink geraniums are used repeatedly to pull this garden together. Two corner arrangements of hollyhocks, callas and turf lily partially frame the garden. The plants, in pots and boxes, are arranged in tiers so all flowers are visible. A concrete floor provides walking and seating areas.

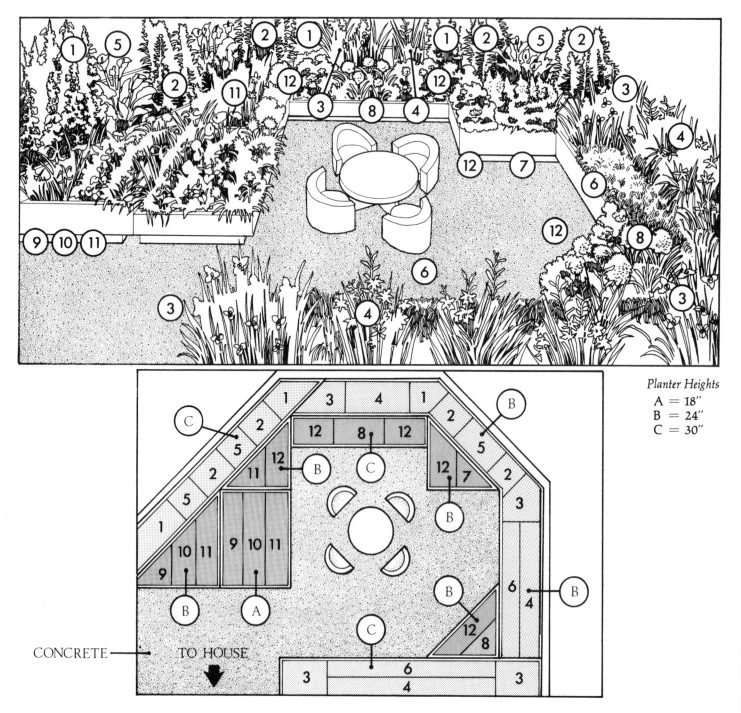

Planter Heights
A = 18"
B = 24"
C = 30"

CONCRETE

TO HOUSE

1. *Hibiscus syriacus*
   'Redheart'
   Shrub Althea
   Shrub/Deciduous
   Hardy to −10F
   To 15 feet; heart-shaped leaves; open-faced white flowers with red center. Difficult to grow and transplant.

2. **Penstemon 'Firebird'**
   Beard-tongue
   Perennial
   Summer
   To 30 inches; tall spikes of bright red flowers. Grow in full sun or light shade. Needs acid soil.

3. **Tigridia 'Grandiflora'**
   Shell Flower
   Bulb/Hardy
   Summer
   Hardy to 10F
   To 36 inches; grassy foliage; solid-color petals, speckled center. Does not like too much sun; needs evenly moist soil. Dig up and store in colder regions.

4. *Montbretia crocosmiiflora*
   Bulb/Hardy
   Summer
   To 48 inches; grassy foliage; lilylike red or orange flowers. Divide every third year.

5. *Zantedeschia elliottiana*
   Golden Calla Lily
   Bulb/Tender
   Summer
   Hardy to 20F
   To 24 inches; handsome green leaves dotted white; tall spikes of yellow flowers. Grows well in light shade. Dig up and store in colder regions.

6. *Ophiopogon japonicus*
   Dwarf Lilyturf
   Ground Cover/Evergreen
   Hardy to 5F
   To 10 inches; grassy rosettes with spines of tiny lilac flowers. Grows in sun or shade.

7. *Ornithagalum arabicum*
   Star-of-Bethelem
   Bulb
   Spring
   Hardy to 10F
   To 24 inches; clusters of small white flowers with black centers. Does well in sun or light shade in any soil.

8. **Agapanthus**
   'Rancho Dwarf'
   Lily-of-the-Nile
   Bulb/Tender
   Summer
   Hardy to 30F
   To 36 inches; grassy leaves; white flowers in clusters. Will grow in most soils.

9. *Sprekelia formosissima*
   Aztec Lily
   Bulb/Tender
   Fall
   Hardy to 30F
   To 24 inches; long and thin dark green foliage; brilliant red flowers. Needs full sun and even moisture.

10. *Anthurium andreanum*
    Flamingo Plant
    Perennial
    To 24 inches; broad leaves; waxy, spathe-shaped red flowers. Spectacular tropical plant.

11. *Vallota purpurea*
    Scarborough Lily
    Bulb/Tender
    Summer/Fall
    Hardy to 40F
    To 18 inches; grassy foliage; stems crowded with red flowers. Likes light shade. Needs good drainage.

12. **Geranium (Carefree type)**
    Perennial
    Summer
    To 18 inches; abundant masses of pink flowers.

1. Hibiscus syriacus 'Redheart'

2. Penstemon 'Firebird'

3. Tigridia 'Grandiflora'

4. Montbretia crocosmiiflora

5. Zantedeschia elliottiana

6. Ophiopogon japonicus

7. Ornithagalum arabicum

8. Agapanthus 'Rancho Dwarf'

9. Sprekelia formosissima

10. Anthurium andreanum

11. Vallota purpurea

12. Geranium (Carefree type)

76 / Rock Garden

This is a basic rock garden
with stone steps used for a
path through the flowers. The
rocks are selected for their
varying heights—low, medium,
high—and the plants are tucked
between them. This garden will
be sparse in the first year, but
after a few years it develops its
full beauty. Though this plan
is for a man-made rock garden,
the same appearance can be
achieved on a natural rocky
site.

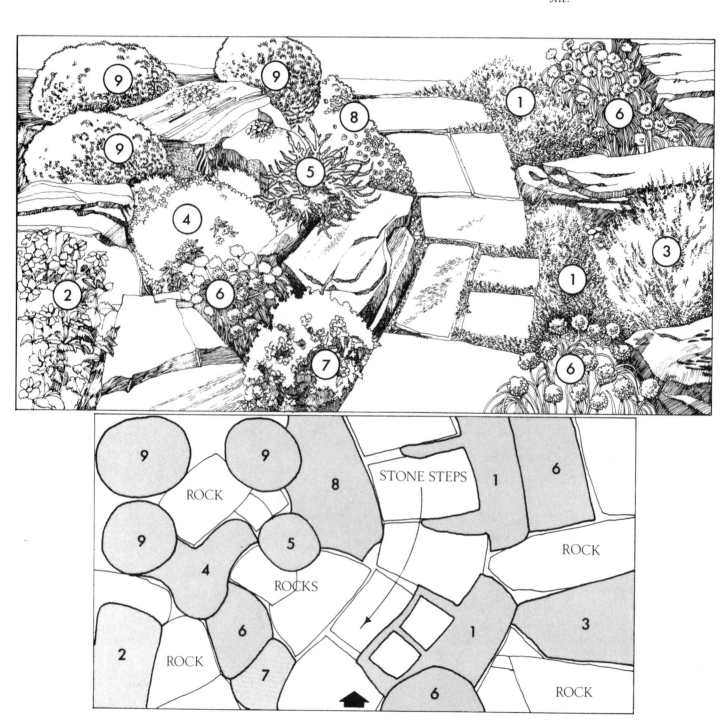

1. **Arenaria verna caespitosa**
Moss Sandwort
Perennial
Spring
To 3 inches; leaves flat, narrow, and dark green; flowers tiny and white. Prostrate. Okay to walk on occasionally. Mix a little sand in soil.

2. **Anemone 'Robustissima'**
Perennial
Summer/Fall
To 36 inches; leaves five-lobed; flowers bright pink. Needs rich sandy soil, some shade. Water often and mulch each year. Magnificent cut flowers.

3. **Perovskia atriplicifolia**
Russian Sage
Perennial
Summer
To 36 inches; oval, oblong leaves; lavender-blue flowers; spreading habit. Needs full sun.

4. **Lithospermum diffusum 'Heavenly Blue'**
Gromwell
Shrub/Evergreen
Hardy to −20F
To 10 inches; blue flowers. Low growing. Likes rich, well-drained, acid soil. Also called Lithodora.

5. **Calluna 'J. H. Hamilton'**
Heath
Shrub/Evergreen
Hardy to −10F
To 8 inches; one of the best pink flowering heaths. Needs sun to flower. In shade makes an excellent ground cover.

6. **Armeria 'Royal Rose'**
Thrift
Perennial
Spring
To 10 inches; grasslike leaves; deep rose-pink flowers. Needs sandy soil and full sun.

7. **Arabis 'Flore Pleno'**
Rock Cress
Perennial
Spring
To 12 inches; double white flowers. Allow soil to dry out between waterings.

8. **Brunnera macrophylla**
Heartleaf Brunnera
Perennial
Spring
To 12 inches; green dwarf mound; bright blue flowers in late spring. Dislikes wet soil.

9. **Artemisia schmidtiana 'Silver Mound'**
Satiny Wormwood
Ground Cover/Deciduous
Hardy to −20F
To 8 inches; leaves gray and fernlike; flowers small and yellow. Likes a dry sunny spot. Dies down in winter.

1. Arenaria verna caespitosa

2. Anemone 'Robustissima'

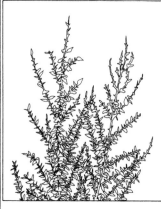

3. Perovskia atriplicifolia

4. Lithospermum diffusa 'Heavenly Blue'

5. Calluna 'J.H. Hamilton'

6. Armeria 'Royal Rose'

7. Arabis 'Flore Pleno'

8. Brunnera macrophylla

9. Artemisia schmidtiana 'Silver Mound'

77 / Rooftop Garage Garden

This sleek simple garden features planter beds of brilliant color. Dramatic blue and fiery red flowers are used to create a handsome scene atop a roof. A white gravel roof topping serves as surface.

MGV NOV 76

1. *Buddleia davidii*
   'Empire Blue'
   Butterfly Bush
   Shrub/Evergreen
   Hardy to −10F

To 84 inches; leaves narrow; purplish-blue flowers in clusters in summer. Use very rich mulch, water well. Magnificent color into fall.

2. *Cotoneaster apiculata*
   Cranberry Cotoneaster
   Shrub/Deciduous
   Hardy to −10F

To 36 inches; leaves bright green; flowers pinkish; berries red in summer. Grows in weeping fashion.

3. *Caryopteris clandonensis*
   'Heavenly Blue'
   Bluebeard
   Shrub/Deciduous
   Hardy to −10F

To 48 inches; toothed leaves; lavender flowers in clusters in fall. Sometimes called Blue Spirea. Likes sandy light soil. Prune in early spring.

4. **Calendula 'Sunny Boy'**
   Pot Marigold
   Annual
   Summer

To 6 inches; leaves fleshy and narrow; flowers to 3 inches, double and orange. Dwarf variety creates mounds of bright golden orange.

5. *Aubrieta deltoidea*
   Purple Rockcress
   Perennial
   Spring

To 4 inches; leaves small; flowers in a large variety of colors.

6. *Iberis sempervirens*
   Evergreen Candytuft
   Shrub/Evergreen
   Hardy to −35F

To 12 inches; leaves dark green; flowers white, minute and in 2-inch clusters. Cascades well. An outstanding bloomer.

7. **Petunia (Giant Double**
   type)
   Annual
   Summer

To 14 inches; leaves fleshy; flowers to 3 inches, double and in pinks, reds, and whites. Easily grown.

8. **Chrysanthemum**
   'Diener's Double'
   Perennial
   Summer/Fall

To 28 inches; leaves narrow and toothed; flowers white.

1. Buddleia davidii 'Empire Blue'

2. Cotoneaster apiculata

3. Caryopteris clandonsis 'Heavenly Blue'

4. Calendula 'Sunny Boy'

5. Aubrieta deltoidea

6. Iberis sempervirens

7. Petunia (Giant Double type)

8. Chrysanthemum 'Diener's Double'

78 / Rose Garden

This rather formal garden is built on a modified cross banked with masses of different roses. The center structure, a gazebolike enclosure, breaks the plan and also provides supports for the many climbing roses. Charming lattice fences are also used.

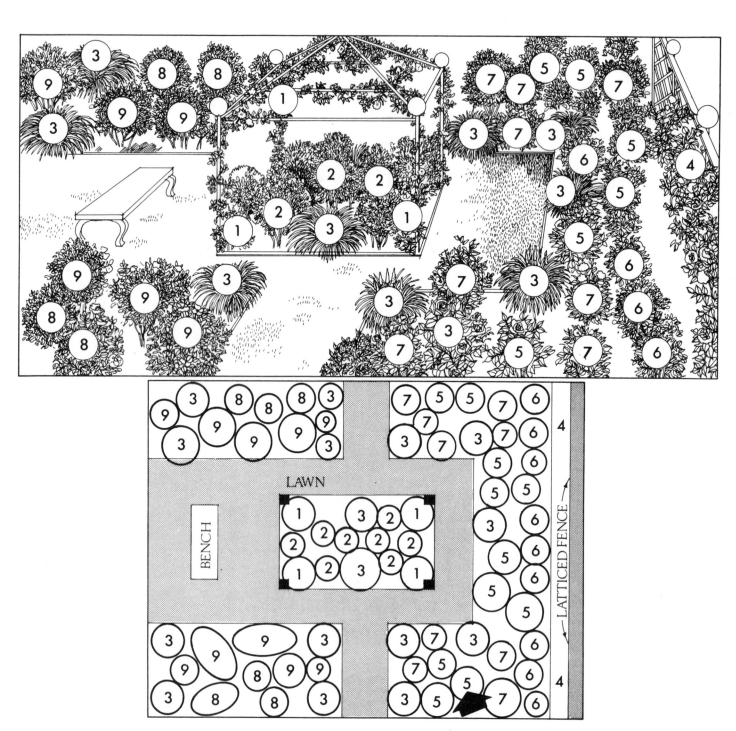

LAWN

BENCH

LATTICED FENCE

1. Rosa 'Dainty Bess'
Shrub/Deciduous
Hardy to −10F
To 10 feet; leaves compound; one layer of pink petals surrounds maroon stamen. Hybrid tea climber. Prune lightly. Attach to arbor diagonally for fuller bloom.

2. Rosa 'Dainty Bess'
Shrub/Deciduous
Hardy to −10F
To 4 feet; same variety as above. Both shrub and climber are hardy and resist mildew.

3. Liriope 'Majestic' Creeping Lilyturf
Groundcover/Evergreen
Hardy to −10F
To 6 inches; leaves small and grasslike; flowers white or blue. One of the few ground covers that does not object to foot traffic. Keeps moisture.

4. Rosa 'Thor'
Shrub/Deciduous
Hardy to −20F
To 10 feet; leaves compound; profuse flowers scarlet and large, with fifty or more petals. Resists most maladies. Not good for cutting.

5. Rosa 'Chrysler Imperial'
Shrub/Deciduous
Hardy to −10F
To 30 inches; leaves compound; flowers double and red, and developing from long tapering buds. Hybrid tea type.

6. Rosa 'Pink Grootendorst'
Shrub/Deciduous
Hardy to −5F
To 60 inches; flowers pink, carnation-like. Resists usual rose problems. Prune canes high to stand above the 'Chrysler Imperial'; they will branch out and remain strong. Rugosa type.

7. Rosa 'Lilac Charm'
Shrub/Deciduous
Hardy to 10F
To 30 inches; leaves dark green; flowers single and lilac with yellow stamen, 2 to 3 inches wide, full blooming. Floribunda type.

8. Rosa 'Town Crier'
Shrub/Deciduous
Hardy to 10F
To 48 inches; leaves compound; flowers gold-yellow on long stems. Keep well pruned in winter to create more blooms. Hybrid tea type.

9. Rosa 'Frau Dagmar Hartop'
Shrub/Deciduous
Hardy to −20F
To 36 inches; leaves compound and glossy; single, bright pink flowers; yellow stamens. Fans out.

1. Rosa 'Dainty Bess'

2. Rosa 'Dainty Bess'

3. Liriope 'Majestic'

4. Rosa 'Thor'

5. Rosa 'Chrysler Imperial'

6. Rosa 'Pink Grootendorst'

7. Rosa 'Lilac Charm'

8. Rosa 'Town Crier'

9. Rosa 'Frau Dagmar Hartop'

79 / Seaside Garden

A serpentine path defines the plan for this garden by the sea. Tucked along the way are mounds of digitalis and rugosa roses. Silver-frost artemisia borders the walk to pull the garden together. This is a low-maintenance plan.

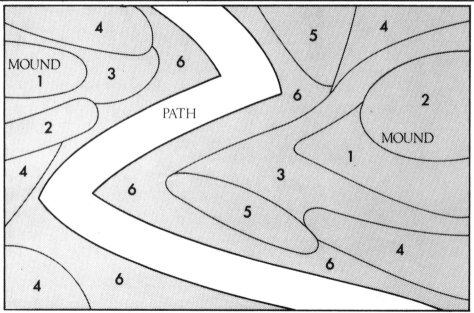

1. **Achillea 'Coronation Gold' Yarrow**
Perennial
Summer
To 40 inches; tall spikes of gold flowers.

2. *Rosa* **'Flamingo'**
Shrub/Deciduous
Hardy to —10F
To 60 inches; flowers open-faced, pink and long-blooming. For maximum bloom, do not fertilize.

3. *Digitalis grandiflora* **Yellow Foxglove**
Biennial
Summer
To 60 inches; leafy stems, spikes of yellow flowers. Keep soil evenly moist.

4. *Erigeron glaucus* **Brown Fleabane**
Perennial
Spring/Summer
To 12 inches; pale green oval leaves; violet flower heads. Does best in well-drained soil.

5. *Armeria maritima laucheana* **Common Thrift**
Perennial
Summer
To 6 inches; narrow grasslike leaves; deep rose flowers. Does best in well-drained sandy soil with minimal feeding.

6. *Artemisia albula* **'Silver Frost' Satiny Wormwood**
Ground Cover/Semievergreen
Hardy to —35F
To 14 inches; popular silver-gray foliage plant. Excellent drainage is essential. Dies down in winter.

1. Achillea 'Coronation Gold'

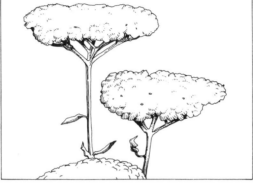

2. Rosa 'Flamingo'

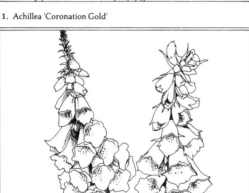

3. Digitalis grandiflora

4. Erigeron glaucus

5. Armeria maritima laucheana

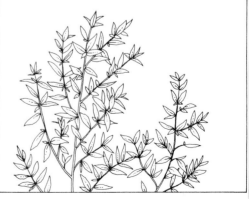

6. Artemisia albula 'Silver Frost'

80 / Semiformal Garden

Using wood posts or tree trunks to contain plants, this rustic garden plan offers a lot of color in a small area. Giant hibiscus shrubs are the backbone of the plan and the lawns offer a complementary foil for the colorful blooms. Lovely veronica frames the garden at the end. This garden will do well on a small or large site.

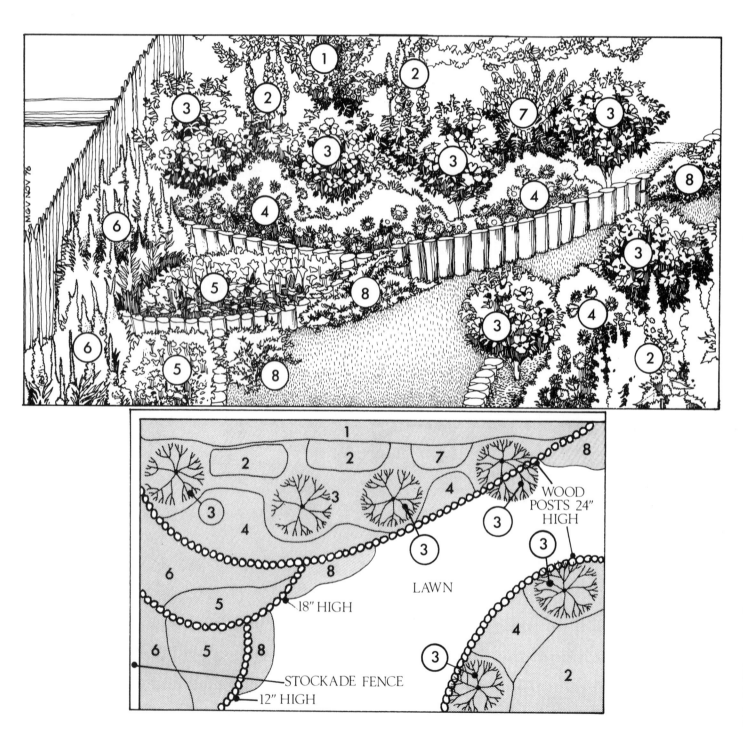

MGV NOV 76

WOOD POSTS 24" HIGH

18" HIGH

LAWN

STOCKADE FENCE
12" HIGH

1. **Campsis tagliabuana 'Mme Galen'**
   Clinging Vine
   Vine/Semievergreen
   Perennial
   Hardy to −10F
   Summer/Fall
   Climbs to 30 feet; dense foliage; trumpet-shaped fiery red-orange flowers in summer. Must have sun. Also called Bignonia.

2. **Delphinium 'King Arthur'**
   Perennial
   Summer
   To 60 inches; masses of low-lobed leaves; spires of dramatic blue-lavender flowers. Mix in 'Summer Skies' for a two-tone blue effect. Often needs staking.

3. **Hibiscus syriacus 'Crimson Wonder'**
   Rose-of-Sharon
   Shrub/Deciduous
   Hardy to −10F
   To 40 inches; shrubby and upright; large single red flowers. One of the giant blossoming variety. Spectacular bloom. Likes a warm sunny spot. Water freely.

4. **Aster 'Blue Radiance'**
   Michaelmas Daisy
   Perennial
   Summer/Fall
   To 36 inches; ferny foliage; masses of small blue flowers with yellow centers. Grows in rounded form.

5. **Campanula carpatica**
   Bellflower
   Perennial
   Summer/Fall
   To 12 inches; oval leaves; vivid violet-blue flowers in masses above foliage which move around in the slightest breeze.

6. **Veronica 'Minuet'**
   Perennial
   Summer
   To 18 inches; grayish-green slender leaves; spike of small pink flowers. Easily grown, likes rich loamy soil.

7. **Dicentra exima**
   Fringed Bleeding-heart
   Perennial
   Summer
   To 20 inches; ferny green foliage; pink bell-shaped flowers. Much improved. Many-bloom stalks have bright pink all over.

8. **Hedera helix 'Tribairn'**
   Baltic Ivy
   Ground Cover/Evergreen
   Hardy to −35F
   To 60 inches; fine cut-leaf ivy.

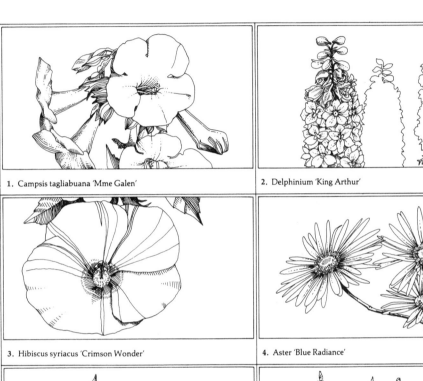
1. Campsis tagliabuana 'Mme Galen'

2. Delphinium 'King Arthur'

3. Hibiscus syriacus 'Crimson Wonder'

4. Aster 'Blue Radiance'

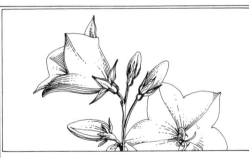
5. Campanula carpatica

6. Veronica 'Minuet'

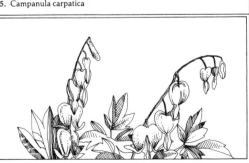
7. Dicentra exima

8. Hedera helix 'Tribairn'

81 / Service Garden

This inexpensive garden admirably serves the purpose of hiding a service area. Using hanging begonias over the garbage area and hydrangeas at one side, there is almost a total cover of any unsightly areas. To balance the plan, clematis adjoins the arrangement. This is a simple garden to maintain.

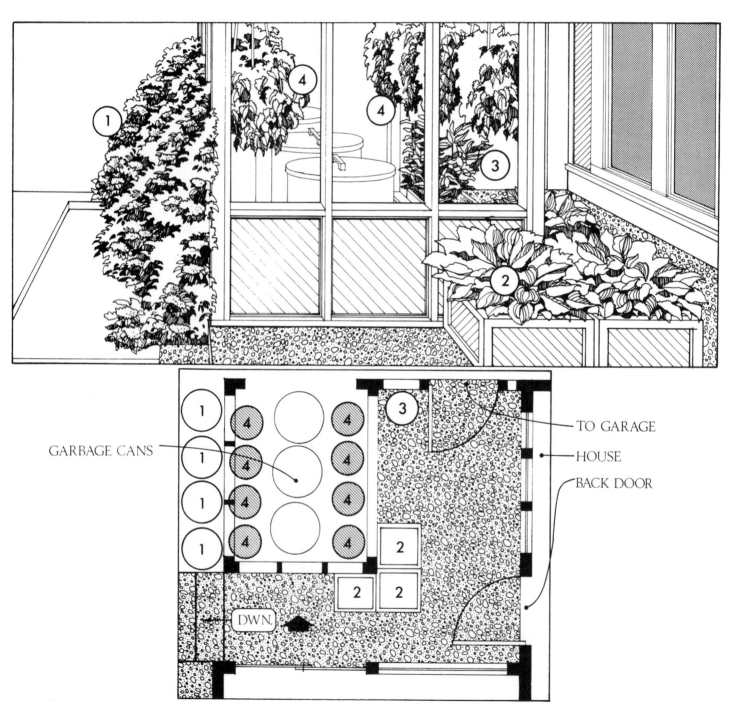

GARBAGE CANS

TO GARAGE

HOUSE

BACK DOOR

DWN.

1. *Hydrangea petiolaris*
   Climbing Hydrangea
   Vine/Deciduous
   Perennial
   Summer
   Hardy to −10F
Climbs to 35 feet; oval leaves; large white flowers in branched clusters. Needs sandy loamy soil and good drainage.

2. **Hosta 'Thomas Hogg'**
   Plantain Lily
   Perennial
   Fall
To 20 inches; variegated leaves; stellar foliage plant. Keep damp.

3. *Clematis tangutica*
   Golden Clematis
   Vine/Semievergreen
   Perennial
   Hardy to −10F
   Summer/Fall
Climbs to 10 feet; scalloped leaves; handsome golden-orange flowers. Small but persistent. Loves lime.

4. *Begonia pendula*
   Bulb/Tender
   Summer
Cascades to 4 feet; leafy with exquisite pendulous flowers, many colors and varieties. Prolific bloomer in summer. Grow in leaf mold and soil mix; feed lightly with 15–30–15 fertilizer.

1. Hydrangea petiolaris

2. Hosta 'Thomas Hogg'

3. Clematis tangutica

4. Begonia pendula

82 / Spring Garden (all red)

Using a hedge effect of red flowering peach, red weigela and red-flowered quince at one end of the garden, this arrangement mirrors the lawn and walkway at the opposite end. A row of azaleas follows the quince, succeeded by a row of tulips and a row of primulas and finally a row of red hyacinths. A lawn provides a contrasting green foil to complete the plan.

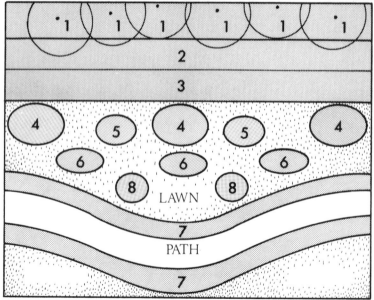

1. Prunus persica 'Cardinal'
Flowering Peach
Tree/Deciduous
Hardy to −10F
To 25 feet; leaves oblong; flowers rose-red. Handsome and easy to grow, but affected by polluted air.

2. Weigela florida
'Bristol Ruby'
Shrub/Deciduous
Hardy to −10F
To 72 inches; leaves oblong; flowers red and tubular. Needs plenty of water, sun, good drainage.

3. Cydonia oblongo 'Spitfire'
Common Quince
Tree/Deciduous
Hardy to −10F
To 20 feet; leaves small and green; flowers crimson and very abundant. Attractive branching habit. Prune to 6 feet.

4. Azalea (Exbury hybrids)
Shrub/Deciduous
Hardy to −10F
To 60 inches; leaves oblong; flowers in globe-shaped clusters, yellow, pink, or orange. Use cool, moist, acid soil.

5. Tulipa 'Orange Favorite'
Bulb/Hardy
Spring
To 24 inches; leaves narrow and basal; flower on end of stem, large, cuplike, usually with green streaking. Plant 4 inches deep. Parrot type.

6. Primula acaulis (hybrid)
Primrose
Annual
Spring
To 8 inches; oblong rosette leaves; flowers red and scarlet on stalks. Water freely; very strong growing. Withstands inclement weather well.

7. Anemone fulgens annulata
grandiflora
Peacock Anemone
Bulb/Hardy
Spring
To 12 inches; leaves very narrow; flowers bright scarlet. Likes attention. Work soil thoroughly and mulch. Plant 2 inches deep.

8. Hyacinthus 'Jan Bos'
Hyacinth
Bulb/Hardy
Spring
To 24 inches, leaves narrow and basal, flowers red, in showy cluster on stem. Plant 3 inches deep.

1. Prunus persica 'Cardinal'

2. Weigela florida 'Bristol Ruby'

3. Cydonia oblongo 'Spitfire'

4. Azalea (Exbury hybrids)

5. Tulipa ' Orange Favorite'

6. Primula acaulis (hybrid)

7. Anemone fulgens annulata grandiflora

8. Hyacinthus 'Jan Bos'

83 / Summer Garden (for temperate climates)

Defined with a gravel path, this garden reaches peak color in midsummer. There is an abundance of plant material and flower forms are specifically selected to provide a handsome design-upon-design effect, by the use of round and star-shaped blossoms, rosette plants and leafy giants.

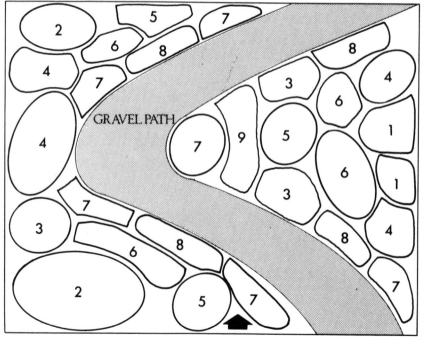

GRAVEL PATH

1. **Celosia 'Golden Fleece'**
   Cockscomb
   Annual
   Summer
   To 36 inches; leaves large, ribbed, and oblong; yellow flowers in clusters. Grows easily in any soil. Good dried flowers.

2. **Celosia 'Tango'**
   Cockscomb
   Annual
   Summer
   To 36 inches; narrow leaves to 2½ inches long; orange flowers in plumes. Grows easily in any soil. Good dried flowers. Very hardy.

3. **Celosia 'Crusader'**
   Cockscomb
   Annual
   Summer
   To 10 inches; leaves bronze and narrow; flowers in red plumes. One of the dwarf forms ideal for edging accent. This is low-growing and has dark foliage. Clumps well.

4. **Canna 'Ambassador'**
   Bulb/Tender
   Summer/Fall
   To 48 inches; leaves large and bronze; flowers large and cherry pink. Must be dug up and stored over winter. Plant bulbs 3 to 4 inches deep.

5. **Canna 'Primrose Yellow'**
   Bulb/Tender
   Summer/Fall
   To 24 inches; foliage bushy and dark green; yellow flowers in clusters. Must be dug up and stored over winter. Plant bulbs 3 to 4 inches deep.

6. **Tagetes**
   'Diamond Jubilee'
   Marigold
   Annual
   Summer/Fall
   To 24 inches; foliage bushy and dark; flowers spherical, 4 inches wide, and yellow. Easy to grow. Excellent for cutting. Use only the yellow of this variety; orange is too strong for this garden plan. Cut to force more blooms.

7. **Zinnia 'Minipink'**
   Annual
   Summer/Fall
   To 4 inches; leaves oblong; flowers double and lovely pink. Leave space between plants so they can bush out. Watch for mildew. Thumbelina type.

8. **Ageratum 'Blue Mink'**
   Annual
   Summer
   To 10 inches; leaves oblong and dark green; blue flowers in clusters. Pinch back plants so that they grow compact.

9. **Celosia 'Floradale'**
   Cockscomb
   Annual
   Summer
   To 16 inches; leaves narrow; flowers red in a large central plume with smaller plumes on side branches. Grows easily in any soil. Good for dried flowers. Long-lasting blooms.

1. Celosia 'Golden Fleece'

2. Celosia 'Tango'

3. Celosia 'Crusader'

4. Canna 'Ambassador'

5. Canna 'Primrose Yellow'

6. Tagetes 'Diamond Jubilee'

7. Zinnia 'Mini-Pink'

8. Ageratum 'Blue Mink'

9. Celosia 'Floradale'

84 / Swimming Pool Garden

In a U-shape, this plan frames a swimming pool with square planters at varying heights. Rudbeckia, geraniums, and petunias are the dominant flowers. One accent red maple tree is used at right of the pool. Though there are not too many flowers, this simple plan works well.

1. **Clematis montana 'Alba'**
   Anemone Clematis
   Vine/Evergreen
   Perennial
   Hardy to −5F
   Spring
   To 20 feet; lobed leaves; masses of white flowers. Likes alkaline soil; needs some sun.

2. **Ampelopsis**
   'Beverly Bowers'
   Boston Ivy
   Vine/Deciduous
   Perennial
   Hardy to −10F
   To 20 feet; large crinkle-type leaves. Makes dense screen. Not particular about soil.

3. **Azalea mucronalatum**
   Korean Rhododendron
   Shrub/Deciduous
   Hardy to −10F
   To 72 inches; yellow to bronze leaves in fall; masses of showy lavender flowers in early spring. Likes acid soil.

4. **Rudbeckia gloriosa**
   Gloriosa Daisy
   Perennial
   Summer
   To 48 inches; leaves oblong; flowers usually golden-yellow with brown center. Long-lasting cut flowers. No special requirements.

5. **Geranium (Double-dip type)**
   Perennial
   Summer
   To 16 inches; leaves round and dark green; flowers 5 inches wide, red and pink and abundant.

6. **Petunia 'Razzle Dazzle'**
   Annual
   Summer
   To 16 inches; red-and-white flowers in masses.

7. **Lobularia 'Rosie O'Day'**
   Sweet Alyssum
   Annual
   Summer/Fall
   To 6 inches; leaves small and green; flowers rose-pink and abundant. Grows quickly. Keep weeded. Reseeds itself.

8. **Antirrhinum**
   (Rocket hybrid mix)
   Snapdragon
   Annual
   Summer
   To 36 inches; flowers red, pink, orange. Likes moist soil, sun.

9. **Acer palmatum dissectum**
   Threadleaf Japanese Maple
   Tree/Deciduous
   Hardy to −5F
   To 20 feet; leaves palmate, highly disected and scarlet in autumn. A small handsome tree that grows readily with little care.

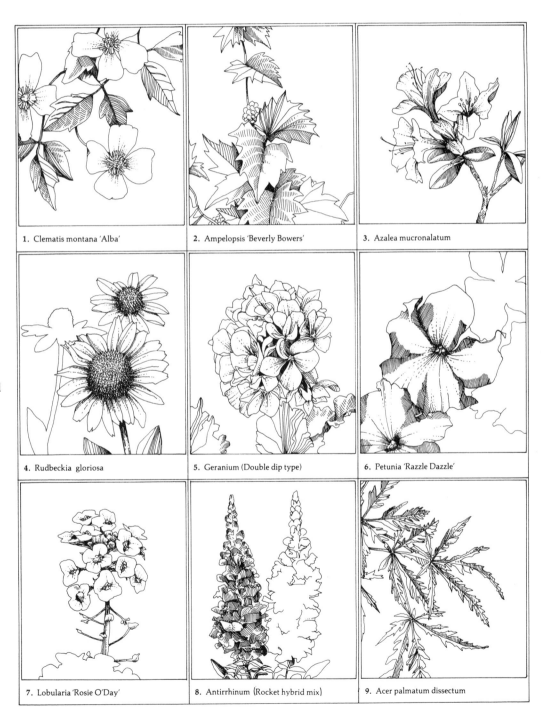

1. Clematis montana 'Alba'

2. Ampelopsis 'Beverly Bowers'

3. Azalea mucronalatum

4. Rudbeckia gloriosa

5. Geranium (Double dip type)

6. Petunia 'Razzle Dazzle'

7. Lobularia 'Rosie O'Day'

8. Antirrhinum (Rocket hybrid mix)

9. Acer palmatum dissectum

85 / Terrace Garden

Quarry tile is dramatically contrasted with lawn in this plan. Dwarf pomegranate trees are placed in tubs at the entrance area. Viburnum opulus is the low-growing plant in the foreground and lythrum provides vertical accent. The design is formal yet pleasing and can be used in a small or large site.

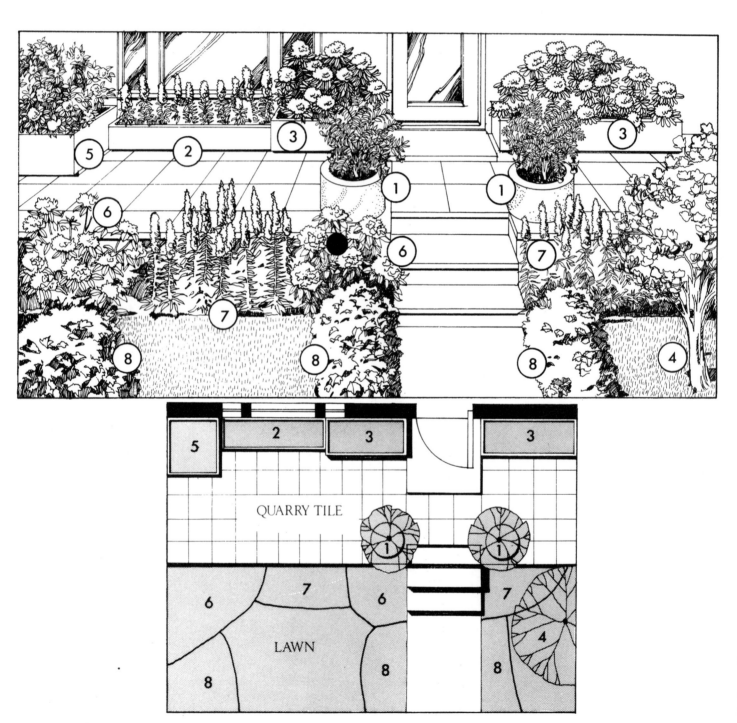

1. *Punica granatum*
   Pomegranate
   Tree/Deciduous
   Hardy to 20F
   To 15 feet; leaves lance-shaped; flowers red; fruit reddish. Likes sandy soil. Allow soil to dry out between waterings.

2. *Matthiola incana annua*
   Stock
   Annual
   Summer
   To 12 inches; leaves narrow; flowers white to red to blue, in dense spikes. Good fragrant garden plant.

3. *Daphne cneorum*
   Rose Daphne
   Shrub/Evergreen
   Hardy to −20F
   To 12 inches; leaves oblong; flowers pink, fragrant and abundant. Needs cool moist conditions.

4. *Magnolia soulangiana*
   Saucer Magnolia
   Tree/Deciduous
   Hardy to −10F
   To 15 feet; leaves broad; flowers white to pink. Popular variety.

5. *Syringa laciniata*
   Cutleaf Lilac
   Shrub/Deciduous
   Hardy to −10F
   To 60 inches; leaves bright green; flowers blue or pink. Prefers lime soil. Prune severely in early spring.

6. *Rhododendron carolinianum*
   Carolina Rhododendron
   Shrub/Evergreen
   Hardy to −10F
   To 72 inches; narrow leaves to 3 inches long; flowers bell-shaped and rose-purple to white. Use acid-type soil, keep moist.

7. *Lythrum 'Morden's Pink'*
   Loosestrife
   Perennial
   Summer
   To 36 inches, leaves narrow; large pink clumps of flowers on spikes. Likes moisture and sun.

8. *Viburnum opulus 'Nanum'*
   European Cranberry Bush
   Shrub/Deciduous
   Hardy to −35F
   To 48 inches; leaves lobed; pink flowers in clusters; berries red. Grows in practically any soil; tolerates light shade.

1. Punica granatum

2. Matthiola incana annua

3. Daphne cneorum

4. Magnolia soulangiana

5. Syringa laciniata

6. Rhododendron carolinianum

7. Lythrum 'Morden's Pink'

8. Viburnum opulus 'Nanum'

86 / Textured Garden

This plan accentuates shape, form, and leaf texture in a "walk and touch" garden. The stepping stones are an essential part of the plan not only for walking but also to create pattern. When beginning this garden, use bark in bare areas; eventually plants will fill in to create a visual textured treat.

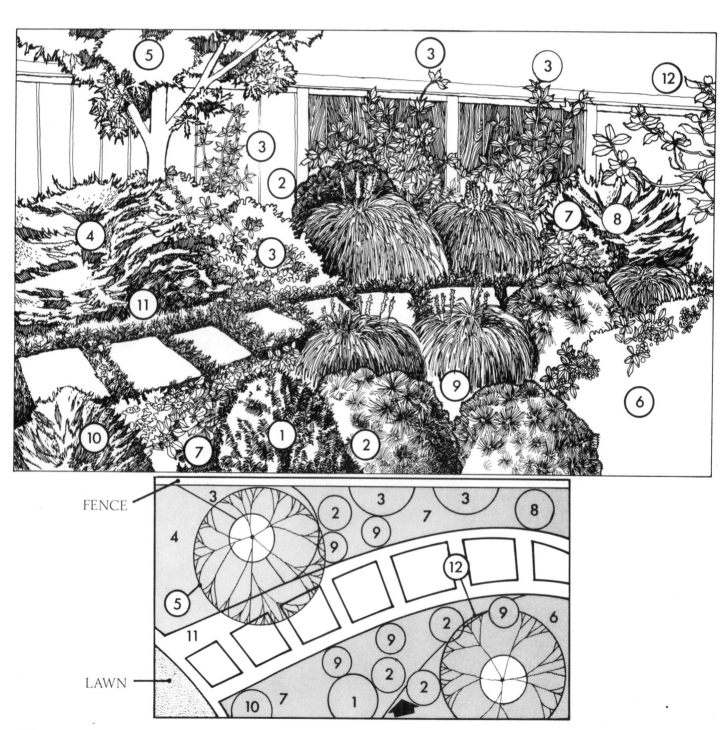

FENCE

LAWN

1. **Taxus cuspidata capitata**
   Japanese Yew
   Tree/Evergreen
   Hardy to −10F
   To 50 feet; leaves needlelike
   and dark green; flowers inconspicuous; berries red. Will
   grow in almost any soil. Good
   for hedges and screens.

2. **Pinus mugo**
   Swiss Mountain Pine
   Shrub/Evergreen
   Hardy to −35 F
   To 25 feet; bright green needles in bunches of two; cones
   to 2½ inches long. A good ornamental. Easy to train to
   shape.

3. **Lonicera heckrottii**
   Everblooming
   Honeysuckle
   Vine/Evergreen
   Perennial
   Hardy to −10F
   Summer
   Climbing vine to 10 feet;
   leaves light green and shiny;
   flowers bright pink with yel-
   low center. Not as rampant as
   other varieties; usually can be
   easily contained. Delightful
   fragrance. Used to be called
   'Winchester.'

4. **Juniperus horizontalis**
   'Wiltoni'
   Creeping Juniper
   Shrub/Evergreen
   Hardy to −35F
   To 12 inches; leaves scalelike,
   minute, and bluish-green;
   berries blue. Prefers a some-
   what alkaline soil.

5. **Acer palmatum dissectum**
   Threadleaf Japanese
   Maple
   Tree/Deciduous
   Hardy to −5F
   To 20 feet; leaves palmate
   and highly disected, scarlet in
   autumn. A handsome small
   tree that grows readily with
   little care.

6. **Cotoneaster salicifolia**
   floccosus
   Shrub/Semievergreen
   Hardy to −5F
   To 15 feet; leaves 3 inches
   long and oblong; flowers
   white in 2-inch clusters; berries bright red. Can take
   abuse.

7. **Plumbago larpentae**
   Shrub/Semievergreen
   Hardy to −10F
   To 12 inches; small, leathery
   leaves turn mahogany in fall;
   blue flowers in clusters.
   Grows well, even in adverse
   conditions. Feed lightly.

8. **Juniperus chinensis**
   'Maneyi'
   Chinese Juniper
   Tree/Evergreen
   Hardy to −10F
   To 60 feet; blue-green, linear
   leaves; brown berries. Needs
   an alkaline soil.

9. **Ophiopogon japonicus**
   Dwarf Lilyturf
   Ground Cover/Evergreen
   Hardy to −5F
   To 10 inches; leaves dark
   green, and to 10 inches;
   flowers lilac and small, fruit
   blue and pea-sized. Grows
   in sun or shade.

10. **Juniperus scopulorum**
    'Sutherland'
    Tree/Evergreen
    Hardy to −5F
    To 30 feet; leaves yellow-
    green and scalelike; flowers
    inconspicuous; fruit blue. Col-
    orful in fall and winter.

11. **Arenaria verna caespitosa**
    Moss Sandwort
    Perennial
    Spring
    To 3 inches; leaves flat, nar-
    row, and dark green; flowers
    tiny and white. Can walk on
    it occasionally. Mix some
    sand into soil.

12. **Cornus florida**
    'Spring Song'
    Dogwood
    Tree/Deciduous
    Hardy to −10F
    To 40 feet; green leaves to 2
    inches; flowers prolific and
    rose-red. Popular.

1. Taxus cuspidata capitata

2. Pinus mugo

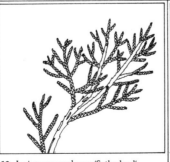

3. Lonicera heckrottii

4. Juniperus horizontalis 'Wiltonii'

5. Acer palmatum dissectum

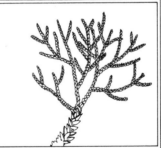

6. Cotoneaster salicifolia floccosus

7. Plumbago larpentae

8. Juniperus chinensis 'Maneyi'

9. Ophiopogon japonicus

10. Juniperus scopulorum 'Sutherland'

11. Arenaria verna caespitosa

12. Cornus florida 'Spring Song'

87 / Tree Form Garden

With a center island of ground cover, this unusual plan uses tree form or standards throughout, with a border of weigela to provide bushy accent. By its very nature, the garden is formal in design and will take several years to reach its peak beauty.

1. **Wisteria floribunda 'Longissima Alba' Japanese Wisteria**
Vine/Deciduous
Perennial
Hardy to —10F
Spring
To 10 feet; leaves oblong; flowers white, in pendent clusters. Does best in poor sandy soil. Grow to standard form.

2. **Viburnum juddii**
Shrub/Deciduous
Hardy to —10F
To 72 inches; foliage dark green; blue-white flowers in round clusters. Grows in most soil; will tolerate light shade. Grow to standard form.

3. **Prunus tenella 'Fire Hill'**
Tree/Deciduous
Hardy to —10F
To 48 inches; leaves narrow and willowlike; red-rose flowers appear before the leaves. Candelabra-shaped. Grow to standard form.

4. **Syringa palibiniana**
Shrub/Deciduous
Hardy to —20F
To 10 feet; leaves oval, lilac flowers in 5-inch-long clusters. Grows symmetrically. Outstanding in June. Grow to standard form.

5. **Cotoneaster apiculata Cranberry Cotoneaster**
Shrub/Deciduous
Hardy to —10F
To 60 inches; bright green leaves; flowers pinkish; bright red berries. Grows in a weeping fashion, cascading downward. Grow to standard form.

6. **Rosa 'The Fairy'**
Shrub/Deciduous
Hardy to —20F
To 48 inches; layers of green leaves composed of oblong leaflets, roses light pink.

7. **Weigela florida 'Springtime'**
Shrub/Deciduous
Hardy to —10F
To 60 inches; leaves oblong, flowers pink and abundant. Used here as low background around the perimeter. Prune to desired height.

8. **Thymus serpyllum Woolly Thyme**
Ground Cover/Evergreen
Hardy to —35F
To 3 inches; leaves small and very green; flowers purplish. Use clumps of *Thymus serpyllum* and *T. lanuginosus* for a gray and green effect. Likes sandy loam with a little lime.

9. **Thymus lanuginosus**
Ground Cover/Semievergreen
Hardy to —10F
To 3 inches; leaves small, gray, and hairy; flowers purplish. Likes sandy loam with a little lime.

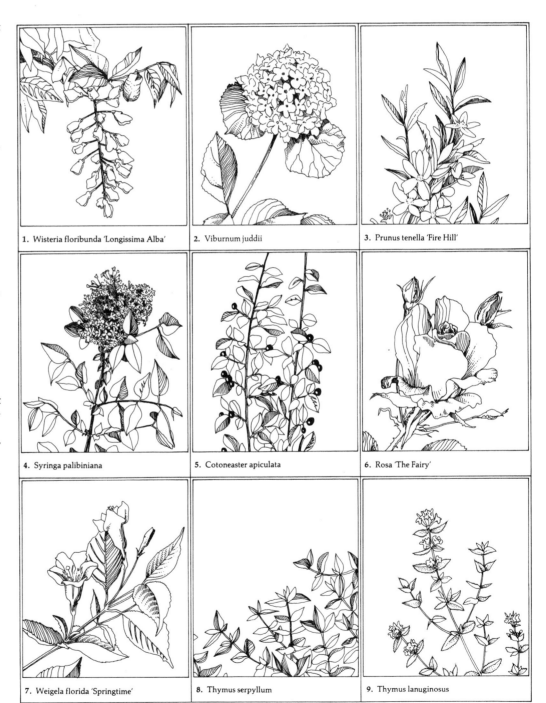

1. Wisteria floribunda 'Longissima Alba'   2. Viburnum juddii   3. Prunus tenella 'Fire Hill'

4. Syringa palibiniana   5. Cotoneaster apiculata   6. Rosa 'The Fairy'

7. Weigela florida 'Springtime'   8. Thymus serpyllum   9. Thymus lanuginosus

88 / Vacation Home Garden

This simple garden was designed for the vactioneer. Fingers of lawn are bordered with low-care plants that are at their peak in spring. Hydrangeas are used in the center foreground and tall salvia serves as a vertical element to balance the low bushy drifts of violas. This works well as a vacation garden because the plants are low maintenance. To enlarge this plan, merely make a mirror image of it.

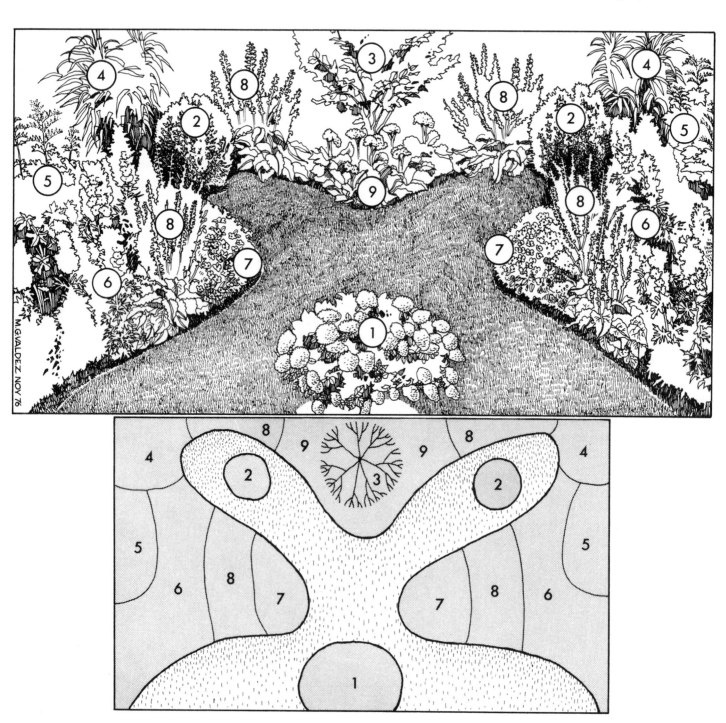

M.G.VALDEZ NOV 76

206

1. **Hydrangea paniculata 'Grandiflora'**
   Tree/Deciduous
   Summer
   Hardy to —10F
   To 30 feet; oval leaves to 5 inches; pink flowers in large profuse clusters. Magnificent. This blossoms so profusely it may need branch support.

2. **Daphne burkwoodii 'Somerset'**
   Shrub/Deciduous
   Spring
   Hardy to —10F
   To 36 inches; leaves narrow; flowers pink, star-shaped and in 6-inch clusters. Elegant and airy; nurse it along at first.

3. **Fagus sylvatica**
   European Beech
   Tree/Deciduous
   Hardy to —10F
   To 80 feet; young leaves yellow, mature leaves light green; flowers inconspicuous. Prospers in loamy limestone soil.

4. **Arundo donax 'Variegata'**
   Giant Reed
   Grass
   To 10 feet; leaves long and narrow, green with white stripes. Likes moisture.

5. **Macleaya cordata**
   Plume Poppy
   Perennial
   Summer
   To 96 inches; leaves with fingerlike lobes, to 8 inches wide; cream colored flowers in spikes.

6. **Malva alcea fastigiata**
   Hollyhock Mallow
   Perennial
   Summer/Fall
   To 30 inches; leaves palm-shaped; red flowers in clusters. Easy to grow, likes moisture.

7. **Viola 'Catherine Sharp'**
   Tufted Pansy
   Perennial
   Spring/Summer
   To 12 inches; leaves wavy; flowers purple with slender spur. Need fairly rich soil and partial shade.

8. **Salvia haematodes**
   Gentian Salvia
   Perennial
   Summer
   To 36 inches; leaves narrow; spires of blue flowers.

9. **Bergenia ciliata**
   Heart-Leaf Bergenia
   Perennial
   Spring
   To 12 inches; leaves large and broad; clusters of pink flowers. Loves water. Will form solid mass of green leaves. Often listed as Saxifraga.

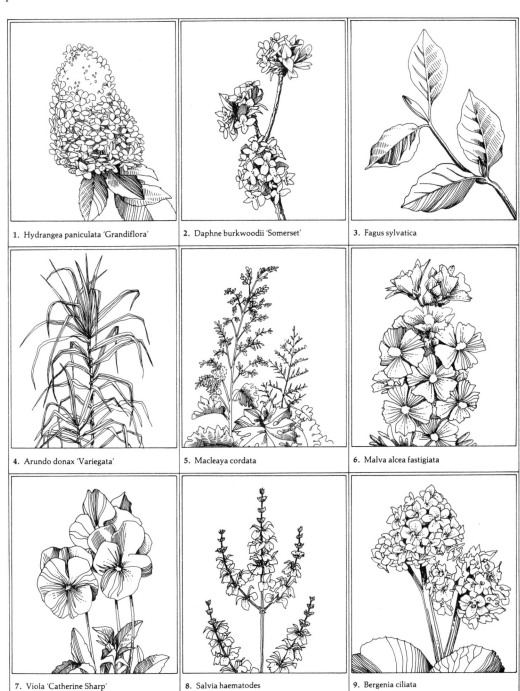

1. Hydrangea paniculata 'Grandiflora'   2. Daphne burkwoodii 'Somerset'   3. Fagus sylvatica

4. Arundo donax 'Variegata'   5. Macleaya cordata   6. Malva alcea fastigiata

7. Viola 'Catherine Sharp'   8. Salvia haematodes   9. Bergenia ciliata

89 / Vegetable Garden

Vegetable gardens can be both functional and beautiful, as shown in this handsome plan. The basic circular design with islands provides easy access to the vegetables and at the same time an interesting pattern. This is not a large garden and yet it provides ample produce and melons for an average family. The plot covers only a 15- by 20-foot area. Fruit trees at the rear provide a horizontal line and asparagus at each end are used for vertical thrust.

M.G. VALDEZ NOV. 76

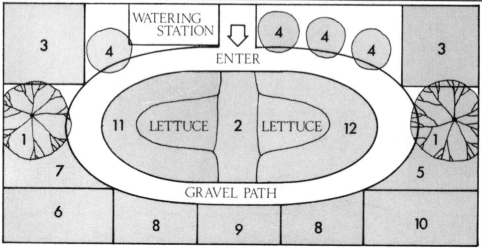

1. *Prunus armeniaca* 'Chinese Golden'
To 5 feet. Plant two different varieties for cross-pollination. Fruits ripen in August. Need lots of water. Also use peach or apple varieties or whatever suits your region.

2. Asparagus 'Mary Washington'
Buy one-year-old plants (crowns) from suppliers. Plant in 10-inch trenches. Set crowns 16 inches apart. Cut spears when 8 inches high, using a knife. Needs compost or manure in soil.

3. Corn 'Golden Cross'
Matures in 85 days. Corn is wind-pollinated. Plant in rows of 3 or 4, never in a single line. Must have copious water. Space plants 12 to 15 inches apart.

4. Tomato 'Burpee Big Boy'
Matures in 75 days. Set pre-starts 16 to 18 inches apart. Plant deep so first leaves are just above soil. Substitute a variety best suited for your region.

5. Eggplant 'Long Tom'
Matures in 75 to 80 days. Buy prestarts and set 16 inches apart. Some plants need staking. Cannot tolerate low temperatures (minimum 70F).

6. Green Pepper 'Yolo Wonder'
Matures in 75 to 80 days. Buy prestarts and set 20 inches apart. Must have copious water. Blossoms drop when night temperatures are below 60F and above 75F.

7. Squash 'Baby Crookneck'
Matures in 50 days. Space plants 20 to 24 inches apart. Grow vertically with support. Likes heat and moisture.

8. Watermelon 'Wide Ranger'
Matures in 100 days. Plant seed 1 inch deep. Germinates in 15 days. Space plants 18 inches apart.

9. Muskmelon 'Sweetie'
Matures in 80 days. Plant seeds 1 inch deep. Germination in 10 days. Set plants 15 inches apart. Needs water and heat.

10. Bean 'Tendercut'
Matures in 55 days; bush type. Seeds won't germinate in cold soil. Germination in 14 days. Plant seed 2 inches deep; space plants 2 to 3 inches apart.

11. Carrot 'Nantes Coreless'
Matures in 70 to 75 days. Sow seed ½ inch deep. Germination in 15 days. Thin plants to 2 inches apart. Needs plenty of water.

12. Beet 'Detroit Dark Red'
Matures in 65 days. Plant 12 inches apart, then thin to 2 inches apart. Prefers cool temperatures.

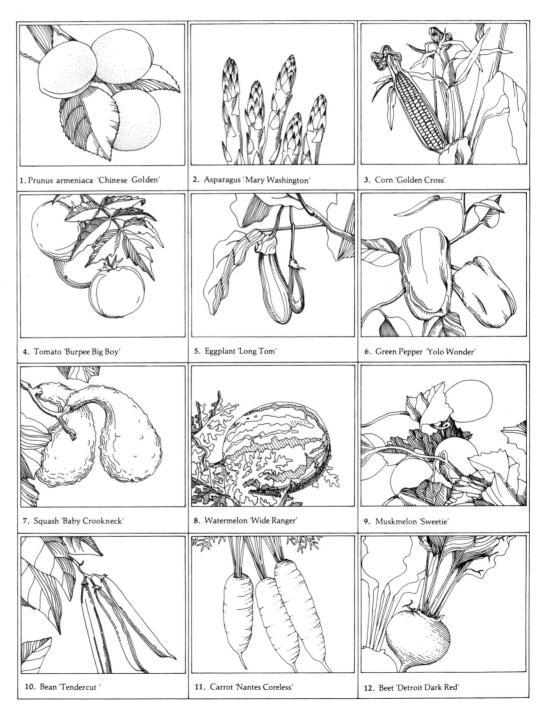

1. Prunus armeniaca 'Chinese Golden'
2. Asparagus 'Mary Washington'
3. Corn 'Golden Cross'
4. Tomato 'Burpee Big Boy'
5. Eggplant 'Long Tom'
6. Green Pepper 'Yolo Wonder'
7. Squash 'Baby Crookneck'
8. Watermelon 'Wide Ranger'
9. Muskmelon 'Sweetie'
10. Bean 'Tendercut'
11. Carrot 'Nantes Coreless'
12. Beet 'Detroit Dark Red'

90 / Walk-through Garden

Pools and paths and wood bridges are melded in this serpentine garden plan. Annuals, perennials, shrubs and trees provide something to see at every turn. Designed for walking, this garden suits its purpose beautifully.

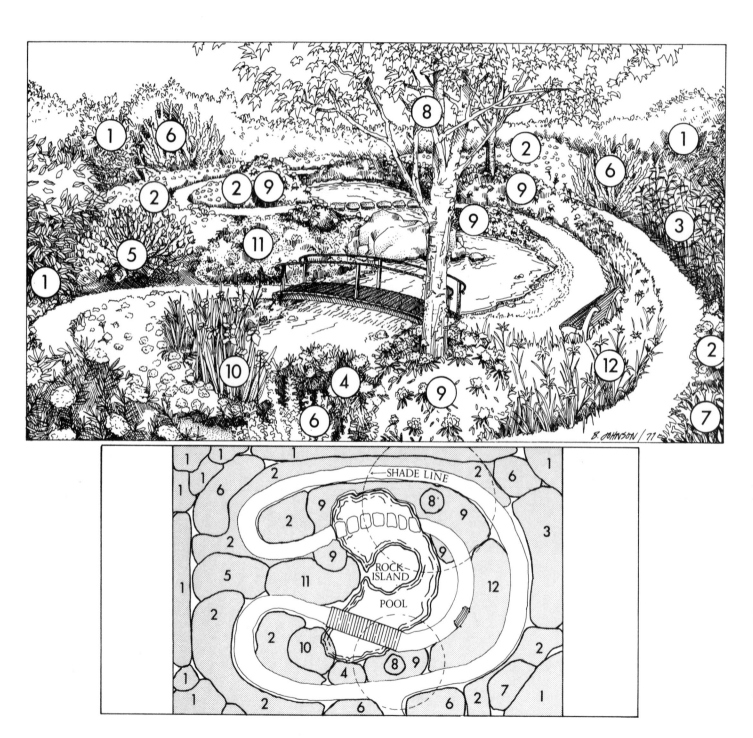

B. JOHNSON / 71

1. **Rhamnus frangula**
Alder Buckthorn
Shrub/Deciduous
Hardy to −35F
To 18 feet; dark lustrous green leaves; good dense habit; vigorous growth. Good in any soil.

2. **Tagetes 'Aztec'**
Marigold
Annual
Summer
To 30 inches; divided leaves; solitary yellow or orange flowers. A popular variety with a good yield.

3. **Phyllostachys nigra**
Black Bamboo
Hardy to −10F
To 25 feet; graceful form and beautiful blackish green leaves. Likes moisture; very porous soil.

4. **Daphne cneorum**
Rose Daphne
Shrub/Evergreen
Hardy to −20F
To 12 inches; small leaves; fine pink flowers in spring.

5. **Magnolia soulangiana**
Saucer Magnolia
Tree/Deciduous
Hardy to −10F
To 15 feet; leaves 6 to 8 inches; masses of pink flowers in spring.

6. **Forsythia intermedia 'Spring Glory'**
Shrub/Deciduous
Hardy to −10F
To 72 inches; tall spines of yellow flowers in spring. Prune only after blooming.

7. **Kolkwitzia amabilis**
Beauty Bush
Shrub/Deciduous
Hardy to −20F
To 10 feet; leaves turn reddish in fall; pale pink flowers in spring. Rather showy.

8. **Acer griseum**
Paperback Maple
Tree/Deciduous
Hardy to −10F
To 25 feet; compound leaves with leaflets. Outstanding because of its ornamental bark.

9. **Rhododendrum (hybrid)**
Shrub/Evergreen
Hardy to −10F
To 60 inches; handsome masses of colorful flowers. Bright pinks and red are recommended for this garden: use 'Roseum Elegans' and 'Winsome.'

10. **Iris kaempferi**
Japanese Iris
Bulb/Hardy
To 48 inches; beardless, blue, pink, or white blooms in summer. Likes wet feet. Try acid-type food.

11. **Phlox paniculata**
Garden Phlox
Perennial
Spring/Summer
To 30 inches; masses of pink or red flowers. Needs staking. Subject to mildew.

12. **Hemerocallis (Hyperion type)**
Lemon Lily
Perennial
Spring
To 36 inches; large, everblooming, fragrant yellow flowers grow into a big clump. A great favorite.

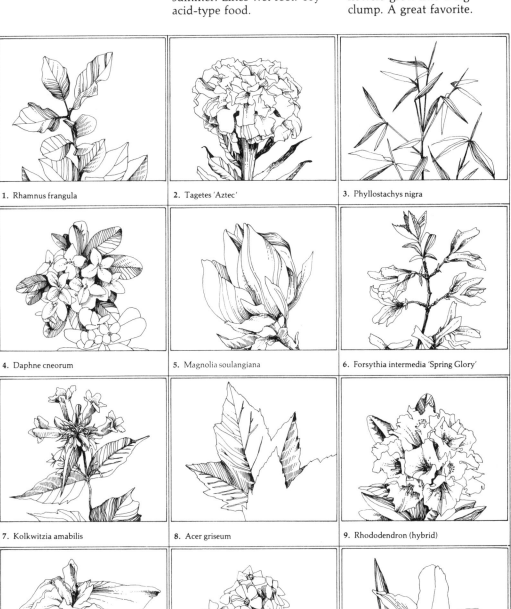

1. Rhamnus frangula   2. Tagetes 'Aztec'   3. Phyllostachys nigra

4. Daphne cneorum   5. Magnolia soulangiana   6. Forsythia intermedia 'Spring Glory'

7. Kolkwitzia amabilis   8. Acer griseum   9. Rhododendron (hybrid)

10. Iris kaempferi   11. Phlox paniculata   12. Hemerocallis (Hyperion type)

91 / Walkway Garden

Using a monochromatic color scheme, this plan offers a distinctive walkway garden. A few plants, green lawns, colorful borders and a handsome brick path make this a totally charming, low-maintenance garden.

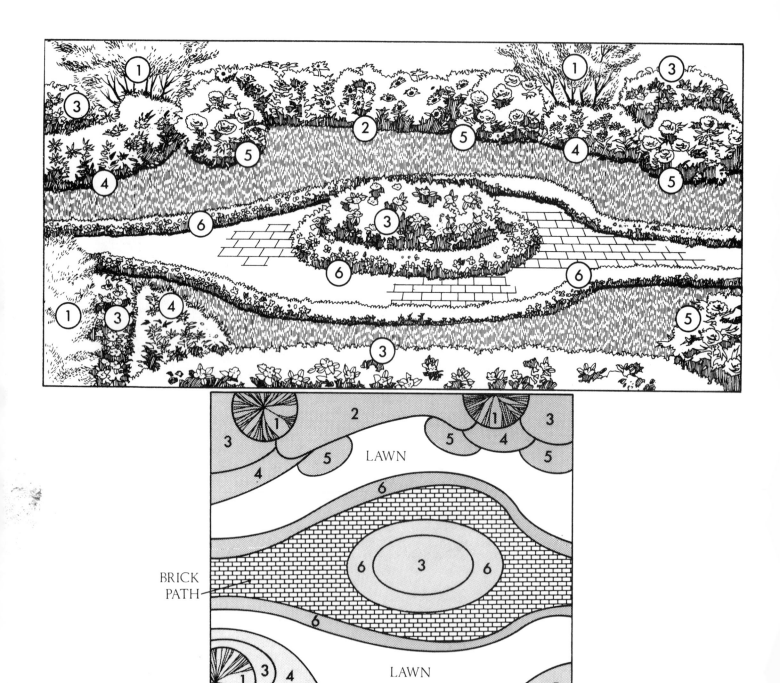

LAWN

BRICK PATH

LAWN

1. *Tamarix pentandra rubra* **'Summer Glow'**
   Salt Cedar
   Shrub/Evergreen
   Hardy to −20F
   To 8 feet; ferny foliage; masses of pink flowers. Good along coast, withstands salt spray. Prune each spring.

2. **Echinacea 'The King'**
   Coneflower
   Perennial
   Summer
   To 48 inches; weedy type, toothed leaves; large lavender flowers. Likes sun and sandy soil; tolerates wind.

3. **Rosa**
   'Frau Dagmar Hartop'
   Shrub/Deciduous
   Hardy to −20F
   To 36 inches; bushy green leaves; masses of pink flowers. Good shape.

4. **Chrysanthemum**
   'Clara Curtis'
   Perennial
   Summer
   To 24 inches; masses of single pink flowers bloom from midsummer to frost. Low growing, bushy.

5. **Paeonia 'Mrs. Franklin D. Roosevelt'**
   Peony
   Shrub/Deciduous
   Hardy to −10F
   To 40 inches; bushy green foliage; large pink blossoms. Keeps shape and color.

6. *Vinca rosea*
   Madagascar Periwinkle
   Annual
   Summer/Fall
   To 10 inches; pointed leaves; pale pink flowers. Good ground cover; easy to grow.

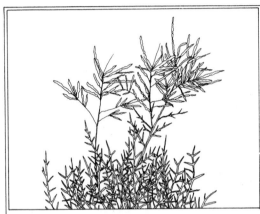
1. Tamarix pentandra rubra 'Summer Glow'

2. Echinacea 'The King'

3. Rosa 'Frau Dagmar Hartop'

4. Chrysanthemum 'Clara Curtis'

5. Paeonia 'Mrs. Franklin D. Roosevelt'

6. Vinca rosea

92 / Wall Garden

Rather formal in appearance, this charming wall garden relies on varying levels for a dramatic effect. Cedars provide privacy and a background for the flowers. Brick or concrete can be substituted for the flag-stone floor.

1. **Jasminum mesyni**
   Primrose Jasmine
   Vine/Perennial
   Hardy to —20F
   Summer
   To 10 feet; large yellow flowers in spring and summer. Tolerates some shade.

2. **Cupressocyparis leylandii**
   Leland Cypress
   Tree/Evergreen
   Hardy to 10F
   To 50 feet; small scalelike leaves; pyramidal. A cross between *Chamaecyparis* and *Cupressus*.

3. **Rhododendron**
   'David Gable'
   Shrub/Evergreen
   Hardy to —10F
   To 48 inches; fine, pink-flowering rhododendron. Acid-loving. Must have good drainage; likes morning sun.

4. **Hebe traversii**
   Bigleaf Hebe
   Shrub/Evergreen
   Hardy to 30F
   To 72 inches; spreading branches, dark green glossy leaves; tiny blue flowers. Does best in dry, almost sandy soil.

5. **Leptospermum scoparium**
   'Keatley'
   Tea Tree
   Tree/Evergreen
   Hardy to 30F
   To 15 feet; small leaves; showy, pink flowers. Good in sandy soil.

6. **Santolina chamaecyparissus**
   Lavender Cotton
   Ground Cover/Evergreen
   Hardy to —5F
   To 24 inches; silvery-gray woolly leaves; yellow flowers.

7. **Calluna vulgaris**
   Heather
   Shrub/Evergreen
   Hardy to —10F
   To 18 inches; lovely foliage; fine pink flowers in summer. Needs sun for flowers; makes excellent ground cover in shade.

8. **Plumbago capensis**
   Leadwort
   Shrub/Deciduous
   Hardy to 30F
   To 24 inches; dense leafy plant; fine crop of blue flowers.

9. **Pinus resinosa**
   Red Pine
   Tree/Evergreen
   Hardy to —35F
   To 75 feet; long flexible needles; reddish bark. Dependable and durable.

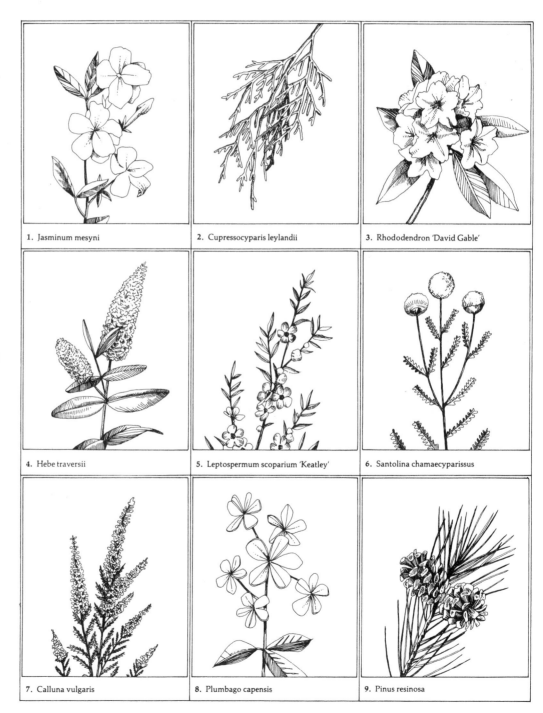

1. Jasminum mesyni

2. Cupressocyparis leylandii

3. Rhododendron 'David Gable'

4. Hebe traversii

5. Leptospermum scoparium 'Keatley'

6. Santolina chamaecyparissus

7. Calluna vulgaris

8. Plumbago capensis

9. Pinus resinosa

93 / Water Garden

This elegant plan is enhanced
by raised platforms surrounded
by varieties of water lilies. It
is a dramatic visual setting for
dining.

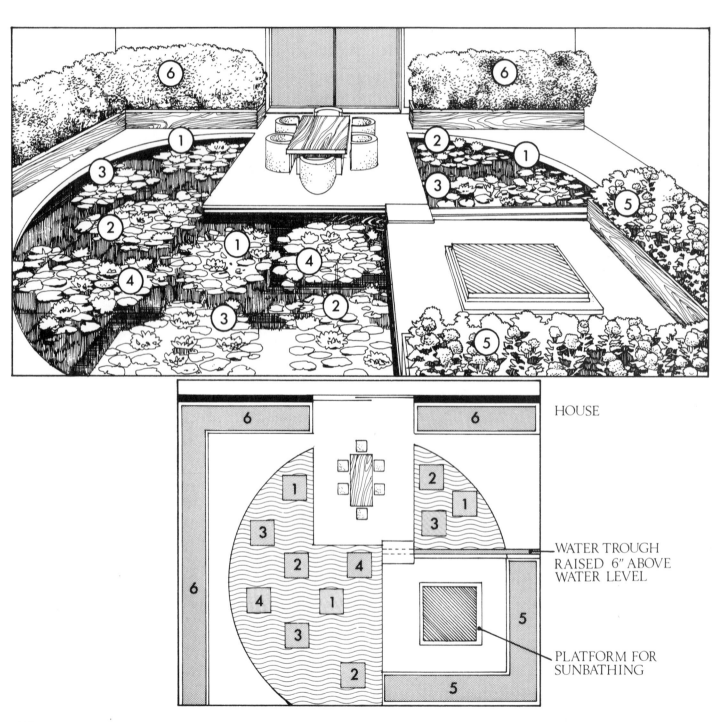

HOUSE

WATER TROUGH
RAISED 6" ABOVE
WATER LEVEL

PLATFORM FOR
SUNBATHING

1. **Nymphaea 'Gloriosa'**
   Water Lily
   Perennial
   Summer
   Flowers deep carmine-rose, to 5 inches wide. Hardy type.

2. **Nymphaea 'August Koch'**
   Water Lily
   Perennial
   Summer
   Huge, profuse, wisteria-violet blooms, to 9 inches wide. Tender tropical type.

3. **Nymphaea 'Pink Opal'**
   Water Lily
   Perennial
   Summer
   Attractive deep pink flowers, to 5 inches wide. Stand above water line. Hardy.

4. **Nymphaea 'Gladstone'**
   Water Lily
   Perennial
   Summer
   Largest of the whites; to 8 inches wide. Needs plenty of room. Hardy type.

5. *Sedum spectabile*
   Showy Sedum
   Perennial
   Summer/Fall
   To 15 inches; leaves gray-green; flowers red in clusters. Can tolerate shade if necessary. Keep evenly moist.

6. *Gypsophila paniculata*
   Baby's-breath
   Perennial
   Spring/Summer
   To 18 inches; fine lacy leaves; branching habit; tiny white or rose flowers.

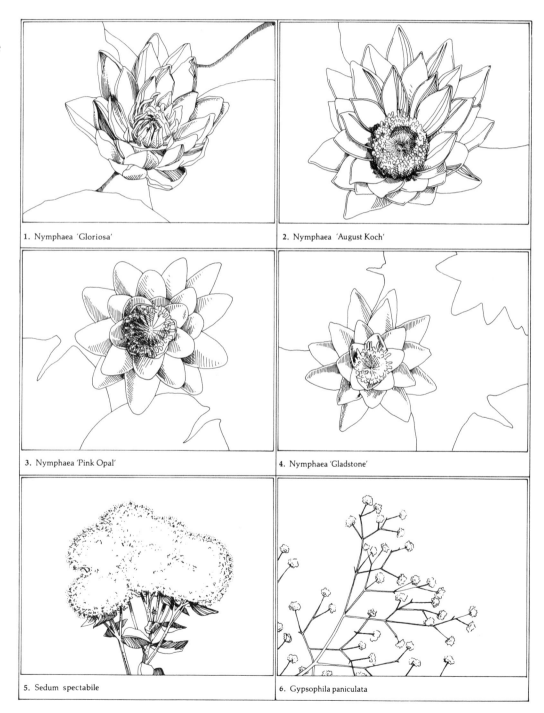

1. Nymphaea 'Gloriosa'

2. Nymphaea 'August Koch'

3. Nymphaea 'Pink Opal'

4. Nymphaea 'Gladstone'

5. Sedum spectabile

6. Gypsophila paniculata

94 / West Coast Shade Garden

This graceful plan employs circular ramps with bordering ribbons of color and four mass plantings of pink rhododendrons. A white weeping cherry dominates the pool area. Dramatic blue gentian is used only once, midway between the pink rhododendrons and the pool, to create a dramatic thrust. The garden is planned on three levels to create an exciting landscape, and it is all in shade!

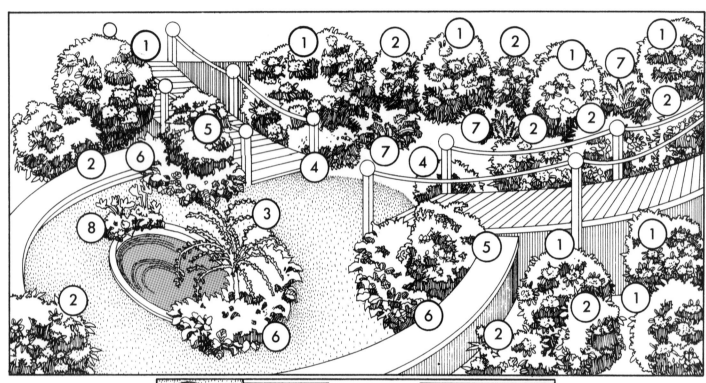

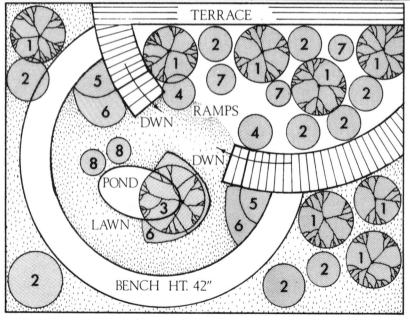

1. **Rhododendron 'Nova Zembla'**
   Shrub/Evergreen
   Hardy to −10F
   TO 15 feet; leaves oblong; flowers showy. A great number of forms, sizes, and colors are available. Use pinks and reds. Prefers acid soil, loose loam.

2. **Azalea (Exbury hybrids)**
   Shrub/Deciduous
   Hardy to −10F
   To 15 feet; leaves oblong; flowers in various colors, in round clusters. Use cool, moist, acid soil.

3. *Prunus subhirtella*
   White Weeping Cherry
   Tree/Deciduous
   Hardy to −10F
   Spring
   To 60 inches; branches curving downward; flowers abundant and white. Good small tree that grows easily in most gardens.

4. *Gentiana makinoi*
   Gentian
   Perennial
   Summer
   To 18 inches; leaves lance-shaped; tubular flowers pale blue. Requires good drainage, moist soil, coolness.

5. **Fuschia (upright type)**
   Perennial
   Summer
   To 60 inches; leaves oblong; flowers showy, pendent, in a variety of colors. Use acidy loose loam; responds to feeding. Water freely.

6. **Hosta 'Thomas Hogg'**
   Plantain Lily
   Perennial
   Fall
   To 20 inches; leaves broad, long, and green with silver edging; lavender flowers on spikes. Keep damp.

7. *Osmunda claytoniana*
   Interrupted Fern
   Fronds to 48 inches; no flowers.

8. *Cyclamen neopolitanum*
   Neopolitan Cyclamen
   Bulb/Hardy
   Fall
   To 8 inches; leaves dark green, broad, lobed; flowers reddish-pink. Once established, produces good color.

1. Rhododendron 'Nova Zembla'

2. Azalea (Exbury hybrid)

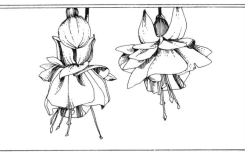
3. Prunus subhirtella

4. Gentiana makinoi

5. Fuschia (upright type)

6. Hosta 'Thomas Hogg'

7. Osmunda claytoniana

8. Cyclamen neopolitanum

95 / Wildflower Garden (Midwestern)

Native May apples (Podophyllum) under an existing tree are center stage for this plan and leafy ferns furnish a green background. Blazing stars (liatris) are the vertical thrust in the upper right rear area, and in the foreground shooting stars (dodocatheon) furnish color. This is a small but adequate wildflower garden with little or no maintenance. The stone path—a sweeping arc—defines the two areas.

M. G. VALDEZ

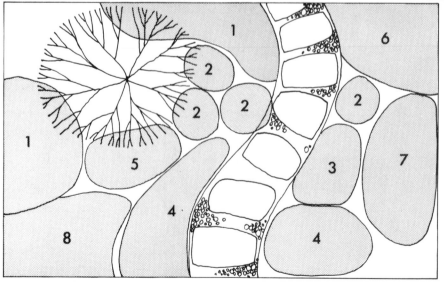

1. *Achillea millefolium*
   Yarrow
   Perennial
   Fall
To 10 inches; leaves feathery; flowers small. Prospers in the poorest of soils.

2. *Polypodium virginianum*
   Polypody
   Fern
To 20 inches; fronds leathery and bright green. Likes a moist shady place.

3. *Dicentra cucullaria*
   Dutchman's-breeches
   Perennial
   Spring
To 10 inches; leaves compound; flowers white in drooping clusters. Likes humusy rich soil and shade.

4. *Dodecatheon meadia*
   Shooting-star
   Perennial
   Spring
To 16 inches; leaves 6 inches long in rosette habit; flowers deep rose. Tempermental; likes rich soil and shade.

5. *Podophyllum peltatum*
   May Apple
   Perennial
   Spring
To 20 inches; leaves large and rounded; flowers small and waxy white. Grows in rich moist soil. Spreads rapidly.

6. *Liatris pycnostachya*
   Gay-feather
   Perennial
   Summer
To 36 inches; leaves narrow; flowers purple in dense clusters. Likes damp shady conditions.

7. *Rudbeckia hirta*
   Black-eyed Susan
   Annual
   Summer
To 36 inches; leaves and stems rough and hairy; flowers yellow with brown center. Grows easily in most soils.

8. *Geranium maculatum*
   Wood Geranium
   Perennial
   Summer
To 24 inches; leaves deeply lobed; flowers violet. Needs rich soil and plenty of moisture and sun.

1. Achillea millefolium

2. Polypodium virginianum

3. Dicentra cucullaria

4. Dodocatheon meadia

5. Podophyllum peltatum

6. Liatris pycnostachya

7. Rudbeckia hirta

8. Geranium maculatum

96 / Wildflower Garden (Northeastern)

Existing birch trees at the right and a branching tree at the left contain this wildflower garden. A bark path meanders through the plants, and native trilliums and iris are used for color accent. The plants, in two separate groups, are chosen to make gardening easy.

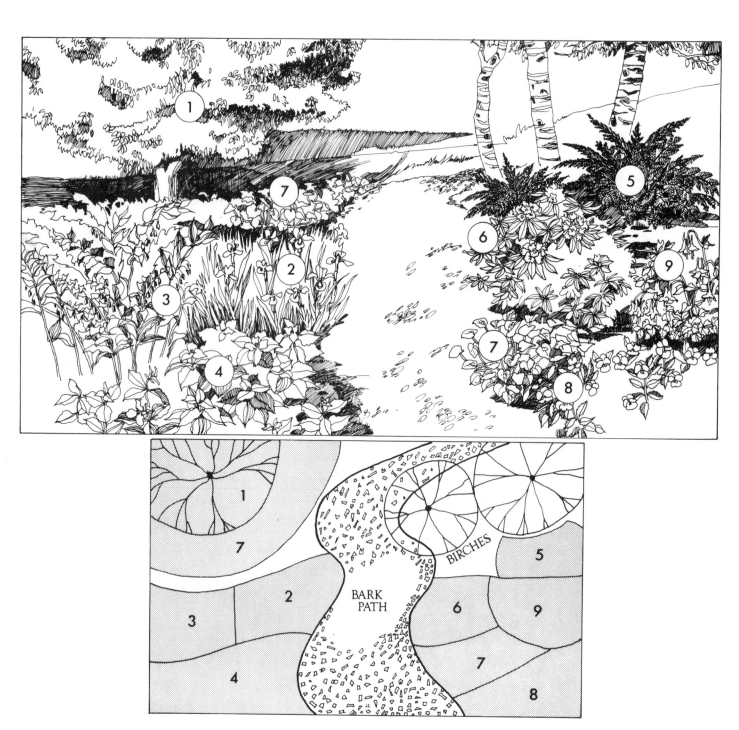

1. **Cornus florida**
Dogwood
Tree/Deciduous
Hardy to −10F
To 40 feet; leaves oblong to 6 inches and turn in autumn; flowers have large white bracts; fruit scarlet. One of the best ornamental trees; many varieties.

2. **Iris verna**
Wild Iris
Bulb/Hardy
Spring/Summer
To 8 inches; leaves long and narrow; flowers violet blue to white. Prefers loose loam with good drainage.

3. **Polygonatum biflorum**
Solomon's Seal
Perennial
Summer
To 36 inches; leaves 4 inches long and 2 inches wide; flowers in groups of one to four, drooping and greenish. Likes a moist soil.

4. **Trillium grandiflorum**
Perennial
Spring
To 18 inches; leaves flat and broad; flowers white to pink. Difficult to transplant; likes woodsy acid soil.

5. **Osmunda cinnamomea**
Cinnamon Fern
To 36 inches; leaves to 60 inches long, turn cinnamon-brown as spores mature. A good fern for moist and shady locations.

6. **Rhododendron nudiflorum**
Pinxterbloom
Shrub/Deciduous
Hardy to −10F
To 72 inches; leaves to 3 inches; flowers pink to white and funnel-shaped. Needs cool, moist, acid soil. Prune occasionally; cut out old canes.

7. **Asarum canadense**
Wild Ginger
Ground Cover/Evergreen
Hardy to −10F
To 12 inches; leaves heart-shaped, to 7 inches wide; flowers brownish purple. An excellent ground cover that likes shade and moisture.

8. **Viola incognita**
Violet
Perennial
Spring/Summer
To 3 inches; roundish leaves with pointed tip; flowers small and white.

9. **Aquilegia canadensis**
American Columbine
Perennial
Spring/Summer
To 20 inches; leaves compound; flowers spurred in red or yellow. A lovely native wildflower; needs a rather dry sandy soil.

1. Cornus florida

2. Iris verna

3. Polygonatum biflorum

4. Trillium grandiflorum

5. Osmunda cinnamomea

6. Rhododendron nudiflorum

7. Asarum canadense

8. Viola incognita

9. Aquilegia canadensis

97 / Wildflower Garden (Southeastern)

There are only six plants in this plan, but they are repeated several times to create a lush garden. Built on a terrace design there is good balance, with an old tree serving as the background. Stepping stones lead to the top and ferns dot the landscape.

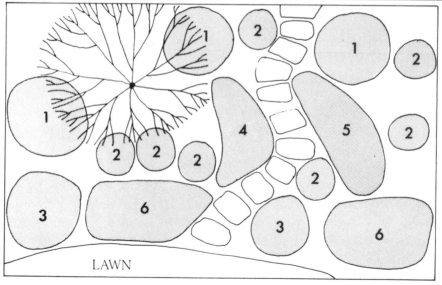

LAWN

1. *Rhododendron carolinianum*
Carolina Rhododendron
Shrub/Evergreen
Hardy to −10F
To 72 inches; leaves 3 inches and brownish on underside; flowers pale rose-purple. Likes acid soil. An amenable plant.

2. *Polystichum acrostichoides*
Christmas Fern
Fern
To 30 inches; fronds dark green and evergreen. Likes good moisture.

3. *Rhododendron vaseyi*
Pinkshell Azalea
Shrub/Deciduous
Hardy to −10F
To 72 inches; leaves small and bright green; flowers light rose in early May. Good autumn leaf color. Likes wet locations.

4. *Aquilegia canadensis*
American Columbine
Perennial
Spring/Summer
To 20 inches; leaves lobed, nodding flowers of yellow sepals and red spurs on stalks. Likes a rather dry, sandy soil.

5. *Shortia uniflora*
Nippon Bells
Perennial
Spring
To 8 inches; leaves heart-shaped; flowers white. Likes shade and a humusy soil.

6. *Silene caroliniana*
Wild Pinks
Perennial
Summer
To 10 inches; leaves bluish-green; flowers white to deep pink in clusters. Likes somewhat dry locations.

1. Rhododendron carolinianum

2. Polystichum acrostichoides

3. Rhododendron vaseyi

4. Aquilegia canadensis

5. Shortia uniflora

6. Silene caroliniana

98 / Wildflower Garden (sunken)

Railroad ties create natural divisions between hardy native plantings in abundant lush color. Two existing trees are the anchor of this garden, and banks of phlox and silene act as colorful accents. There is a bark path for easy maintenance.

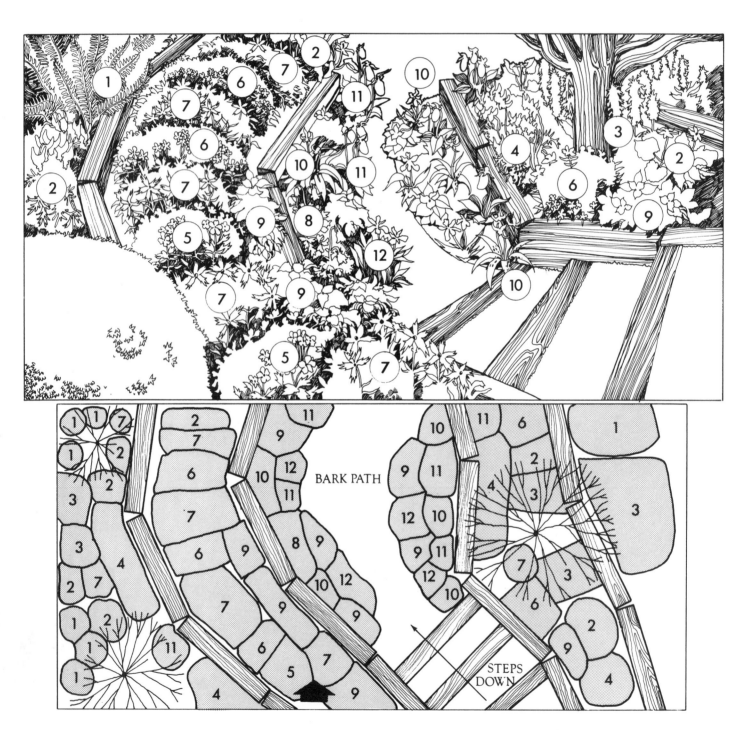

1. *Matteuccia pensylvanica*
   Ostrich Fern
   To 50 inches; fronds 72 inches long. Easily grown in most soils; do not overwater.

2. *Sanguinaria canadensis*
   Bloodroot
   Perennial
   Spring
   To 8 inches; leaves basal, palmate, to 12 inches wide; white flowers on 8-inch stalks. Needs acid, moist soil.

3. *Lobelia cardinalis*
   Cardinal Flower
   Perennial
   Summer/Fall
   To 24 inches; leaves oblong, toothed; flowers bright red, 1½ inches across. Likes moisture. Mulch plants in winter.

4. *Dicentra cucullaria*
   Dutchman's-breeches
   Perennial
   Summer
   To 10 inches; leaves basal and compound; flowers spurred and white. Needs lime in soil for bloom.

5. *Geranium maculatum*
   Wood Geranium
   Perennial
   Summer
   To 24 inches; leaves deeply lobed; flowers rose-purple, 1 inch across. Likes a rich soil and good sunlight.

6. *Phlox divaricata*
   Wild Phlox
   Perennial
   Summer
   To 18 inches; leaves oblong, to 2 inches; flowers violet-blue to mauve, 1½ inches wide. Needs sun and well-drained soil.

7. *Silene virginica*
   Fire-Pink-Catchfly
   Perennial
   Spring/Summer
   To 18 inches; lance-shaped leaves to 5 inches long; nodding red flowers with notched petals. Likes dry sunny conditions; dislikes transplanting.

8. *Aquilegia canadensis*
   Columbine
   Perennial
   Spring/Summer
   To 20 inches; leaves compound; flowers red or yellow with red spurs. Needs a rather dry sandy soil.

9. *Trillium grandiflorum*
   Perennial
   Spring
   To 18 inches; leaves flat and broad; flowers white to pink. Difficult to transplant; likes woodsy, acid soil.

10. *Erythronium americanum*
    Fawn Lily
    Perennial
    Spring
    To 12 inches; leaves mottled; flowers creamy white, 1¼ inches long. Plant in clumps in rich, woodsy soil. Needs good drainage.

11. *Cypripedium acaule*
    Lady's Slipper Orchid
    Perennial
    Spring
    To 18 inches; leaves long, narrow and basal; flowers to 5 inches wide, greenish-brown and red. Difficult to transplant; likes acid soil.

12. *Iris cristata*
    Crested Iris
    Bulb/Hardy
    Spring/Summer
    To 6 inches; leaves long and narrow; flowers large and blue. Do not cover bulb with soil or it will rot.

1. Matteuccia pensylvanica

2. Sanguinaria canadensis

3. Lobelia cardinalis

4. Dicentra cucullaria

5. Geranium maculatum

6. Phlox divaricata

7. Silene virginica

8. Aquilegia canadensis

9. Trillium grandiflorum

10. Erythronium americanum

11. Cypripedium acaule

12. Iris cristata

99 / Wildflower Garden (West Coast)

A gravel path crosses this lovely natural garden, which uses drifts of a few low easy-maintenance plants. It can be used in small or large sites.

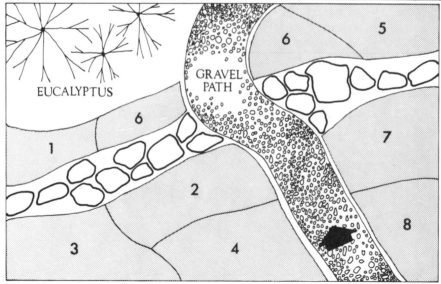

EUCALYPTUS

GRAVEL PATH

228

1. *Mahonia aquifolium*
Grape Holly
Shrub/Evergreen
Hardy to —10F
To 36 inches; five to nine 3-inch leaflets per leaf, glossy dark green on top, lighter below; flowers yellow, and berries blue. Prune or thin plants as necessary to keep in bounds.

2. *Iris douglasiana*
Bulb/Hardy
Spring
To 20 inches; leaves long and narrow; flowers purple to white. Early bloomer, airy and elegant.

3. *Echeveria pulvinata*
Chenille Plant
Perennial
Spring/Summer
To 30 inches; broad leaves to 3½ inches long; flowers red. Good in masses, easy to grow.

4. *Sisyrinchium angustifolium*
Blue-eyed Grass
To 10 inches; leaves grasslike; flowers deep blue. Needs wet soil and full sun.

5. *Cytisus scoparius*
Scotch Broom
Perennial
Spring/Summer
To 10 feet; leaves divided into small opposite leaflets; flowers yellow and pealike. Needs acid soil. Prune after flowers fade.

6. *Iris prismatica*
Bulb/Hardy
Spring
To 36 inches; leaves narrow; flowers in two's or solitary, blue with yellow veins. Grows in wet location.

7. *Lupinus perennis*
Lupine
Perennial
Spring
To 24 inches, leaves palmately lobed; flowers pealike, blue, pink, or white. Transplant only when small. Grows in poor sandy soil if necessary.

8. *Eschscholzia californica*
California Poppy
Perennial
Spring
To 12 inches; leaves very dissected; flowers pale yellow to orange. Thin to 6 inches apart. Likes sandy soil and sun.

1. Mahonia aquifolium

2. Iris douglasiana

3. Echeveria pulvinata

4. Sisyrinchium angustifolium

5. Cytisus scoparius

6. Iris prismatica

7. Lupinus perennis

8. Eschscholzia californica

229

100 / Woodland Garden

This low shady area is filled with native plants of all kinds. The plants are placed informally and pathways are established to simulate a natural wooded site. This garden requires a rather large area but can be used where native plants are already found. It is at its best in spring.

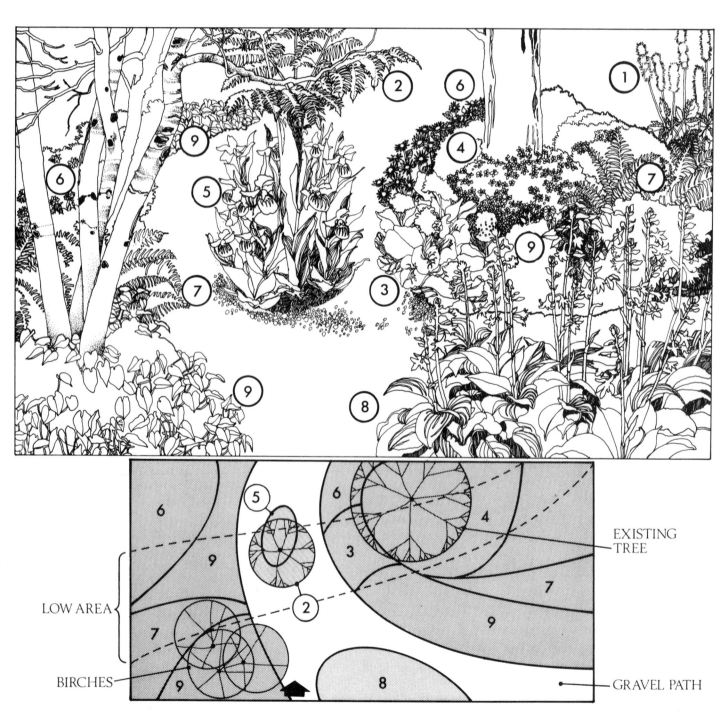

EXISTING TREE

LOW AREA

BIRCHES

GRAVEL PATH

1. **Cimicifuga racemosa**
   Black Snakeroot
   Perennial
   Summer
   To 48 inches; three green, toothed leaflets per leaf; pure white flowers on stalks. A good wildflower that needs somewhat acid soil.

2. **Dicksonia antarctica**
   Tasmanian Tree Fern
   To 40 feet; leaves on 6-foot fronds. Graceful arching habit. Can tolerate abuse.

3. **Bergenia cordifollia**
   Heart-Leaf Bergenia
   Perennial
   Spring
   To 12 inches; leaves thick roundish, and large; pink flowers in clusters. Loves water. Forms solid mass of green leaves. Often listed in catalogs as Saxifraga.

4. **Phlox divaricata**
   Wild Phlox
   Perennial
   Spring
   To 18 inches; leaves oblong; flowers large, fragrant, and violet-blue. Good-growing corner plant. Needs well-drained soil and lots of sun.

5. **Cypripedium spectabile**
   Lady's Slipper Orchid
   Perennial
   Spring
   To 24 inches; leaves parallel ribbed; flowers rose-purple to white. Difficult to transplant but beautiful.

6. **Doronicum caucasicum**
   Leopard's-bane
   Perennial
   Spring
   To 15 inches; leaves heart-shaped and toothed; flowers yellow and 3 inches wide. Foliage fades in summer, but plant grows easily.

7. **Osmunda claytoniana**
   Interrupted Fern
   To 36 inches; coarse fronds to 48 inches long. Grows in almost any soil, but needs plenty of moisture.

8. **Hosta plantaginea**
   Fragrant Plaintain Lily
   Perennial
   Summer/Fall
   To 30 inches; leaves broad, basal, to 10 inches long; flowers white, tubular, to 5 inches long and fragrant. Likes rich soil.

9. **Epimedium pinnatum**
   sulphureum
   Persian Epimedium
   Ground Cover/Evergreen
   Hardy to —10F
   To 9 inches; leaves light green and heart-shaped; flowers yellow in showy clusters. A superior plant that stays green all year.

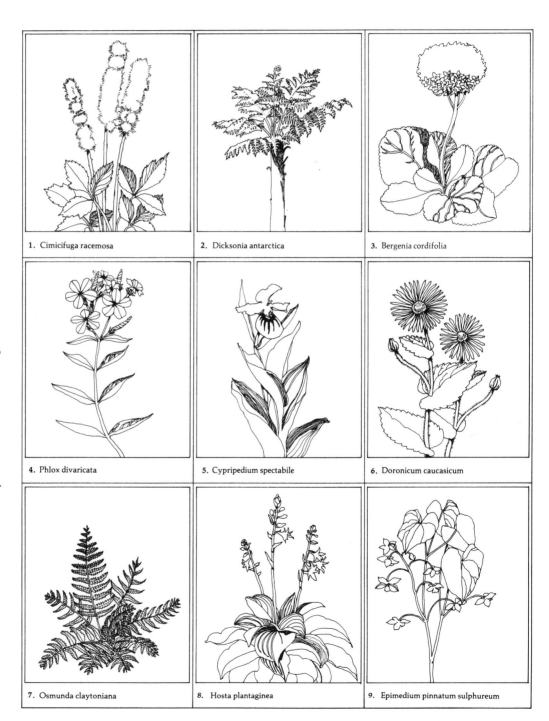

1. Cimicifuga racemosa
2. Dicksonia antarctica
3. Bergenia cordifolia
4. Phlox divaricata
5. Cypripedium spectabile
6. Doronicum caucasicum
7. Osmunda claytoniana
8. Hosta plantaginea
9. Epimedium pinnatum sulphureum

Seven / Protecting the Garden

OUR GARDENS require time, patience, and money to create, and obviously, labor so it is only common sense to protect the beauty we have made. We have talked a little already about insect prevention and watering of plants. Here we offer more ways to keep plants healthy and free of pests and disease.

There are several ways of avoiding harmful chemicals in the garden: helpful insects, birds, companion plantings, botanical repellents and old-fashioned methods of combating pests that bother plants.

INSECT PREDATORS

Natural control uses the insects that feed on other insects. When these insects are laboratory grown (and many are now available), the process is known as biological control.

The popular ladybug is really a beetle, entirely predacious and feeds on aphids, mealybugs, whiteflies, scale insects, larvae and eggs of other insects. Both adults and larvae of the lady beetle are predators and the larvae has an even heartier appetite than the adult beetle we are familiar with. The larvae are flat and dark with orange, blue, and black patches; the deeply segmented body is covered with spines and is tapered towards the end and propelled by six legs. The larvae look nothing like their parents. Ladybugs and their eggs come in convenient cases from mail-order suppliers, four by five inches, and can—if weather prevents you from placing them immediately outdoors—be left in their cases for several days. Place a little water in the box and place it in the refrigerator for use later. To "plant" ladybugs in the garden, dampen the ground and set them in place by the handful. Be sure to release them where there is food (aphids). Will the ladybugs stay in your garden? Enough will offer help against insect pests.

Aphis lions, which are widely distributed through the country, include the ant lions or doodlebugs, dobson flies, and the beautiful lacewings. Lacewings belong to the nerved-winged order of insects and have veined gauze-like wings. They are usually nocturnal and are good controllers; they feed on scale insects, thrips, aphids, mealybugs, and caterpillars. The larvae of the lacewings are called aphis lions and are voracious feeders. Damsel bugs and the well known praying mantids are other beneficial garden insects to help you keep your garden free of pests and chemicals.

Despite the aversion to spiders, many of them are highly beneficial to the garden. A spider's diet consists mainly of insects, and spiders get their food by hunting or spinning webs to snare insects. They take live specimens and even though this includes some helpful insects, spiders are worth their weight in gold because they generally stay within the garden.

There are also insect parasites to help you protect your garden. Generally, the larvae of the parasite enters the body of the host and there sustains itself on tissues until it is nearly grown. When the host expires, the parasite may continue its existence in the dead body or may appear and pupate elsewhere. The parasitic wasps that belong to the order *hymenoptera* are valuable parasites, as are the *braconids*. The host of braconids include some very troublesome pests: satin moths, coddling moths, tent caterpillars, cutworms, aphids, and beetles.

The ichneumon fly, another wasp, is smaller than the braconid and can inhabit many species of hosts. These flies resemble common houseflies. Chalcids are another group of parasites—tiny insects about 1/32-inch in length and they may be black with a metallic sheen.

Trichogrammas now available from insectaries are another species of wasp that is a potent destroyer of many insect eggs. It eventually kills its host long before the host can damage a plant. The trichogramma itself will not harm or feed on vegetation. When you receive the tiny wasps from suppliers they will be almost ready to hatch. Place the opened containers in the area you want controlled. One package will contain from two thousand to four thousand microscopic parasites, enough for five acres. Do not blanket your area with these wasps, because they can eliminate butterflies. Use them judiciously.

The cost of all these beneficial workers is minimal, far less than chemical poisons and sprays. More importantly, these garden helpers do not harm the environment.

BOTANICAL REPELLENTS

The botanical repellents include pyrethrum, rotenone, quassia, and ryania and are being sold in conventional spray form. However, check labels to be sure the botanicals are not being used in combination with poisons.

Pyrethrum is derived from a chrysanthemum species, called *C. cinerariiaefolium* or *C. roseum*. It is a handsome daisylike flower, pink or white. The pulverized flowers are toxic and highly effective in the garden against aphids, whitefly and leaf hoppers. It is sold in powdered form. Some people may be allergic to this powder so be on guard and do not use it if this is the case.

Rotenone comes from derris root—a woody climber with purple and white flowers. The roots are ground into an effective powder that wards off aphids, spider mites, and even the common housefly.

Ryania, a Latin American shrub, is a dust or spray solution made from roots and woody stems and wards off many pests.

Quassia, a tree native to South America, contains intensely bitter roots and bark that repel several kinds of insects when crushed, mixed with water, and sprayed on plants.

Hellebore, a common garden flower in Roman times, is also used as an insect repellant. The pulverized roots and rhizomes contain *helleborin*, which has a burning, acrid taste.

Most of these botanical repellents are available from suppliers and should be used when necessary in the garden. Never use poisonous sprays. Check the Appendix for suppliers of both insects and botanical aids.

OLD-FASHIONED REMEDIES

Handpicking insects is a primitive way of control of insects, but is effective in a small garden. And if you are fighting snails use a snail bait with a covered snail-bait station—a small box or some device with an entrance but where a dog or cat cannot get at the bait. A recent remedy noted by the United States Department of Agriculture suggests beer in bottle caps to combat snails. Sometimes this works but often it does not.

Look for snail bait without metaldehyde; the alternatives are not harmful to animals or humans and are still effective against snails and slugs. Be sure to read the ingredients on the canister or package.

You can eliminate a great many harmful insects with a simple solution of one-half laundry soap and one-half water. Spray plants and then hose them with clear water. Do not use detergents. Soap-and-water sprays eliminate red spider, mealybugs, and some scale. And don't forget common rubbing alcohol as a deterrent against insect pests. Simply apply the alcohol on cotton swabs direct to the insect. Works like a charm.

SAFETY EQUIPMENT

There is a great deal of safety equipment on the market now for gardening use to protect you against fumes, dusts, and so forth. Actually, if you are not using chemicals you do not need fancy equipment, although a paper mask is effective when dusting or spraying some botanicals.

A good pair of garden gloves is essential to protect your hands in the garden and to make working with soil and plants easier. Select heavy duty canvas gloves rather than the one-size-fits all cloth ones.

DRIP-SYSTEM WATERING

We have discussed conventional watering, but if possible drip-system watering is the best way to really get water to the plant's roots. These systems have become quite popular in the last decade and rightly so. Water is a vital resource and conservation of this precious commodity is necessary by all Americans, and especially by gardeners. Hoses and sprinklers waste water because they do not put water where you want it—at the plant roots; the water is sprayed in a haphazard fashion with over 60 percent being wasted.

Drip watering is a system that slowly and steadily applies moisture directly to plant roots. Drip-watering systems consist of various manufactured parts—emitters, tubing, holding stakes, sprayers and soakers and now come in kits at hardware stores or nurseries. This system can be connected to any water outlet easily. The emitter releases water drop by drop—and you position the emitter where you want it—near the plant. There is no excessive spraying and no need to stand and hold a hose and water a plant. It takes almost 20 minutes of direct hose watering to penetrate the soil 16 inches to the plants roots where water is needed. So you also save a great deal of your time.

You can use drip systems for shrubs, trees, flower beds, and so on. Plants will grow faster than they do with standard watering methods and certainly grow better, with more foliage and more flowers.

Agricultural experts believe that 33 percent of the soil in the root zone of crops must be wetted for peak growth and that the crop performance improves as the amount of root soil wetted increases to 60 percent or more. Frequent drip irrigation provides an evenly moist soil that does not fluctuate by being too wet nor too dry. Weed growth is inhibited by drip watering too, because only the roots rather than large surfaces are being watered. And drip watering dispenses water slowly at a rate that the soil can absorb. Water flows by capillary action through the soil and the soil is not drowned as it is with regular hosing or sprinkler watering.

The drip system can be automated by valves, moisture-sensing devices, and other devices such as timers. You can even install a fertilizer injector into the system to provide proper amounts of nutrients for your plants.

Good as they are, drip systems should not be considered miracle-workers; some things can go wrong with the system, the main problem being clogged emitters. Because the emitters are small, they can become clogged with minute particles of organic matter. This clogging can reduce the rate of emission of the water. The fine-mesh filters and emitters can be replaced easily, or self-flushing emitters are the answer. (Sprinklers too regularly clog with organic matter).

The basic system involves a large pipe of about ½- to ¾-inch in diameter carrying water to the site, and a series of smaller main lines connecting to the larger pipe; these are usually ¼-inch to ⅜-inch in diameter. The lateral lines are placed parallel to the plants on or just below the surface of the ground. The water is supplied through the lateral lines through the emitters (there are many different kinds—spray, drip, mist, and so on).

Drip-system watering is the really excellent way to water your plants and a fine way of conserving water.

APPENDICES

1 / PLANT SOCIETIES

YOU CAN write to these plant societies for information on membership, which usually includes a bulletin or magazine (monthly or semi-monthly). Some societies have library books available, distribute seed, and hold conventions.

Prices listed are membership fees as of January, 1993.

American Boxwood Society ($15)
Blandy Experimental Farm
P.O. Box 85
Boyce, VA 22620

American Camellia Society ($17.50)
Dr. C. David Schiebert
P.O. Box 1217
Fort Valley, GA 31030-1217

American Conifer Society ($20)
Maxine Schwarz
P.O. Box 242
Severna Park, MD 21146

American Dahlia Society ($8)
Michael Martinolich
159 Pine St.
New Hyde Park, NY 11040

American Fuchsia Society ($12.50)
San Francisco County Fair Bldg.
Ninth Ave. & Lincoln Way
San Francisco, CA 94122

American Hemerocallis Society ($18)
Elly Launius
1454 Rebel Dr.
Jackson, MS 39211

American Hibiscus Society ($13)
P.O. Drawer 321540
Cocoa Beach, FL 32932

American Hosta Society ($12.50)
Jack A. Freedman
3103 Heatherhill Dr.
Huntsville, AL 35802

American Iris Society ($9.50)
Carol Ramsey
6518 Beachy Ave.
Wichita, KS 67206

American Peony Society ($7.50)
Greta M. Kessenich
250 Interlachen Rd.
Hopkins, MN 55343

American Rhododendron Society ($25)
Paula L. Cash
14885 S.W. Sunrise Ln.
Tigard, OR 97224

American Rose Society ($25)
P.O. Box 30,000
Shreveport, LA 71130

Azalea Society of America ($15)
Marjorie Taylor
P.O. Box 6244
Silver Spring, MD 20901

Cactus & Succulent Society of
    America ($20)
Virginia F. Martin
2631 Fairgreen Ave.
Arcadia, CA 93130

The Delphinium Society ($6)
Shirley E. Bassett Takakkaw
Ice House Wood
Oxted, Surrey, RH8 9DW, England

Gardenia Society of America ($5)
Lyman Duncan
P.O. Box 879
Atwater, CA 95301

Herb Society of America ($35)
9019 Kirtland Chardon Rd.
Mentor, OH 44060

Hobby Greenhouse Association ($10)
Janice L. Hale
8 Glen Terr.
Bedford, MA 01730

Hydroponic Society of America ($25)
Gene Brisbon
P.O. Box 6067
Concord, CA 94524

International Camellia Society ($9)
Edith Mazzei
1486 Yosemite Cir.
Concord, CA 94521

International Clematis Society
Hildegard Widmann-Evison
Buford House, Tenbury Wells
Worcester WR15 8HQ, England

International Geranium Society ($12.50)
Mrs. Robin Schultz
5861 Walnut Dr.
Eureka, CA 95501

International Lilac Society, Inc. ($10)
Walter W. Oakes
P.O. Box 315
Rumford, ME 04276

Magnolia Society ($15)
Phelan A. Bright
907 S. Chestnut St.
Hammond, LA 70403-5102

National Chrysanthemum Society ($12)
Galen L. Goss
5012 Kingston Dr.
Annandale, VA 22003

National Fuchsia Society ($14)
Mrs. Mildred Elliott
15103 McRae
Norwalk, CA 90650

North American Lily Society ($12.50)
Dorothy B. Schaefer
P.O. Box 476
Waukee, IA 50263

Perennial Plant Association ($35)
Steven Still
3383 Schirtzinger Rd.
Columbus, OH 43026

2 / PLANT INFORMATION SOURCES

THE FOLLOWING GROUPS are also good sources of information on plant conservation and general horticultural subjects. Write them for membership information and fees.

Brooklyn Botanic Garden
1000 Washington Ave.
Brooklyn, NY 11225

The Farallones Institute
The Rural Center
15290 Coleman Valley Rd.
Occidental, CA 95465

Gardens for All
Dept. FG
180 Flynn Ave.
Burlington, VT 05401

Herb Society of America
300 Massachusetts Ave.
Boston, MA 02115

National Audubon Society
950 Third Ave.
New York, NY 10022

National Wildlife Federation
1412 16th St., N.W.
Washington, DC 20036

Sierra Club
530 Bush St.
San Francisco, CA 94108

3 / STATE AGRICULTURAL EXTENSION SERVICES

THIS SERVICE is the combined effort of the county government, the state college or university responsible for agriculture, and the U.S. Department of Agriculture. Telephone numbers and addresses for these services will be found under the county government listings in your local telephone directories. The Agricultural Extension Service is the most up-to-date and extensive source of information on horticultural subjects in the United States. Circulars or bulletins answering frequently asked questions about gardening are generally available in printed form for the asking. Addresses of these offices follow:

Auburn University
Auburn, Alabama 36830

College of Agriculture
University of Arizona
Tucson, Arizona 85721

University of Arkansas
Box 391
Little Rock, Arkansas 72203

Agricultural Extension Service
2200 University Ave.
Berkeley, California 94720

Colorado State University
Fort Collins, Colorado 80521

College of Agriculture
University of Connecticut
Storrs, Connecticut 06268

College of Agricultural Sciences
University of Delaware
Newark, Delaware 19711

University of Florida
217 Rolfs Hall
Gainesville, Florida 32601

College of Agriculture
University of Georgia
Athens, Georgia 30602

University of Hawaii
2500 Dole St.
Honolulu, Hawaii 96822

College of Agriculture
University of Idaho
Moscow, Idaho 83843

College of Agriculture
University of Illinois
Urbana, Illinois 61801

Agricultural Administration Building
Purdue University
Lafayette, Indiana 47907

Iowa State University
Ames, Iowa 50010

Kansas State University
Manhattan, Kansas 66502

College of Agriculture
University of Kentucky
Lexington, Kentucky 40506

Louisiana State University
Knapp Hall, University Station
Baton Rouge, Louisiana 70803

Department of Public Information
University of Maine
Orono, Maine 04473

University of Maryland
Agricultural Division
College Park, Maryland 20742

Stockbridge Hall
University of Massachusetts
Amherst, Massachusetts 01002

Department of Information Service
109 Agricultural Hall
East Lansing, Michigan 48823

Institute of Agriculture
University of Minnesota
St. Paul, Minnesota 55101

Mississippi State University
State College, Mississippi 39762

1-98 Agricultural Building
University of Missouri
Columbia, Missouri 65201

Office of Information
Montana State University
Bozeman, Montana 59715

Dept. of Information
College of Agriculture
University of Nebraska
Lincoln, Nebraska 68503

Agricultural Communications Service
University of Nevada
Reno, Nevada 89507

Schofield Hall
University of New Hampshire
Durham, New Hampshire 03824

College of Agriculture
Rutgers, State University
New Brunswick, New Jersey 08903

New Mexico State University
Drawer 3AI
Las Cruces, New Mexico 88001

State College of Agriculture
Cornell University
Ithaca, New York 14850

North Carolina State University
State College Station
Raleigh, North Carolina 27607

North Dakota State University
State University Station
Fargo, North Dakota 58102

Ohio State University
2120 Fyffe Road
Columbus, Ohio 43210

Oklahoma State University
Stillwater, Oklahoma 74074

Oregon State University
206 Waldo Hall
Corvallis, Oregon 97331

Pennsylvania State University
Armsby Building
University Park, Pennsylvania 16802

University of Rhode Island
16 Woodwall Hall
Kingston, Rhode Island 02881

Clemson University
Clemson, South Carolina 29631

South Dakota State University
University Station
Brookings, South Dakota 57006

University of Tennessee
Box 1071
Knoxville, Tennessee 37901

Texas A & M University
Services Building
College Station, Texas 77843

Utah State University
Logan, Utah 84321

University of Vermont
Burlington, Vermont 05401

Virginia Polytechnic Institute
Blacksburg, Virginia 24061

Washington State University
115 Wilson Hall
Pullman, Washington 99163

West Virginia University
Evansdale Campus
Appalachian Center
Morgantown, West Virginia 26506

University of Wisconsin
Madison, Wisconsin 53706

University of Wyoming
Box 3354
Laramie, Wyoming 82070

Federal Extension Service
U.S. Department of Agriculture
Washington, D.C. 20250

4 / MAIL-ORDER SUPPLIERS

WRITE to these suppliers for information on prices, shipping, and available plants and products. Catalogs are generally free, but send a self-addressed stamped envelope.

PLANTS, GENERAL

Burgess Seed & Plant Co.
905 Four Seasons Rd.
Bloomington, IL 61701

Henry Field's Heritage Gardens
1 Meadow Ridge Rd.
Shenandoah, IA 51601-0700

Gurney Seed & Nursery Co.
Yankton, SD 57079

Herbst Brothers Seedsmen, Inc.
1000 N. Main St.
Brewster, NY 10509

International Growers Exchange, Inc.
16785 Harrison
Livonia, MI 48154

Inter-State Nurseries
Hamburg, IA 51644

J. W. Jung Seed & Nursery Co.
335 S. High St.
Randolph, WI 53957

Kelly Nurseries
P.O. Box 800
Dansville, NY 14437-0800

Krider Nursery
Box 29
Middlebury, IN 56540

Louisiana Nursery
Rt. 7, Box 43
Opelousas, LA 70570

May Nursery Company
P.O. Box 1312
2115 W. Lincoln Ave.
Yakima, WA 98907

Earl May Seed & Nursery Co.
Shenandoah, IA 51603

J. E. Miller Nurseries
Canandaigua, NY 14424

Nichols Garden Nursery
1190 North Pacific Highway
Albany, OR 97321

Spring Hill Nurseries
6523 N. Galena Rd.
P.O. Box 1758
Peoria, IL 61656

Stern Nurseries
Geneva, NY 14456

Tennessee Nursery & Seed Co.
Tennessee Nursery Rd.
Cleveland, TN 37311

Wayside Gardens Co.
Hodges, SC 29695

White Flower Farm
Litchfield, CT 06759

SPECIALTY PLANT SUPPLIERS

Begonias

Antonelli Bros.
2545 Capitola Rd.
Santa Cruz, CA 95062

Fairyland Begonia and Lily Garden
1100 Griffith Rd.
McKinleyville, CA 95521

Bulbs, Corms, Tubers

P. DeJager & Sons, Inc.
188 Asbury St.
S. Hamilton, MA 01982

John Scheppers, Inc.
63 Wall St.
New York, NY 10005

Chrysanthemums

Dooley Gardens
Rt. 1
Hutchinson, MN 55350

Huff's Gardens
P.O. Box 187
Burlington, KS 66839

Sunnyslope Gardens
8638 Huntington Dr.
San Gabriel, CA 91775

Thon's Garden Mums
4811 Oak St.
Crystal Lake, IL 60012

Daylilies

American Daylily & Perennials
P.O. Box 210
Grain Valley, MO 64029

Lenington-Long Gardens
7007 Manchester Ave.
Kansas City, MO 64133

Saxton Gardens
1 First St.
Saratoga Springs, NY 12866

Seawright Gardens
134 Indian Hill
Carlisle, MA 01741

Wimberlyway Gardens
7024 N. W. 18th Ave.
Gainesville, FL 32605-3237

Fruits, Berries, Nuts

Ahrens Strawberry Nursery
R.R. 1
Huntingburg, IN 47542

Allen Co.
P.O. Box 310
Fruitland, MD 21826-0310

Ames' Orchard & Nursery
6 E. Elm St.
Fayetteville, AR 72703

Brittingham Plant Farms
P.O. Box 2538
Salisbury, MD 21801

Chestnut Hill Nursery
Rt. 3, Box 267
Alachua, FL 32615

Cumberland Valley Nurseries, Inc.
P.O. Box 471
McMinnville, TN 37110

Dean Foster Nurseries
511 S. Center St.
P.O. Box 127
Hartford, MI 49057

Hollydale Nursery
P.O. Box 26
Pelham, TN 37366

Johnson Orchard & Nursery Co.
Rt. 5, Box 29J
Ellijay, GA 30540

Nourse Farms, Inc.
Box 485 RFD
S. Deerfield, MA 01373

Raintree Nursery & Northwoods
  Nursery
391 Butts Rd.
Morton, WA 98356

Rayner's
P.O. Box 1617
Salisbury, MD 21801
  (berries)

Stark Brothers Nurseries
Box X9851G
Louisiana, MO 63353

Gesneriads

Fischers Greenhouses
Linwood, NJ 08221

Lyndon Lyon
14 Mutchier St.
Dolgeville, NY 11329

Gladiolus

Michigan Bulb Co.
1950 Waldorf N. W.
Grand Rapids, MI 49550

Noweta Gardens
St. Charles, MN 55972

Pleasant Valley Glads
P.O. Box 494
Agawam, MA 01001

Waushara Gardens
Plainfield, WI 54966

Houseplants

Alberts & Merkel Bros, Inc.
P.O. Box 537
Boynton Beach, FL 33435

Cook's Geraniums
712 N. Grand
Lyons, KS 67554

Fischer Greenhouse
Oak Ave.
Linwood, NJ 08221
  (African violets)

Glasshouse Works
Church St., Box 97
Stewart, OH 45778-0097

Greenlife Gardens
101 County Line Rd.
Griffin, GA 30223

Grigsby Cactus Gardens
2354 Bella Vista Dr.
Vista, CA 92084

Robert B. Hamm
10065 River Mist Way
Rancho Cordova, CA 95670

Kartuz Greenhouses
1408 Sunset Dr.
Vista, CA 92083

Lauray of Salisbury
Undermountain Rd.
Rt 41
Salisbury, CT 06068

Logee's Greenhouses
55 North St.
Danielson, CT 06239

Lyndon Lyon Greenhouses
14 Mutchler St.
Dolgeville, NY 13329-0249
  (African violets)

Merry Gardens
P.O. Box 595
Camden, ME 04843

Rainbow Gardens
1444 E. Taylor St.
Vista, CA 92084

Rhapis Gardens
105 Rhapis Rd.
Box 287
Gregory, TX 78359

Shady Hill Gardens
821 Walnut St.
Batavia, IL 60510
   (geraniums)

Sunset Nurseries
4007 Elrod Ave.
Tampa, FL 33616
   (bamboo)

Tinari Greenhouses
Box 190
2325 Valley Rd.
Huntingdon Valley, PA 19006
   (African violets)

Volkmann Brs.
2714 Minert St.
Dallas, TX 75219
   (African violets)

Irises

Comanche Acres Iris Gardens
R.R. 1, Box 258
Gower, MO 64454

Cooley's Gardens, Inc.
Box 126
Silverton, OR 97381

Mid-America Iris Gardens
P.O. Box 12982
Oklahoma City, OK 73157

Schreiner's Gardens
3625 Quinaby Rd. N.E.
Salem, OR 97303

Gilbert H. Wild & Sons
Sarcoxie, MS 64862

Lilies

B & D Lilies
330 P St.
Port Townsend, WA 98368

Borbeleta Gardens
15974 Canby Ave., Rt. 5
Fairbault, MN 55021

Fairyland Begonia and Lily Garden
1100 Griffith Rd.
McKinleyville, CA 95521

Oregon Bulb Farms
14071 N. E. Arndt Rd.
Aurora, OR 97002

Rex Bulb Farms
P.O. Box 774
Port Townsend, WA 98368

Orchids

Fennell Orchid Jungle
26715 S. W. 157th Ave.
Homestead, FL 33031

Arnold J. Klehm
44 W. 637 Rt. 72
Hampshire, IL 60140

Oakhill Gardens
Box 25
Binnie Rd.
Dundee, IL 6061X

Rod McLellan Co.
1450 El Camino Real
South San Francisco, CA 94080

Orchids by Hausermann, Inc.
2N-134 Addison Rd.
Villa Park, IL 60181

Perennials

Bluebird Nursery
Box 460
Clarkson, NE 68629

Bluestone Perennials
7211 Middle Ridge Rd.
Madison, OH 44057

Busse Gardens
Rt. 2, Box 238
Cokato, MN 55321
  (peonies, hostas, daylilies, perennials)

Caprice Farm Nursery
15425 S. W. Pleasant Hill Rd.
Sherwood, OR 97140
  (tree peonies, hostas, daylilies)

Carroll Gardens
P.O. Box 310
Westminster, MD 21157

Crownsville Nursery
P.O. Box 797
Crownsville, MD 21032

Fairway Enterprises
114 The Fairway
Albert Lea, MN 56007

Holbrook Farm and Nursery
Rt. 2, Box 223B
Fletcher, NC 28732

Klehm & Son Nursery
Rt. 5, Box 197 Penny Rd.
S. Barrington, IL 60010

Lamb Nurseries
E. 101 Sharp Ave.
Spokane, WA 99202

Milaegers
4838 Douglas Ave.
Racine, WI 53402

Putney Nursery, Inc.
Rt. 5
Putney, VT 05346

Rice Creek Gardens
1315 66th Ave. N.E.
Minneapolis, MN 55432

Rocknoll Nursery
9210 U.S. 50
Hillsboro, OH 45133-8546

Savory's Gardens
5300 Whiting Ave.
Edina, MN 55435
  (hostas)

Siskiyou Rare Plant Nursery
2825 Cummings Rd.
Medford, OR 97501

Spring Hill Nurseries
6523 N. Galena Rd.
P.O. Box 1758
Peoria, IL 61656

Gilbert H. Wild & Son
Sarcoxie, MO 64862
  (peonies, daylilies)

Rhododendrons, Azaleas

The Bovees Nursery
1737 S. W. Coronado
Portland, OR 97219

Cardinal Nursery
Rt. 1, Box 316
State Rd., NC 28676

Carlson's Gardens
Box 305
South Salem, NY 10590

Greer Gardens
1280 Goodpasture Island Rd.
Eugene, OR 97401

Roses

Armstrong Nurseries
Ontario, CA 91764

Fred Edmunds Roses
6235 S. W. Kahle Rd.
Wilsonville, OR 97070

Jackson & Perkins Co.
Medford, OR 97501

The Mini Farm
Rt. 1, Box 501
Bon Aqua, TN 37025

Mini-Roses
P.O. Box 4255, Station A
Dallas, TX 75208

Moore Miniature Roses
2519 Visalia Ave.
Visalia, Ca 93277

Nor'East Miniature Roses, Inc.
58 Hammond St.
Rowley, MA 01969
P.O. Box 473
Ontario, CA 91762

Pixie Treasures Miniature Rose
   Nursery
4121 Prospect Ave.
Yorba Linda, CA 92686

Roses of Yesterday and Today
802 Brown's Valley Rd.
Watsonville, CA 95076

Star Roses
West Grove, PA 19390

Water lilies

Lilypons Water Gardens
301 Flower Rd.
Lilypons, MD 21717
                  or

301 Lilypons Rd.
Brookshire, TX 77423
                  or
301 Lilypons Way
P.O. Box 1130
Thermal, CA 92274
   (use nearest address)

Paradise Gardens
16 May St.
Whitman, MA 02382

Perry's Water Gardens
191 Leatherman Gap Rd.
Franklin, NC 28734

S. Scherer & Sons
Waterside Rd.
Northport, NY 11768

Slocum Water Gardens
1101 Cypress Gardens Blvd.
Winter Haven, FL 33880-6099

Three Springs Fisheries
120 Main Rd.
Lilypons, MD 21717

William Tricker Inc.
Box 398
Saddle River, NJ 07458
                  or
Box 7845
Independence, OH 44131

Van Ness Water Gardens
2460 North Euclid Ave.
Upland, CA 91786

OTHER SPECIALTY SUPPLIERS

Fox Hill Farm
444 W. Michigan Ave.
Box 9
Parma, MI 49269
   (herbs)

John Messelaar Bulb Co., Inc.
P.O. Box 269
Ipswich, MA 01938

Mohn's, Inc.
P.O. Box 2301
Atascadero, CA 93423
   (perennial hybrid poppies)

Musser Forests, Inc.
P.O. Box 340
Indiana, PA 15701
   (evergreen & hardwood seedling trees)

Plumeria People
P.O. Box 820014
Houston, TX 77282-0014

Prairie Nursery
P.O. Box 365
Westfield, WI 53964
   (prairie flowers, grasses)

Sandy Mush Herb Nursery
Rt 2
Leicester, NC 28748

Shady Oaks Nursery
700 19th Ave. N.E.
Waseca, MN 56093
   (northern & shade plants)

Swan Island Dahlias
P.O. Box 800
Canby, OR 97013

TyTy Plantation
Box 159
TyTy, GA 31795
   (cannas, southern bulbs)

Mary Walker Bulb Co.
P.O. Box 256
Omega, GA 31775
   (southern specialties)

SEEDS, GENERAL

Banana Tree
715 Northampton St.
Easton, PA 18042
   (tropical ornamentals)

John Brudy Exotics
3411 Westfield
Brandon, FL 33511-7736
   (unusual tropicals)

W. Atlee Burpee & Co.
300 Park Ave.
Warminster, PA 18974

The Cook's Garden
Box 65
Londonderry, VT 05148
   (salad & imported vegetables)

The Country Garden
Rt. 2, Box 455A
Crivitz, WI 54114
   (cut flowers)

Henry Field Seed & Nursery Co.
407 Sycamore St.
Shenandoah, IA 51602

Gurney Seed & Nursery Co.
Yankton, SD 57079

Harris Seeds Garden Trends, Inc.
961 Lyell Ave.
Rochester, NY 14606

Hastings
P.O. Box 4274
Atlanta, GA 30302-4274

Jackson & Perkins Co.
P.O. Box 1028
Medford, OR 97501

Le Jardin du Gourmet
Box 32
West Danville, CT 05873
   (herbs, shallots)

J. W. Jung Seed & Nursery Co.
335 S. High St.
Randolph, WI 53957

Kitazawa Seed Company
356 West Taylor St.
San Jose, CA 95110

Liberty Seed Co.
P.O. Box 806
New Philadelphia, OH 44663

Earl May Seed & Nursery Co.
208 N. Elm St.
Shenandoah, IA 51603

Nichols Garden Nursery
1190 N. Pacific Hwy.
Albany, OR 97321
    (vegetables)

George W. Park Seed Co.
P.O. Box 31
Greenwood, SC 29647

Pinetree Garden Seeds
R.R. 1, Box 397
New Gloucester, ME 04260
    (small quantity vegetables)

Clyde Robin Seed Co., Inc.
P.O. Box 2855
Castro Valley, CA 94546

Select Seeds
81 Stickney Hill Rd.
Union, CT 06076
    (heritage perennials and annual
    flowers)

Shepherd's Garden Seeds
7839 W. Zayante Rd.
Felton, CA 95018
    (European vegetables)

R. H. Shumway's
P.O. Box 1
Graniteville, SC 29829
                or
P.O. Box 777
Rockford, IL 61105
    (use near address)

Stokes Seeds
Stokes Bldg
Buffalo, NY 14240

Thompson & Morgan, Inc.
Jackson, NJ 08527

Otis S. Twilley Seed Co.
P.O. Box 65
Trevose, PA 19047

Wildflower Seed Co.
P.O. Box 406
St. Helena, CA 94574
    (specialty wildflower seed mixtures)

BENEFICIAL INSECTS

The following insectaries provide natural enemies of insect pests:

American Biological Supply Co.
1330 Dillon Heights Ave.
P.O. Box 3149
Baltimore, MD 21228

Beneficial Insectary
14751 Oak Run Rd.
Oak Run, CA 96069

BioLogic
Box 177 Springtown Rd.
Willow Hill, PA 17271

Carolina Biological Supply Co.
Burlington, NC 27215

Nature's Control
Box 35
Medford, OR 97501

Rincon Vitova
Box 45
Oak View, CA 93022

GARDEN TOOLS AND EQUIPMENT

Country Home Products
Box 89
Cedar Beach Rd.
Charlotte, VT 05445

Cumberland General Store
Rt. 3
Crossville, TN 38555

Denman & Co.
2913 Saturn St.
Brea, CA 92621

John Houchins & Sons, Inc.
801 N. Main
Schulenburg, TX 78956

LaMotte Chemical Co.
P.O. Box 329
Chestertown, MD 21620

A. M. Leonard
6665 Spiker Rd.
Piqua, OH 45356

Mantis Mfg.
1458 County Line Rd.
Huntingdon Valley, PA 19006

Walter Nicke
19 Columbus Tpk.
Hudson, NY 12534

Smith & Hawken Tool Co.
68 Homer
Palo Alto, CA 94301

Troy Bilt Mfg.
102nd St. & 9th Ave.
Troy, NY 12180

Yardman
5389 W. 130th
Cleveland, OH 44111

5 / BOOKS FOR FURTHER READING

THE BOOKS in the following list are the ones that I have referred to over and over through the years. Some are old classics, some are revised editions, and some are relatively new. Most are available at libraries and at bookstores with good gardening sections. If you have trouble locating any, you may try checking with a local plant society; they often make books available or can refer you to places to find them. Because of space I cannot list all the books I would like to, especially the recent plethora of big color garden books, so if your favorite book is missing it is not deliberate. What you will find here are the books that I have found to be most helpful in my many years of gardening.

LANDSCAPING AND PLANNING BOOKS

Brookes, John. *The Book of Garden Design.* New York: Macmillan Publishing Co., 1991.

Eckbo, Garrett. *Urban Landscape Design.* New York: McGraw-Hill, 1964.

Hyams, Edward. *English Cottage Gardens.* New York: Viking Penguin, 1988.

Ireys, Alice Recknagel. *Garden Design.* Englewood Cliffs, NJ: Prentice Hall, 1991.

Ireys, Alice Recknagel. *Designs for American Gardens: A Guide with Complete Plans, Growing Information, and Hundreds of Recommended Plants.* Englewood Cliffs, NJ: Prentice Hall, 1991.

Johnson, Hugh. *The Principles of Gardening.* New York: Simon & Schuster, 1984.

Malitz, Jerome. *Personal Landscapes.* Portland, OR: Timber Press, 1989.

Nelson, William R. *Planning Design: A Manual of Theory and Practice.* Champaign, IL: Stipes Publishing Co., 1985.

Reader's Digest, ed. *Reader's Digest Practical Guide to Home Landscaping.* Pleasantville, NY: Reader's Digest Association, 1972.

Saito, Katsuo. *Japanese Gardens.* New York: Tuttle, Charles E., Company, 1971.

Smith, Ken. *Home Landscaping in the Northeast & Midwest.* New York: Price Stern Sloan, Inc., 1985.

Smith, Ken. *Southern Home Landscaping.* New York: Price Stern Sloan, Inc., 1982.

TREES AND SHRUBS

Bird, Richard. *Flowering Trees & Shrubs.* Hauppauge, NY: Barron's Educational Series, Inc., 1989.

Frederick, William H., Jr. *100 Great Garden Plants.* Portland, OR: Timber Press, 1986.

Gardiner, James M. *Magnolias.* Chester, CT: Globe Pequot, 1989.

Harris, Richard W. *Arboriculture: Care of Trees, Shrubs & Vines in the Landscape, 2nd ed.* Englewood Cliffs, NJ: Prentice Hall, 1991.

Hessayon, D. G. *The Tree & Shrub Expert.* New York: Sterling Publishing Company, Inc., 1990.

The Hillier Manual of Trees & Shrubs. North Pomfret, VT: Trafalgar Square, 1991.

Taffler, Stephen. *Climbing Plants & Wall Shrubs.* North Pomfret, VT: Trafalgar Square, 1991.

Wyman, Donald. *Trees for American Gardens.* New York: Macmillan Publishing Co., 1969.

Zucker, Isabel. *Flowering Shrubs and Small Trees.* New York: Grove/Weidenfeld, 1990.

REGIONAL BOOKS

Foley, Daniel J. *Gardening by the Sea.* Orleans, MA: Parnassus Imprints, 1982.

Hunt, William L. *Southern Garden, Southern Gardening.* Durham, NC: Duke University Press, 1982.

Schuler, Stanley, *How to Grow Almost Everything.* New York: Evans & Co., 1965.

PERENNIALS AND ANNUALS

Clausen, Ruth Rogers, and Nicholas H. Ekstrom. *Perennials for American Gardens.* New York: Random House, 1989.

Garden Way Staff. *Using Annuals & Perennials.* Longmeadow Press, 1990.

McGourty, Frederick. *The Perennial Gardener.* Boston, Houghton Mifflin, 1991.

McGourty, Frederick. *Perennials & Their Uses.* Brooklyn, NY: Brooklyn Botanic Garden, 1989.

Sunset Magazine & Book Editors. *Garden Color: Annuals & Perennials.* Menlo Park, CA: Sunset Publishing Corp., 1981.

Wilson, Helen Van Pelt. *New Perennials Preferred.* New York: Macmillan Publishing Co., 1992.

VINES, GROUND COVERS, AND LAWNS

Foley, Daniel J. *Ground Covers for Easier Gardening.* Mineola, NY: Dover Publications, 1972.

Fretwell, Barry O. *Clematis.* Deer Park, WI: Capability's Books, 1989.

Wyman, Donald. *Shrubs and Vines for American Gardens.* New York: Macmillan Publishing Co., 1970.

BULBS

Glattstein, Judy. *The Gardener's World of Bulbs.* Brooklyn, NY: Brooklyn Botanic Garden, 1991.

Horton, Al. *All About Bulbs.* San Ramon, CA: Ortho Books, 1986.

James, Theodore. *Flowering Bulbs Indoors & Out.* New York: Macmillan Publishing Co., 1991.

Whiteside, Katherine. *Classic Bulbs: Hidden Treasures for the Modern Garden.* New York: Random House, 1992.

LILIES

Bird, Richard. *Lilies.* Book Sales, Inc., 1991.

Brown, M. Jefferson. *A Plantsman's Guide to Lilies.* New York: Sterling Publishing Co., 1991.

Jefferson-Brown, Michael. *The Lily: For Garden, Patio & Display.* North Pomfret, VT: Trafalgar Square, 1988.

VEGETABLES AND FRUITS

Garden Way Staff. *Fruits & Vegetables: One Thousand and One Gardening Questions Answered.* Powmall, VT: Storey Communications, Inc., 1990.

Hagy, Fred. *The Practical Garden of Eden: Beautiful Landscaping with Fruits & Vegetables.* New York: Overlook Press, 1990.

Hill, Lewis. *Fruits and Berries for the Home Garden, revised edition.* Powmall, VT: Storey Communications, Inc. 1992.

Rogers Gessert, Kate. *The Beautiful Food Garden: Creative Landscaping with Vegetables, Herbs, Fruits & Flowers.* Powmall, VT: Storey Communications, Inc., 1987.

Solomon, Steve. *Growing Vegetables West of the Cascades.* Seattle, WA: Sasquatch Books, 1989.

WATER GARDENING

Leverett, Brian. *Water Gardens: Step by Step to Success.* North Pomfret, VT: Trafalgar Square, 1991.

Swindells, Philip. *The Water Garden.* New York: Sterling Publishing Co., 1990.

Uber, William C. *Water Gardening Basics.* Upland, CA: Dragonfly Press, 1988.

DISEASES AND PESTS

Carr, Anna. *Rodale's Color Handbook of Garden Insects.* Emmaus, PA: Rodale Press, 1983.

Chaube, H. S. *Plant Disease Management: Principles & Practice.* Boca Raton, FL: CRC Press, Inc., 1991.

Debach, Paul. *Biological Control of Natural Enemies, Second Edition.* Cambridge, UK: Cambridge University Press, 1991.

Hart, Rhonda, M. *Bugs, Slugs & Other Thugs: Controlling Garden Pests Organically.* Powmall, VT: Storey Communications, Inc., 1991.

Ware, George W. *The Pesticide Book.* Thomson Publications, 1989.

PLANT PROPAGATION

Clarke, Graham & Alan Toogood. *The Complete Book of Plant Propagation.* New York: Sterling Publishing Co., Inc., 1990.

Hartmann, Hudson T. and Dale E. Kester. *Plant Propagation—Principles and Practices, Fifth Edition.* Englewood Cliffs, NJ: Prentice-Hall, 1990.

Hill, Lewis. *Secrets of Plant Propagation*. Powmall, VT: Storey Communications, Inc., 1985.

Thompson, Peter. *Creative Propagation: A Grower's Guide*. Portland, OR: Timber Press, 1989.

ORGANIC GARDENING

Blake, Francis. *Organic Farming & Growing*. North Pomfret, VT: Trafalgar Square, 1991.

Hamilton, Geoff. *Organic Gardening*. New York: Random House, 1992.

Pike, Dave. *Organic Gardening: Step by Step to Growing Success*. Trafalgar Square, 1991.

Smith, Keith. *Backyard Organic Gardener*. Lothian Publishers, 1990.

Sunset Editors. *An Illustrated Guide to Organic Gardening*. Menlo Park, CA: Sunset Publishing Corp., 1991.

PATIO GARDENING

Kramer, Jack. *Patio Gardening*. New York: Price Stern Sloan, Inc., 1980.

Williams, Robin. *The Complete Book of Patio & Container Gardening*. New York: Sterling Publishing Co., Inc., 1991.

Yang, Linda. *The Terrace Gardener's Handbook: Raising Plants on a Balcony, Terrace, Rooftop, Penthouse or Patio*. Portland, OR: Timber Press, 1982.

CONTAINER GARDENING

Hillier, Malcolm. *Book of Container Gardening*. New York: Simon & Schuster, 1991.

Joyce, David. *Hanging Baskets, Window Boxes, & Other Container Gardens: A Guide to Creative Small-Scale Gardening*. New York: Summit Books, 1991.

Taloumis, George. *Container Gardening*. New York: Brooklyn Botanic Garden, 1989.

CITY GARDENING

Colby, Deirdre. *City Gardening*. New York: Simon & Schuster, 1988.

Riker, Tom. *City & Suburban Gardens: Frontyards, Backyards, Terraces, Rooftops & Window Boxes*. Englewood Cliffs, NJ: Prentice-Hall, 1977.

Young, Linda. *The City Gardener's Handbook*. New York: Random House, 1990.

GREENHOUSE GARDENING

Edwards, Jonathan. *Greenhouse Gardening: Step by Step to Growing Success*. North Pomfret, VT: Trafalgar Square, 1991.

Hessayon, D. G. *Be Your Own Greenhouse Expert*. New York: Sterling Publishing Co., Inc., 1991.

INDOOR GARDENING

Crockett, James. *Crockett's Indoor Garden*. Boston, MA: Little Brown & Co., 1978.

Herwig, Rob. *How to Grow Healthy Houseplants*. Los Angeles, CA: Price Stern Sloan, 1979.

Herwig, Rob. *Growing Houseplants*. New York: Facts on File, Inc., 1992.

Herwig, Rob. *The Treasury of Houseplants*. New York: Macmillan, 1979.

ORCHIDS

Kramer, Jack. *The World Wildlife Fund Book of Orchids*. New York, Abbeville Press, 1989.

Leroy-Terquem, Gerald & Parisot, Jean. *Orchids: Care & Cultivation*. New York: Sterling Publishing Co., Inc., 1991.

Northern, Rebecca. *Home Orchid Growing, Fourth Edition*. Englewood Cliffs, NJ: Prentice-Hall, 1990.

Rentoul, J. N. *Expanding Your Orchid Collection*. Lothian Publishers, 1990.

ROSES

Ray, Richard & MacCaskey, Michael. *Roses*. New York: Price Stern Sloan, Inc., 1984.

Ross, Dean. *The Ross Guide to Rose Growing*. Lothian Publishers, 1991.

Toogood, Alan. *Roses in Gardens*. New York: Sterling Publishing Co., Inc., 1990.

PRUNING

Cook, Alan D. *Pruning Techniques*. Brooklyn, NY: Brooklyn Botanic Gardens, 1991.

Joyce, David. *The Complete Guide to Pruning & Training Plants*. New York: Simon & Schuster, 1992.

Rudman, Jack. *Climber & Pruner*. Syosset, NY: National Learning Corp., 1991.

Plant names change frequently as taxonomists continue their work with plants. No doubt by the time this book goes to press, there may be some changes in botanical names. For our reference we have used HORTUS III, 1976 Edition, Macmillan Publishers.

Every effort has been made by the author and the publisher to provide accurate, up-to-date information in the lists of sources. The publisher welcomes responses from readers on any additions or changes. Please send letters to:

Jack Kramer
2225 Crayton Rd.
Naples, FL 33940

6 / PLANT HARDINESS ZONES

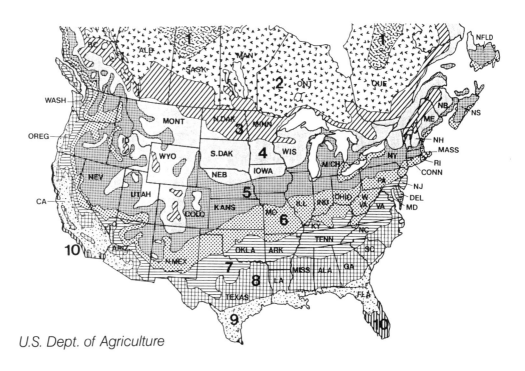

U.S. Dept. of Agriculture

Zone 1: below −50°
Zone 2: −50 to −40°
Zone 3: −40 to −30°
Zone 4: −30 to −20°
Zone 5: −20 to −10°

Zone 6: −10 to 0°
Zone 7: 0 to 10°
Zone 8: 10 to 20°
Zone 9: 20 to 30°
Zone 10: 30 to 40°

This is the Plant Hardiness Zone Map published by the U.S. Department of Agriculture. It is based on average annual low temperatures. A few other versions of zone maps are sometimes encountered and may differ from this one. However, this is the map that is generally used by growers and gardeners.

While this map (combined with zone information in the Botanical Names/ Common Names Listing found on page 426) can help you decide which plants are best suited for your part of the country, microclimates can sometimes create vast temperature differences within a specific zone. For this reason, I have included temperature hardiness information for most trees and shrubs in the alphabetical listings.